DICTIONARY OF URBAN AND REGIONAL PLANNING

DICTIONARY OF URBAN AND REGIONAL PLANNING

Incorporating:
Housing, Transport Planning, Landscaping, Urban Design, Planning Techniques, Services, Environment, Demography, Geography, Economics, Agriculture, Education and Training, Finance, Law, Administration

Editor
S. K. Kulshrestha

KALPAZ

Published by

Kalpaz Publications
C-30, Satyawati Nagar,
Delhi – 110052
Ph.: 011-47034999, 9811692060
www.kalpazpublications.com
E-mail: kalpaz@hotmail.com

Distribution Network
gyanbooks.com
India, USA, Canada, UK, Australia, France

ISBN: 978-81-7835-472-9 (HB)

Reprint in India, 2024
First Published, 2006

Printed at: Gyan Press, Delhi.

Dictionary of Urban and Regional Planning
Editor: S.K. Kulshrestha

Dedicated to
All Engaged in Planning
and
Development of Human Settlement

PREFACE

This compilation of about 2,700 terms, related to urban and regional planning, is the outcome of 38 years' of teaching varied courses like planning techniques, planning principles, city and metropolitan regional planning, and models in regional planning. Preparations of Master Plans of 13 cities and participation in several research studies have also formed the base for this effort.

The basic objective of this collection is to provide a dictionary of terms in urban and regional planning and other related disciplines in simple language for the benefit of the academicians, researchers, practitioners, and administrators. This was felt necessary because most of the laws, while providing legal definition of the terms refer to a particular section of the law, which must be referred to before getting a clear understanding. In other cases, the explanations of terms are written in a legal language that takes care of all loopholes or situations making the definition very complex. Definitions of terms given by various planning and development agencies, also, are according to their particular needs making them very specific. Literature also does not provide a tailor-made definition of terms and a combination of definitions by several authors gives a satisfying explanation. Practically all terms, therefore, have been edited and I do not claim to have written them.

Urban and regional planning is a multi-disciplinary subject and it synthesises inputs from various disciplines during the processes of planning, and development. It is desirable and convenient if explanations of various terms from such disciplines, as applied to planning, are available in one volume. Accordingly, this compilation provides terms from the following 15 disciplines / specialised fields, and one multidisciplinary class with abbreviation as indicated in italic letters:

Abbreviations

A	:	Administration (Urban)
AG	:	Agriculture
D	:	Demography
E	:	Environment
EC	:	Economics (Urban and Regional)
ET	:	Education and Training
F	:	Finance
H	:	Housing
L	:	Law
LA	:	Landscaping
M	:	Multidisciplinary
P	:	Planning (Urban and Regional)
S	:	Services (water supply, sewerage and drainage and solid waste management)
T	:	Transport Planning
TQ	:	Techniques (Planning) and
UD	:	Urban Design.

System of Referencing Followed

For classification of the terms by disciplines, the above abbreviations have been used in parenthesis after the term.

Example:

City: *(P)*

or

Curriculum: *(ET)*

When a term has more than one meaning or it is a multidisciplinary, various definitions have been separated by (a), (b).. . etc.

Example:

Market: *(P)* (a) The actual and potential consumers of a commodity or service, (b) A designated place where sale and purchase of commodities and services takes place, (c) A designated place where sale and purchase of specialised commodities takes place for example vegetable market, paper market, steel market, (d) A designated place where sale and purchase of commodities and services takes place on a specific day of a week or time of a day e.g. Sunday market, week-end market, or night market.

or

Development: *(M)* (a) Spatially, a process of change in physical conditions and quality of life of people in an area, initiated by spatial planning interventions (b) Economically, a product of planned investment in various sectors of economy and the resultant economic welfare of the people, (c) Socially, a process of change in the society caused by impact of socio-economic and physical changes on the behavior, attitudes and beliefs of the people.

In case a term has more than one sub-points, for better clarity, they have been separated by (i), (ii), (iii).....

Example:

Covered Area: *(P)* The area of a plot, expressed as percentage of the total plot area, that is permitted to be covered and built upon and includes the ground area covered by the building immediately above the plinth level and does not include (i) garden, well, pool, open to air swimming pool, open to sky unenclosed platform, fountain, (ii) compound wall, gate, un-storeyed portico, uncovered stair case, ramps, *chajja*, (iii) pump house, watchman's booth, utility structures meant for serving the building, and (iv) covered or open drainage.

Or

Urban Area: *(M)* .... (b) An area that fulfils the following conditions: (i) has a minimum population of 5, 000, (ii) at least 75 per cent of male working population is engaged in non agricultural pursuits, and (iii) has a density of population of at least 400 persons per sq. km.

For cross-references, the following four expressions have been used:

1. also ..... (followed by a term)
   Indicating that the following term also has the same meaning as the term being defined.

   Example:
   Real-estate Market: *(P)* ...., also *Property Market*

2. see ... (followed by a term)
   Indicating that the following term will provide the definition of this term.
   Example:
   Real Property: *(P)* see *Real Estate.*

3. see also ..... (followed by a term)
   Indicating that the following term, though different in meaning, will provide additional information related to the term and, therefore, for better understanding, it will be useful to refer the same.
   Example:
   Regional Periphery: *(P)* .... see also *Regional Core, Sub-region.*

4. see ....term-(a) or (b)
   Indicating that the meaning of the following term given under (a) or (b), as the case may be, will provide of definition of this term.
   Example:
   Resettlement: *(P)* see *Rehabilitation-(a).*

The following Acts, master plans, government documents, and other unpublished materials have beer referred during the course of this compilation:

Building Byelaws for the Union Territory of Delhi, 1976;

Bureau of Indian Standards, National Building Code;

Bureau of Indian Standards, Requirements of Cluster Planning for Housing- Guide (IS-13727: 1993);

Bureau of Indian Standards, Requirements of Low Income Housing- Guide (IS-8888 Part-1: 1993);

Census of India, 2001;

Government of India, UDPFI Guidelines;

Gujarat Town Planning and Urban Development Act, 1976;

Internet (about 1,175,000 sites under key words 'planning' 'glossary');

Maharashtra Regional and Town Planning Act, 1966;

Model Regional and Town Planning and Development Law, TCPO;

Pondicherry Building Bye-laws and Zoning Regulations, 1972;

Pondicherry Town and Country Planning Act, 1969;

Rajasthan Town and Country Planning Bill, 1994;

The Air (Prevention and Control of Pollution) Act, 1981;

The Air (Prevention and Control of Pollution) Rules, 1982;

The Assam Slum Area (Improvement and Clearance) Act, 1959;

The Bio-medical Waste (Management and Handling) Rules, 1998;

The Constitution (Seventy-fourth Amendment) Act 1992;

The Constitution (Seventy-third Amendment) Act 1992;

The Environment (Protection) Act, 1986;

The Forest (Conservation) Act, 1980;

The Hazardous waste (Management and Handling) Rules, 1989;

The Water (Prevention and Control of Pollution) Act, 1974;

The Water (Prevention and Control of Pollution) Rules, 1975;

The Wildlife (Protection) Act, 1972;

UNCHS, Multilingual Glossary of Human Settlements Terms;

UP (Regulation of Building Operations) Act, 1958;

UP (Regulation of Building Operations) Directions, 1960;

UP Nagar Mahapalika Adhiniyam, 1958;

Master Plan for Delhi 2001;

Master Plan for Delhi 2021(Draft);

It is hoped that this compilation will serve fellow urban and regional planners, students and others engaged in management and governance of human settlements.

Dr. S. K. Kulshrestha

A

Abadi: *(P)* That part of a village where people live and where socio-economic activities, serving the rural population, are located, see also *Hamlet, Village.*

Abattoir: *(P)* A premises where animals are slaughtered for use as food, also *Slaughterhouse.*

Abiotic: *(E)* A non-living entity, e.g. climate is an abiotic component of ecosystems.

Absentee Landlord: *(P)* A person who owns a property but he himself does not stay there but rents it or leaves it vacant.

Absolute Poverty: *(P)* Condition of poverty that is below the lowest level of income distribution.

Abutting Building: *(P)* A building, located in such a way that a portion of it is adjacent to another building.

Access: *(T)* A way to a plot or building.

Access Mode: *(T)* see *Feeder Service.*

Access Panel: *(S)* A removable panel in a frame, normally secured with screws and mounted on walls or ceiling, to provide access to concealed appurtenances or items that may require maintenance.

Access Road: *(T)* A road providing direct vehicular access to a plot of land and premises.

Accessory Use: *(P)* see *Ancillary Use.*

Accident: *(T)* Any event that happens by chance or unintentionally like collision of vehicles and injury, damage to property or death to passengers.

Accommodate: *(P)* To adjust, adapt, reconcile or bring to agreement an idea or policy in a plan or a proposal.

Accommodation: *(H)* A set of room(s) with necessary facilities attached or shared that is provided to visitors in a hotel or to tenants in a house.

Accrual: *(F)* An estimate of cost that has been incurred but not yet paid by the Agency.

Accrued Expenditures: *(F)* An expenditure incurred by a recipient, for performing a service or supply of goods or other items as per agreement or contract for which payment falls due or for which there is no provision in the current budget.

Accrued Income: *(F)* An income earned by a recipient for performing a service or supply of goods or other items as per agreement or contract for which payment falls due.

Acid Rain: *(E)* Refers to evaporation of water from sea, lakes, and rivers and transformation of such water vapours into Carbonic acids, Sulphuric acid, Nitric acid, and Hydrocloric acid after coming in contact with industrial air pollutants like Carbon-di-oxide, Sulpher-di-oxide, Nitrogen-di-oxide, and Chlorine respectively, and falling down of these acids on the surface of the earth as rain.

Acknowledgment: *(A)* Confirmation of receipt of a document by the person signing for it.

Acquisition Cost of Equipment: *(F)* The final cost of an equipment and includes the net invoice price and the cost of modifications, attachments, accessories, or auxiliary apparatus necessary to make it functional including the other charges, such as the cost of installation, transportation, taxes, duty or protective in-transit insurance.

Acre: *(P)* A measure of area of land, in foot-pound-second system, representing an area equal to 4840 square yard, or about 4000 square metre (historically it represents an area that can be ploughed in one day by a pair of oxen and later on it was limited by statute in England to an area 40 poles long by 4 poles broad where one pole measured 5.5 yard, hence the area of 4840 sq. yd.).

Acropolis: *(P)* The citadel of a Greek town.

Act: *(L)* A legislative enactment after following the due procedure including notification in the official gazette, see also *Bill.*

Action Plan: *(P)* (a) A plan that highlights current issues and emerging trends and specifies the actions to be taken including implementation agencies, their targets, requirement of funds, mobilisation of fiscal resources and a contingency plan, (b) A plan, prepared within the framework of a structure plan, that provides specific actions to be taken, by the implementing agency, pertaining to the development goals, current issues and priorities, see also *Structure Plan.*

Action Taken Report: *(A)* A report that highlights point-by-point action taken by a relevant body on the findings / directions / decisions of a statutory committee / commission.

Active Recreation: *(P)* Leisure activities of people involving vigorous movement of limbs such as swimming, skating, hiking, biking, fitness trails, running, and playing ball-games, also *Recreation (active).*

Activities Permissible: *(P)* see *Permissible Use.*

Activities Permitted: *(P)* see *Permitted Use.*

Activities Prohibited: *(P)* see *Prohibited Use.*

Activity Centre: *(P)* Any area, in a city, where there is substantial concentration of residential, commercial, industrial, recreational or other activities that attract supporting facilities and services and people.

Adaptation: *(P)* The process of accepting and adjusting to changes as to suit new conditions or environment.

Adaptive Re-use: *(P)* The process of transforming an old abandoned or underutilised structure or area into some other form and function than the original, e.g. converting a heritage building into tourist complex or an abandoned quarry site into recreation complex.

ADB: Asian Development Bank.

Add-a-Lane: *(T)* To increase the capacity of a road by creating a new lane through modification of median or shoulder or both.

Adequate Shelter: *(H)* A dwelling unit, located in an area having basic services, access to employment, and transport facility at reasonable cost, and having a minimum space needed by a household for living, privacy, security, light and ventilation, see also *Basic Services, Shelter.*

Adjourn: *(A)* To defer a meeting or proceeding to another time on the same day or another day and, in this case, the resumed meeting shall be considered as continuation of the same adjourned meeting.

Adjournment *Sine Die*: *(A)* Termination of a siting of the House (Lok Sabha, Rajya Sabha, or State Assembly) without any definite date being fixed for the next meeting.

Adjustable Rate of Mortgage: *(F)* see *Mortgage.*

Administer: *(M)* (a) In administration, to manage or look after the designated or assigned task pertaining to public affairs, (b) in housing, to manage or look after an estate, (c) in law, to put into operation the provisions of law.

Administration: *(A)* (a) The executive part of the legislature and includes the government ministries, departments, and agencies, (b) Administrative and regulatory activities of the government pertaining to management of public affairs, also *Public Administration*, see also *Public Affairs.*

Administrator: *(A)* A person who has been empowered to administer by law.

ADT: *(T)* see *Average Daily Traffic.*

Advance: *(F)* A payment made to a recipient, on his request, before it falls due.

Advocacy Planning: *(P)* Practiced in USA, a process of planning having regard to different political, social and economic interests where the planner is required to defend in a convincing manner, like an advocate, the proposed goals, strategies and approaches in front of stakeholders.

Aerial Photography: *(TQ)* The technique of taking photographs from a camera mounted in an airplane or balloon in a vertical or oblique position with respect to the Earth's surface at the time of exposure, see also *Vertical Aerial Photography*, and *Oblique Aerial Photography.*

Aerobic Treatment: *(E)* Treatment of wastes with the help of bacteria that live on oxygen.

Aesthetic: *(P)* Relating to principals of beauty in nature, arts, architecture, and organisation of spaces in a city.

Affidavit: *(L)* A written statement of facts on oath by a party making it and verified by a notary public.

Affinity Among Land Uses: *(P)* A close interaction among a set of land uses that tend to get located together in an area in a formal or informal manner and cause mixed land use pattern.

Affordable Housing: *(H)* A housing programme, designed by using a desirable mix of various types of dwelling units or building materials and implemented in such a way that the amount paid by the occupants as rent or loan-repayment is less than 30% of the occupant's income.

Afforestation: *(E)* The process of establishment of tree-cover on an open area that was not previously under forest or on a designated forest area that has been degraded due to indiscriminate cutting of trees, see also *Reforestation.*

Age Distribution: *(D)* Classification of population according to age groups generally at an interval of 5 years.

Agency: *(A)* An establishment that is performing business for and on behalf of another.

Agency Appraisal: *(F)* An assessment of the legal, organisational and financial soundness of an implementing agency for the purpose of sanctioning development loan by a financial institution, also *Legal Appraisal of Agencies.*

Agenda: *(A)* A list that indicates specific items of business to be considered at a meeting, normally circulated in advance, to all members invited to attend, also *Agenda Papers.*

Agenda Papers: *(A)* see *Agenda.*

Agent: *(A)* A person who acts for or manages the affairs of another.

Age-sex pyramid: *(D)* The graphical presentation of age-sex structure in the form a pyramid comprising two sets of horizontal bars placed side by side, one showing males and the other females in different age groups at 5-years' interval, see also *Age-sex Structure.*

Age-sex Structure: *(D)* The composition of males and females in each age group in a population, see also *Age-sex Pyramid.*

Age-specific Fertility Rate: *(D)* The number of live births in a specific age-group of per 1000 women of that same age-group in a year.

Age-specific Mortality Rate: *(D)* The number of deaths in specific age-group per 1000 population in the same age-group in a given year.

Aggrieved Party: *(L)* An group of persons or individual, who is affected as a consequence of an action or verdict of a local authority, a government body or a court of law

Aging of Population: *(D)* A demographic processes where the proportion of adults and elderly increases in a population and that of the children and adolescents decreases as result of better health care and decline in fertility due to family planning measures.

Agrarian: *(EC)* Concerning land matters in rural areas including land administration, agriculture production and supporting activities and services.

Agrarian Economy: *(EC)* Economy derived from agriculture production and allied activities like horticulture, animal husbandry, and rural industry.

Agrarian Reforms: *(EC)* Reforms covering land matters in rural areas and also social welfare of rural population.

Agreement: *(L)* A set of promises and related conditions, formally and mutually consented by two or more parties, to do something, see also *Memorandum of Understanding.*

Agricultural Labourer: *(D)* A person who works in another person's land for wages in cash or in kind.

Agriculture: *(AG)* The art and science of cultivating soil for production of plants useful to human beings in the form of grains, seeds, fruits including rearing of useful animals, birds and bees for sale or personal use.

Agriculture Belt: *(P)* see *Rural Belt.*

Agriculture Economics: *(EC)* Economics as it relates to agrarian sector.

Agriculture Market: *(P)* A designated place accessible by an all weather road from various villages and located along a major road leading to other urban centres, where, sale and purchase of agriculture produce takes place, also *Mandi.*

Agriculture Marketing: *(EC)* A system of procurement, means of payment, transportation, storage and sale of agriculture production.

Agriculture Pollution: *(E)* Contamination of soil, water and air due to farm and animal husbandry practices such as soil conservation, use of chemical fertilizers and pesticides, and disposal of agriculture and livestock wastes.

Agriculture Sector: *(EC)* The sector of economy contributing to development and employment generation comprising farming, horticulture, dairy farming, animal husbandry, and such other operations.

Agriculture Waste: *(AG)* Wastes generated from processing of agriculture produce.

Agro-based Industry: *(P)* An industry that depends upon input of raw materials from agriculture sector including grains, seeds, fruits, meat, milk, and those from sericulture, also *Agro-industry.*

Agro-industry: *(P)* see *Agro-based Industry.*

***Ahata*:** *(H)* In Arabic, a group of small, generally one-room, dwelling units with common toilets arranged as an enclosure with one entry, for letting out on rent, also *Bara* in Hindi.

Aid Programme: *(F)* Assistance rendered by one country / organisation to another for specified purpose under specific programme like disaster relief, food aid, humanitarian assistance, and economic assistance.

Aided Self-help Housing: *(H)* Housing projects where prospective owners participate in construction of their dwellings and common facilities with financial and technical support from the government or community organisations, see also *Self-help Housing.*

Air Gap: *(S)* A distance between the lowest point of a water inlet / feed pipe to an appliance and its (appliance's) spill-over level.

Air Pollutant: *(E)* Any solid, liquid, or gaseous substance, including noise, present in the atmosphere, due to any process of substances, in such a concentration as may be, or tend to be, injurious to human beings or other living creatures, or plants, or property, or environment.

Air Pollution: *(E)* Presence in the atmosphere of any air pollutant, see also *Air Pollutant.*

Air Quality Standards: *(E)* Prescribed level of pollutants in air that cannot be legally exceeded during a specified time and at a specified place.

Air Rights: *(L)* Legal property rights, with local variations if any, to use, control or occupy the air space over a designated property including the right to ground support (but not ground use) and the right to prevent building in the air space.

Algorithm: *(TQ)* A logical, step by step procedure applied to computing, decision-making or search operations.

Alienation of Property: *(L)* The voluntary transfer or conveyance of real property by one person to another.

Alight: *(T)* To get down from a vehicle that may be bus, train or any other.

Alignment: *(T)* The ground plan of a road, railway or waterway.

All Weather Road: *(T)* A road made of such material that can sustain all weather conditions, and can be used during dry weather, rains, and snowfall.

Alley: *(T)* A narrow pathway between buildings for providing access and not intended for through traffic.

Allocate: *(F)* To distribute funds or other resources according to a plan, set of rules, guidelines, norms, or policy, also *Earmark*.

Allocation of Funds: *(F)* Distribution of funds, by government or a funding agency, for specified purposes such as housing, environmental improvement, poverty alleviation and others.

Allocation of Land: *(P)* Distribution of land for a specified purpose according to an approved layout plan.

Allocation of Resources: *(F)* Scheduling of resources for developmental activities having regard to various constraints.

Allocative Efficiency: *(F)* The extent of optimality in distribution of resources among a number of competing uses.

Allocative Planning: *(P)* A processes of planning, where development proposals and priority of projects are guided by allocation of funds and the specified purposes.

Allot: *(P)* To distribute a thing or property by draw of lots, or in such a way that the recipients have no choice.

Allottee: *(P)* A person to whom an allotment is made.

Allowance: *(F)* A cash payment given by the government or other non-government employers for assisting employees for specific purposes such as house rent, transportation, and medical care.

Alterations: *(P)* (a) A change in structure of a building such as construction of, cutting into, or removal of any wall, partition, column, beam, joist, floor or other support, or (b) changes in the area or height of room, or (c) closing of an existing, or opening of a new door or window, or (d) changes to fixtures or equipments, or (e) changes from one occupancy to another, or (f) a change to or closing of any ingress or egress to a plot, building or area, or (g) any or all of these combinations specifying changes.

Alternative Learning Methods: *(ET)* Learning methods or approaches that are not group-based and include methods such as self-paced learning, computer-assisted learning and on-the-job training.

Alternative Sources of Energy: *(S)* Sources of energy production other than petroleum and electricity such as biomass, sun, and wind, also *Non-conventional Sources of Energy.*

Alternative Technology: *(TQ)* A technology that conserves or minimises the use of non-renewable resources for production of energy, running of transport system, and production of buildings and building materials.

Alternative Work Schedule: *(T)* A programme related to management of peak-period congestion and includes flexible, variable and staggered work-hours with a view to extending the morning and evening peak-periods and reducing the traffic volume.

Alternatives: *(P)* A number of different concepts, solutions or approaches, that address the same set of planning objectives and provide choices at the time of decision-making.

Ambient Air Quality: *(E)* The concentration of pollutants (chemicals and other elements) in the air, discharged from all sources, at a specific place, determined over a set period of time.

Amenities: *(P)* Natural and man-made features in a city or region and include natural landscaped areas, rivers, lakes, open spaces, roads, and utilities, facilities, and services, see also *Utilities, Facilities,* and *Services.*

Amortisation: *(F)* A system of gradual reduction of payment due, as a loan or debt, in installments, as per agreed terms and conditions, in such a way that the amount of current interest and the principal is completely recovered on the payment of the last installment.

Anaerobic Treatment: *(E)* Treatment of wastes with the help of bacteria that do not need oxygen for living.

Ancillary Services: *(P)* The services that support a main activity and their nature changes with the change of the main activity.

Ancillary Use: *(P)* The use of a building, structure or land that is subordinate to, customarily incidental to, and ordinarily found in association with, a principal use, which it serves – for example – small shops, eating places / canteen associated with a large office complex, also *Accessory Use.*

Angan: *(H)* In Hindi, a court yard, see *Court Yard.*

Animals: *(E)* Living beings including amphibians, birds, mammals, and reptiles, and their young as well as, in case of birds and reptiles, their eggs.

Annual Budget: *(F)* An estimate of income and expenditure arising from an annual plan for attaining the specified objectives in one year.

Annual Plan: *(P)* Conceived within the framework of the approved development plan, it is a plan containing the details of new and on-going projects that the development agency intends to implement during the respective financial year and for which fiscal resources shall be mobilised through public and private sources.

Anudan: *(F)* In Hindi, a grant or interest-free loan transferred for development purposes, from the Central government to state government or from state government to the local body

Apartment: *(H)* A self-contained dwelling unit with independent access, comprising one or more rooms forming a portion of a building that may be given on rent or leased out or self-occupied, also *Housing Unit.*

Apartment Building: *(H)* A building or house having two or more apartments with independent access, also *Apartment House*, see also *Apartment.*

Apartment House: *(H)* see *Apartment Building.*

Appreciation: *(H)* An increase in the value of property (building, house, or land) due to inflation, increase in demand, or improvement of accessibility, but not due to additions or alterations to the property.

Apprenticeship Programme: *(H)* A training programme for capacity building of labourers especially in Self-help Projects.

Appropriate Technology: *(TQ)* A technology most suited to local needs that is simple, easily implementable with local resources and labourers and maintained with least operational cost.

Appropriation: *(F)* A legal assignment of grant of money for a legally authorised specific purpose.

Approved: *(P)* Approved by a competent authority having jurisdiction.

Approved Plan: *(P)* A plan approved by a competent authority having jurisdiction.

Aquaculture: *(AG)* A science and art of propagation and cultivation of, for profit or social benefits, the aquatic animals and plant species such as fish, oysters, and weeds.

Aqueduct: *(P)* A man-made channel or conduit for carrying large quantities of water from one place to other including the structure for supporting such a channel.

Aquifer: *(LA)* A body of porous rock, sand or such other material that is saturated with water and releases the same in bore wells, springs and other water bodies.

Arable Land: *(AG)* A land that is used or suitable for growing crops.

Arbitration: *(L)* A quasi-judicial mode of settling the disputes between two parties, by referring them to a nominated person (arbitrator), mutually agreed by all the parities, who decides the issues after hearing both the sides.

Arbitrator: *(L)* A person, generally appointed with the mutual consent of the contending parties for settlement of dispute referred to him. In some cases the court may appoint an arbitrator and the decision of the court shall be final and binding to the contending parties.

Arcade: *(P)* A passageway created by a series of arches supported by columns.

Archaeological Park: *(LA)* An area, designated as such in a Development Plan, that is appropriately landscaped to conserve the historical monuments, buildings, landmarks, sites, natural features and other similar elements and enhance its educational and tourist potential.

Area of Influence: *(P)* (a) The spatial extent of a central function identified by the interaction between places where such function is located and the places from where people derive its benefits, (b) The spatial extent of a the area that is affected by the centripetal and centrifugal forces emanated by the population, economic activities and social facilities located in a large city, also *Sphere of Influence, Zone of Influence.*

Area Plan: *(P)* A plan for development of an area consisting of data, text, maps and other illustrations, pertaining to land use, transportation, utilities, facilities and services as per provisions of the master plan and zoning and sub-division regulations.

Area Sown More Than Once: *(AG)* The area on which crops are cultivated more than once during the agriculture year.

Arid Area: *(G)* see *Arid Region.*

Arid Climate: *(P)* Dry climate with scanty rain.

Arid Landscaping: *(LA)* Landscaping of arid areas using native plant materials suitable for deserts for treating public or private open spaces as well as restricting spread of desert conditions.

Arid Region: *(G)* A dry withered or barren area, due to lack of water, supporting only a few species of plants and animals, also *Desert Area, Arid Area.*

Art Gallery: *(P)* see *Exhibition Centre.*

Arterial Road: *(T)* A road having a right-of-way 50 to 60m., designated for intra-urban through traffic with no frontage access, no standing vehicles, very low cross traffic and minimum spacing of 500 m. between two intersections.

Articulated Bus: *(T)* An high-capacity (60 to 80 seats with additional space for standing passengers) and extra-long (18 –21 m) bus consisting of two distinct sections joint together.

Assimilative Capacity: *(E)* The ability of environment and its sub-components such as rivers, lakes, land and air mass, to carry waste materials without adversely polluting them.

At-grade: *(T)* At the same grade or level as the adjoining property (as opposed to a depressed or elevated road, building or other facility).

Atmosphere: *(E)* An area consisting of an admixture of gases such as Nitrogen (78 %), Oxygen (21%) and others (1%) like Argon, Carbon-di-oxide, Hydrogen, Helium, and Ozone along with some impurities including dust particles, smoke, and micro-organisms. Atmosphere is divided into four zones: Troposphere, Stratosphere, Ionosphere, and Exosphere, see also *Troposphere, Stratosphere, Ionosphere, and Exosphere.*

ATR: *(A)* see *Action Taken Report.*

Attest: *(L)* To bear witness to an act or event.

Attestation: *(L)* The signature of the witnesses attesting the act or event.

Attribute: *(TQ)* (a) In GIS, characteristic of a geographic feature described by numbers, characters, images and CAD drawings, typically stored in tabular format and linked to the feature by a user-assigned identifier, (b) In regional planning, a factor describing the characteristics of a region.

Audiovisuals: *(ET)* Presentation materials and tools used to supplement education and training activities and include power-point, video, audio, slides and transparencies.

Auditorium: *(P)* A building especially designed with all related services and facilities, to serve as an enclosed space to seat audience and a stage for live performances.

Authority: *(A)* A body, appointed under relevant legislation, by central, state, or local government, to perform certain specified functions (including planning and development) and empowered to enforce them.

Authority Having Jurisdiction: *(L)* A body created by a statute, or a person, a committee or an agency authorised by the body created by a statute to act on its behalf, to perform the specified functions.

Auto Rickshaw: *(T)* A three-wheeled vehicle driven with the help of a petrol, diesel or CNG engine and serving a city as a para-transit.

Automatic Sprinkler System: *(S)* An arrangement of pipes and sprinklers for fire fighting purposes, designed to operate automatically, by sensing the smoke/heat of fire in a building, and discharge water upon that fire and may also sound an audible alarm simultaneously.

Autonomous Body: *(A)* see *Quasi-government Body.*

Available Head: *(S)* The height to which water through a supply pipe can reach, at a point of consideration, due to pressure in the mains or generated by overhead tank or any other source.

Avenue: *(LA)* A road lined with trees on either side.

Average Daily Traffic: *(T)* (a) The total volume of traffic on a section of road passing in a period of 24 hours, (b) The average number of trips generated from a specific area during a period of 24 hours.

Average Vehicle Occupancy: *(T)* Average number of passengers traveling in a selected section of road during a selected period of time and it is calculated by dividing the total number of passengers traveling in all vehicles during the selected time period by the total number of vehicles traveling past the selected section.

AVO: *(T)* see *Average Vehicle Occupancy.*

***Awas*:** *(H)* In Hindi, a place for living, a house, see *House.*

B

Back Flow: *(S)* (a) Flow of water or other liquids, into the distributing pipes of a system of supply of potable water from any source other than the intended one, (b) Flow of liquid in the direction reverse of that intended.

Back Siphonage: *(S)* The flowing back of contaminated or polluted water from a plumbing fixture into a potable water supply system due to reduced pressure in such pipes.

Back-to-back Cluster: *(H)* Two housing clusters joined together at the back.

Background Map: *(P)* A map showing basic information about the project area and its environs with a view to support decisions but not intended for official adoption or approval, see also *Map.*

Backwash Effect: *(P)* The phenomenon of stagnation or deterioration in quality of life and level of development in the periphery of a city region due to exploitation of its resources by the regional-core, see also *Regional-core, Regional-periphery.*

Balance of Payment: *(F)* The net balance between the total income and expenditure of a country in its business and trade relations with rest of the world in a given period of time.

Balanced Regional Development: *(P)* A development approach that focuses on minimising the intra-regional inequalities as well as on development of both rural and urban areas in an integrated and mutually supportive manner.

Balcony: *(H)* A space created by horizontal cantilevered projection and secured by handrails or balustrades to serve as a passage or a place for sitting or sleeping outdoors.

Bank: *(F)* A premises for performing the function of keeping, lending and exchanging money and other related financial operations.

***Baoli*:** *(S)* In Hindi, a stepped well.

***Bara*:** *(H)* In Hindi, see *Ahata.*

***Barat Ghar*:** *(P)* In Hindi, a building designed and designated for organising marriage ceremonies and other social functions.

Barrier-free Design: *(P)* Design of building, doorways, pathways, toilets, lifts, transport and such other components in a way that permits easy access and mobility to handicapped individuals.

Barrier-free Zone: *(P)* A zone or area where all facilities, services, roads and buildings have barrier-free design, see also *Barrier-free Design.*

Barsati: *(H)* In Hindi, a habitable room including a kitchen on the roof of a building with or without a toilet.

Base Map: *(P)* A map serving as the foundation for subsequent planning and design operations, showing all features and characteristics of the area, as per requirements of the plan/project, see also *map.*

Basement: *(H)* The lower storey of a building below or partly below the ground level, also *Cellar.*

Basic Activities: *(EC)* Activities located in an area that are influenced by demands generated outside the local area and create further opportunities for growth of local economy, see also *Non-basic Activities, Economic Base.*

Basic Needs: *(P)* A group of needs that are essential for living in a settlement and include clean drinking water, shelter, access, employment, education and health care.

Basic Services: *(P)* A group of interrelated services required, to meet the basic needs of urban poor especially in developing countries, and include common drinking water faucets, toilets, paved roads/ pathways, and drains.

Basic Skills: *(ET)* The fundamental ability required for performance of a particular task or occupation.

Basic Training: *(ET)* The minimum knowledge and skill required for performance of a particular task or function related to a project, a scheme, an organisation or industry.

Basic Village: *(P)* The smallest spatial component of a region comprising the *abadi* area and agriculture fields and other open spaces of a village, see also *Abadi.*

Basin: *(G)* A terrain which is drained by a river or which drains into a particular lake or sea.

Basti: *(P)* In Hindi, (a) a high density, unplanned settlement having a very poor quality of life (b) a slum area in West Bengal.

Bazaar: *(P)* In Urdu, a commercial area in old city core, generally located along a main road in mixed land use pattern, where ground floor, specially the front portion, is shopping and the upper floors are occupied by residential use.

Before-tax Earnings: *(F)* The gross income from salary, commissions, sales, fees, etc., before deductions of income tax.

Behavioural Models: *(TQ)* A group of models that describe the behaviour of a system at a given point of time.

Benami: *(L)* In Hindi, a system of getting virtual ownership of a house through the legal instrument of power of attorney without payment of taxes on sale or purchase of properties.

Benching: *(S)* Sloping surfaces constructed on either side of channels at the base of a man-hole or inspection chamber for the purpose of confining the flow of sewage, avoiding the accumulation of deposits and providing a safe working platform.

Benchmark: *(TQ)* In surveying, a point of reference marked prominently on ground indicating the point of reference from which measurements are made.

Benchmarking: *(TQ)* A systematic and ongoing process of measuring operations, practices, and performance as compared to the others within and outside of the industry/organisation.

Beneficiary: *(P)* A person or an institution, estate, or trustee which receives, or is eligible to receive, certain benefits under a scheme, programme, will, insurance policy, or other contract.

Benefit Evaluation: *(P)* A set of methods of assessing the beneficial impact of an implemented project on the beneficiaries and other actors so that the lesson learnt may guide the formulation and implementation of similar future project, see also *Benefit Monitoring.*

Benefit Monitoring: *(TQ)* A system of information flow from the field on the status of implementation of project and actual deliveries of services to the intended beneficiaries.

Bequeath: *(L)* To dispose of personal property through a will.

Berm: *(LA)* An earthen mound designed to provide visual interest on a site, screening of undesirable views, and reducing noise.

Betterment: *(L)* Increment in property value accruing as a result of public investment such as improvement of accessibility, road condition, and augmentation or provision of facilities or services.

Betterment Fee: *(F)* see *Betterment Levy.*

Betterment Levy: *(F)* A charge imposed on the beneficiaries on the increment in property value accruing as a result of public investment such as improvement of accessibility, road condition, and augmentation or provision of facilities or services, also *Betterment Fee.*

Bhawan / Bhavan: *(P)* In Hindi, a building.

Bicycle Lane: *(T)* see *Cycle Lane.*

Bicycle Path: *(T)* see *Cycle Track.*

Bicycle Track: *(T)* see *Cycle Track.*

Bid: *(L)* A formal offer in writing by a contractor / consultant to perform specified service or task at a quoted price/fees, see also *Bid Price, Bidder.*

Bid Price: *(L)* A sum of money specified in a bid for performing a specified service or task, see also *Bid.*

Bidder: *(L)* A person who submits a bid, see also *Bid.*

Bike Lane: *(T)* see *Cycle Lane.*

Bike Path: *(T)* see *Cycle Track.*

Bikeway: *(T)* see *Cycle Track.*

Bilateral: *(L)* Pertaining to or affecting two parties or countries.

Bilateral Agreement: *(L)* an agreement between two parties or countries for a specified purpose, also *Bilateral Contract.*

Bilateral Assistance: *(F)* A financial or technical assistance given for a specified purpose by one country to another under a bilateral agreement, see also *Bilateral Agreement, Bilateral.*

Bilateral Contract: *(L)* see *Bilateral Agreement.*

Bilateral Institutions: *(F)* An organisation providing financial or technical assistance directly from one country to an organisation in another country, see also *Bilateral.*

Bill: *(L)* A proposed law to be discussed in the Parliament of State Assembly which when passed by the legislature and notified in official gazette is called an Act.

Binder: *(L)* A temporary agreement secured by a payment to evidence good faith, which is valid until a formal agreement takes effect.

Bio-diversity: *(E)* The variety of species, genes, ecosystems, and the ecological processes that are found within a common environment.

Biologicals: *(E)* Preparations made from organisms or micro-organisms or product of metabolism and bio-chemical reaction.

Bio-mass: *(E)* (a) Organic non-fossil materials such as plants, vegetation, or agriculture waste used as feed or building material or source of energy and includes animal droppings also, (b) the total weight of all living organisms in a biological community.

Bio-medical Waste: *(A)* Any waste that is generated during diagnosis, treatment or immunisation of human or animal or in research activities pertaining thereto or in production or testing of biologicals, see also *Biologicals.*

Biosphere: *(E)* The zone of earth extending from deep crest to the lower atmosphere where natural existence of life is possible.

Biota: *(E)* Pertaining to plant and animal life of a particular region.

Biotic: *(E)* Pertaining to life, e.g. plants and soil microorganisms that are biotic components of ecosystems.

Bird Sanctuary: *(P)* A large park or a forest designed and provided with all related facilities to serve as a natural habitat for preservation and breeding of a variety of birds, see also *Sanctuary.*

Birth Rate: *(D)* Ratio of the number of live births per 1000 population in a given year, also *Crude Birth Rate.*

Blight: *(P)* A condition of decay in an area (residential or commercial) due to neglect and lack of maintenance on the part of owners for reasons like low returns from rents and unaffordable cost of repairs and upkeep, also *Urban Blight, Urban Decay.*

Block of Flats: *(H)* A building containing several separate flats, each with an independent entry approached from a common entrance, staircase, lift, or balcony, and sharing other essential services and facilities, see also *Flat.*

Boarding House: *(H)* A building where rooms are let out, for a longer duration than a hotel, to any one and where dining facility is available to any one, living in the house or otherwise.

Body: *(A)* see *Organisation.*

Bond: *(F)* A financial instrument issued by a public agency to raise funds from financial capital market to meet specified development objectives and repayable from anticipated revenues, see also *Municipal Bond.*

Book Value: *(F)* In accounting, it is the value of total assets minus all debts and other liabilities, including the liquidation price of any preferred issues, divided by the number of common shares, in other words, it is the value of total net assets of a company per common share.

BOOT: *(P)* build-own-operate-transfer system of involving private sector in development processes.

Borehole: *(S)* (a) A deep hole sunk into ground to gain soil-related information, (b) A deep hole sunk into ground to get access to subsurface water for a variety of uses.

BOT: *(P)* build-operate-transfer system of involving private sector in development processes.

Botanical Garden: *(LA)* A park landscaped with a variety of plant species for exhibition, nature studies, and botanical research purposes.

Bottleneck: *(T)* A portion of road with lowest capacity along the route due to an obstruction to free-movement of vehicles.

Bottoms-up Procedure: *(P)* see *Grassroots-up Procedure.*

Boulevard: *(UD)* A wide street with rows of trees and aesthetic and functional treatment of pedestrian sidewalks, street furniture, overhead utilities, as well as architectural control of building and advertisement structures.

Boundary: *(P)* (a) A line along which two or more neighbouring areas, zones, administrative units, states, countries, as the case may be.

are joined. A prefix specifies the neighbouring areas such as ward boundary, district boundary, state boundary, and international boundary, (b) A line demarcating an area that specifies the spatial extent of jurisdiction of a legally created body e.g. municipal boundary.

Brackish Water: *(S)* A mixture of fresh and salt water.

Brainstorming: *(TQ)* A procedure of group discussion to generate an extensive list of ideas, thoughts or alternative solutions pertaining to a specific topic or problem through discussion among the participants having knowledge and experience related to the topic, for later evaluation.

Branch: *(S)* Special form of tile and pipe used for making connections to a sewer or water main called as 'T', 'Y', 'T-Y', double 'Y' and 'V' branches according to their respective shapes.

Branch Soil Pipe: *(S)* A pipe connecting one or more soil appliances to the main soil pipe.

Branch Soil Waste Pipe: *(S)* A pipe connecting one or more soil and/ or waste appliances to the main soil waste pipe (one pipe system).

Branch Ventilating Pipe: *(S)* A pipe fitted to prevent loss of water seal from a trap owing to partial vacuum, backpressure, or surging caused by air movement within the pipe system, one end of which is connected to the system adjacent to the trap of an appliance and other to a main-ventilating pipe or a drain-ventilating pipe.

Branch Waste Pipe: *(S)* A pipe connecting one or more waste appliances to the main waste pipe.

Breadwinner: *(EC)* A person who earns and supports himself / herself and his/her dependents and may or may not be the head of the household.

Broker: *(F)* A licensed individual or firm, serving on charging a commission, as an intermediary between a buyer and seller of a commodity, product or service.

Brown Agenda: *(E)* The policies and programmes aimed at improving the quality of urban environment.

BSP: *(S)* see *Branch Soil Pipe.*

BSWP: *(S)* see *Branch Soil Waste Pipe.*

Budget: *(F)* (a) An estimate of income and expenditure arising from a plan for attaining a specified objective within a defined period of time, (b) annual financial statement of the estimated receipts and expenditure of the State or Central Government in respect of a financial year, see also *Annual Budget, Budget Deficit.*

Budget Deficit: *(F)* An excess of expenditure over revenues.

Budget Period: *(F)* A period of 12 months commencing from 1 April of a year and ending on 31 March of next year within which time all budget allocations on the sanctioned projects shall be spent.

Buffer: *(LA)* A landscaped area between two zones provided for the purpose of separating two incompatible land uses and curtailing unwanted view, noise, odour, or dust using plants, walls, berms, or other such elements, also *Buffer Zone, Buffer Strip.*

Buffer Strip: *(LA)* see *Buffer.*

Buffer Zone: *(LA)* see *Buffer.*

Building: *(H)* Any structure, enclosed with external walls and covered with roof, constructed with any material, along with all its components, plumbing and services and used for human habitation or any other purpose and it does not include temporary structures, such as tents and *shamianas* erected for short-term use or for ceremonial occasions.

Building Bulk Regulations: *(L)* A zoning measure that limits size of buildings within a zone by restricting their height, density, location, floor-area ratio and overall shape of the building in relation to the plot area and the surrounding street.

Building Bye-laws: *(L)* Municipal rules, regulations and procedures that, in the interest of public health, safety and welfare, ensure minimum acceptable (i) quality of the design of all types of buildings, (ii) quality of building materials, (iii) structural safety, (iv) provision of sanitation, and (v) other safety and local requirements, also *Building Regulations.*

Building Code: *(H)* A set of regulations and minimum provisions designed to protect health and safety of public with regard to building sufficiency and include development control rules and general requirements for construction of buildings, design of structures, use of materials, electrical installations, plumbing services, signage, and outdoor display structures, also *Housing Code.*

Building Components: *(H)* Elements of a building such as foundations, plinth, walls, floors, roofs, projections, doors, windows, sanitary fittings, heating equipments, elevators, stair case, and fixtures.

Building Cooperative: *(P)* A cooperative society formed for the exclusive purpose of construction of a residential, commercial or any other type of building, and transfer of the titles to individual members, and it generally ceases to exist thereafter.

Building Drain: *(S)* That part of the lowest piping of a drainage system which receives the discharge from soil, waste and other drainage pipes inside the wall of a building and conveys it to the building sewer that begins outside the building wall, also *House drain* (replace 'building' by 'house'), see also *Building Drain Combined, Building Drain Sanitary, Building Drain Storm,*

Building Drain Combined: *(S)* A building drain which conveys both sewage and storm water or other drainage, also *House Drain Combined* (replace 'building' by 'house'), see also *Building Drain.*

Building Drain Sanitary: *(S)* A building drain that conveys sewage only, also *House Drain Sanitary* (replace 'building' by 'house'), see also *Building Drain.*

Building Drain Storm: *(S)* A building drain that conveys storm water or other drainage but no sewage, also *House Drain Storm* (replace 'building' by 'house'). see also *Building Drain.*

Building Height: *(H)* (a) In case of building with flat roof and abating a road - the vertical distance measured from the average level of the centre line of the adjoining street to the highest point of the building adjacent to the street, (b) in case of building with pitched roof and abating a street - the vertical distance measured from the average level of the centre line of the adjoining road to the point where the external surface of the outer wall intersects the finished surface of the sloping roof, (c) in case of building with pitched roof with gables facing the abating a road - the vertical distance measured from the average level of the centre line of the adjoining street to the mid-point between the eves level and the ridge, (d) In case of building not abating a road - the vertical distance measured from the average level of the ground around and continuous to the building to the highest point of the building with flat roof, or to the point where the external surface of the outer wall intersects the finished surface of the sloping roof, or to the mid-point between the eves level and the ridge as the case may be. Architectural features serving no other function except that of decoration are excluded for the purpose of taking height.

Building Industry: *(M)* see *Construction Industry.*

Building Line: *(P)* A line defined on a plot of land, by the by-laws, building regulations, or approved layout plan, up to which the plinth of a building can be lawfully extended.

Building Operations: *(P)* The activity related to (i) erection, re-erection of a building or part there of, (ii) roofing, re-roofing of a building or open space, (iii) any alteration of building as is likely to affect drainage or sanitary arrangement or materially affect its security, or (v) construction of door opening on any street or land not belonging to the owner.

Building Permit: *(P)* An official document issued by the municipality or any other competent authority authorising implementation of the construction project as per approved drawings and specifications.

Building Regulations: *(L)* see *Building Bye-laws.*

Building Renovation: *(P)* Addition, alteration, and reconstruction of the whole or part of a building.

Building Restoration: *(P)* Reconstruction of a building to its original design and appearance.

Building Restrictions: *(P)* A set of limitations imposed by a competent authority on buildings, within a specified area, pertaining to building type, use, location on the plot, style, height, material used and the like.

Building Sewer: *(S)* That part of horizontal piping of a drainage system which extends from the end of the building drain and which receives the discharge of the building drain and conveys it to a public sewer, private sewer, individual sewage-disposal system, or approved point of disposal, also *house sewer* (replace 'building' by 'house').

Building Site: *(P)* A well defined plot of land or area upon which building can be erected as per local building by-laws, also *Site.*

Building Society: *(M)* (a) A financial institution set up for the purpose of providing housing loans, (b) a self-help mutual association that mobilises domestic and corporate funds to finance home ownership on a full recovery basis.

Building Specifications: *(H)* A detailed itemised particulars of different components of a building describing dimensions, plans, material to be used, and other requirements such as construction equipments, quality of work, performance, and installation procedures which form part of the contract document of a construction project.

Building Standards: *(P)* Technical specifications approved by a competent agency for repeated or continuous application in design of buildings and their structures taking into account health and safety considerations with a view to ensuring that the building is fit for the assigned or intended use.

Building Sub-drain: *(S)* That portion of a drainage system which cannot drain by gravity in the building sewer, also *house sub-drain* (replace 'building' by 'house').

Building System: *(H)* (a) Method of construction of buildings that could be using traditional techniques, industrial techniques or both, (b) method of construction of buildings through complete fabrication on modular basis on site, or in a factory, or both.

Building Trap: *(S)* A device, fitting or assembly of fittings installed in the building drain to prevent circulation of air between the drainage of the building and the building sewer, also *house trap* (replace 'building' by 'house').

Built Environment: *(E)* see *Environment-(e).*

Built-in Furniture: *(H)* The permanent fixtures built as an integral part of a building such as cabinets and wardrobe closet.

Built-up Area: *(P)* In the context of a settlement as a whole, an area that is occupied by buildings and structures, see also *Extensively Built-up Area, Substantially Built-up Area.*

Bungalow: *(H)* A detached house, generally not more than 2-storeys high, and surrounded by open space on all the four sides.

Burial Grounds: *(P)* A premises used for burying the dead bodies.

Bus *Adda*: *(T)* In Hindi, an inter-city bus stand.

Bus Bay: *(T)* An additional area designed and designated at a bus stand for buses to pull into to pick up and drop off passengers with a view to minimise disturbance to the flow of traffic.

Bus Depot: *(T)* A premises where the public transport buses are parked during the night period after completing all the trips for the day and includes servicing facility and other related infrastructure.

Bus Lane: *(T)* A separate and exclusively marked lane, out of the road rights-of-way on an arterial or sub-arterial road, restricted to buses only.

Bus Mal: *(T)* In US, a road in a downtown area, designed and designated to movement and parking of buses only, also *Transit Mall.*

Bus Priority Systems: *(T)* A system of management of bus traffic in heavily traveled corridors usually on arterial roads, where facilities like dedicated bus lane and bus bays are provided and where buses get a priority over other vehicles at traffic signals.

Bus Rapid Transit: *(T)* A fixed guided-way transit system in which transit buses operate on right-of-way that is physically or otherwise off-limits to regular vehicular traffic and planned in such a way that the system can be upgraded to light-rail vehicle operations when ridership grows beyond the operational capacity of transit buses.

Bus Terminal: *(T)* A premises managed by public transport agency used for boarding or alighting inter-city or inter-state buses with all related facilities for passengers as well as bus bays and parking of other vehicles used by passengers.

Buspool: *(T)* A system of bus service generally free or at subsidised fare, owned and managed by a single large employer or jointly owned and managed by a group of employers, dedicated to transporting the employees from their place of residence (or a collection point) to place of work and back.

***Bustee*:** *(H)* In Hindi, a human habitation.

BVP: *(S)* see *Branch Ventilating Pipe.*

BWP: *(S)* see *Branch Waste Pipe.*

Bypass: *(T)* A road or a loop, around a built-up area, joined to a major road to facilitate movement of through traffic and reduce congestion for the local traffic.

C

Cab: *(T)* see *Taxi.*

Cadastral Map: *(P)* A map of an area on a scale 1:1000 or below, showing the property boundaries, dimensions, ownership, and value of all subdivisions of land, see also *Map.*

Cadastral Survey: *(P)* An official inventory of boundaries, value and ownership of real estate for the purpose of transfer of title due to sale or purchase and collection of property tax.

Cadastre: *(P)* A public register in which dimensions, value and ownership of all the real estates are recorded.

Calibration: *(TQ)* In GIS, the process of choosing attribute values and computational parameters, based upon real-world situation, so that a model represents the true picture.

Camping Site: *(P)* A premises, located in a recreational or tourist zone and provided with all necessary facilities and services for the purpose of short-duration stay in tents or other temporary structures.

Capacity of Self-help: *(H)* Personal resources and ability of the members of the community to help themselves in a self-help housing programme.

Capacity: *(T)* The maximum number of vehicles passing over a given section of a lane or a road during a given period under a specified speed or level of service.

Capital assets: *(F)* The assets of a permanent nature used in production of income, e.g. land, buildings and machinery.

Capital Base: *(F)* The total paid-up capital and resources.

Capital Budget: *(F)* The annual statement of proposed public expenditure on provision of facilities and infrastructure for which resources are allocated in the budget.

Capital City: *(P)* A city serving as the seat of government of a country or state, which is generally characterised by geographic centrality and nodality as well as concentration of political, economic, judicial, and socio-cultural activities.

Capital Cost: *(F)* The costs associated with the purchase, development or construction of fixed assets such as land, buildings, roads, equipments and vehicles.

Capital Equipments: *(F)* The machines and devices used by an organisation and considered as fixed assets.

Capital Expenditure: *(F)* The money spent on fixed assets e.g. land, buildings, machinery and equipments as well as on major public works like roads, bridges, airport, hospitals, schools and other buildings.

Capital Gains: *(F)* (a) The profit from sales of capital assets calculated as the sale price minus the total cost, (b) An appreciation of value of assets over a period of time.

Capital Intensive: *(P)* An industry or economic activity that is heavily mechanised requiring considerably less workers and where the cost of equipments and plants is more than the labour cost.

Capital Loss: *(F)* The loss incurred from sales of capital assets.

Capital Outlay: *(F)* The direct expenditure for purchase of capital assets and services required for promoting a development programme or objectives of an agency or an enterprise.

Capital Structure: *(F)* The equity and debt securities of an organisation / business together with surplus of resources.

Capital: *(F)* In financial terms, monitory resources available for a venture.

Capital-intensive Technology: *(P)* A technology that requires far greater input on plants and equipments than on labour input, see also *Capital Intensive.*

Cardinal Scale: *(P)* A quantitative scale where equal scale intervals represent equal increase or decrease in the measurement and there are two types of such scales – interval scale and rational scale, see also *Interval Scale, Rational Scale.*

Carpool: *(T)* A system of traffic management where persons traveling to a common point or direction of destination pool their cars and thus reduce traffic volume and parking demand, also *Vanpool,* and *Ridesharing.*

Carriageway: *(T)* The part of road right-of-way designed for movement of vehicular traffic.

Case Study: *(M)* (a) In education and training, a method of teaching with the help of selected examples of live projects from the field for a greater understanding of a subject matter, (b) In planning, analysis of several relevant existing examples with a view to achieving greater understanding of a subject matter and evolving a basis for decision-making, or to finding regularity to evolve replicable models, concepts or theories.

Cash Basis Method of Accounting: *(F)* In this system of accounting the income is reported in the tax-year the money is actually received and similarly, expenses are deducted in the tax-year they are actually incurred.

Cash Crop: *(AG)* A crop produced primarily for marketing.

Cash Flow: *(F)* The net earning of a venture calculated by deducting expenses from the income and for sustainability this should be positive.

Casting Vote: *(A)* The vote cast by the chair person, in a committee meeting, in case of an equality of votes on a matter.

Casual Carpool: *(T)* see *Informal Carpool.*

Catchment Area: *(M)* (a) In geography, the area from where the rain water drains into a river or lake, (b) In case of a facility like school, hospital, or recreation centre, the area from where people come to enjoy its benefits, (c) In case of an industry, the area from where the resources are drawn, (d) In case of a market, the area from where people come to buy or sell commodities.

CBD: *(P)* see *Central Business District.*

CBO: *(P)* community based organisation.

CDS: *(P)* city development strategy.

Cellar: *(H)* see *Basement.*

Cemetery: *(P)* A premises used for burying the dead bodies by the Christian community.

Census Town: *(D)* A place that has (i) a minimum population of 5,000, (ii) at least 75 per cent of male workers engaged in non-agricultural pursuits and (iii) a density of population of at least 400 persons per sq. km. and it may or may not have an urban local body.

Census: *(D)* The periodic, generally every 10 years, official enumeration of population and its demographic, social and economic characteristics including area of settlements and housing conditions.

Central Business District: *(P)* A major commercial area of a large city with high concentration of business activity, having very high land value and where major transportation and communication networks converge, also *CBD.*

Central City: *(P)* The largest city in a large urban agglomeration, usually containing the CBD.

Central Government Office: *(P)* A building or group of buildings used for performing the functions and activities related to the Central Government.

Central Place Functions: *(P)* Those functions that are carried out for the benefit of people spread in an extensive but contiguous area and include manufacturing and sale of higher order goods or provision of specialised facilities and services.

Central Place Theory: *(P)* In a simplified form the theory presents that (i) the central places are towns and cities that manufacture goods and provide services for consumption of the people living within the city and also in other places located at a convenient travel distance and hence these places have their area of influence (the trade area), and (ii) depending upon the nature and concentration of central place functions, a hierarchy, among different settlements located in a region, is evolved. see also *Area of Influence, Central Place Functions.*

Central Places: *(P)* In regional planning, places (towns and cities) that provide goods and services for consumption of the people living within the city and also in other places located at a convenient travel distance in the trade area, where the convenient travel distance is longer for goods and services of higher order (e.g. university) and is shorter for those falling in the lower order (e.g. college).

Central Village: *(P)* A village, located centrally within its catchment area comprising a group of villages, having relatively better education, health and communication facilities and services that serve it and also the other villages in the group.

Centrality: *(P)* The characteristics a settlement that defines its central position, among various other settlements in a region, as determined by its location, accessibility and central functions it performs.

Cess: *(F)* Any tax levied by an authorised body.

CGS: *(M)* The centimetre, gram, and second system of weights and measures.

***Chajja*:** *(H)* In Hindi, a structural overhang provided over openings on external walls for protection from sun and rain.

Change of Mode: *(T)* The changeover from one type of vehicle to another in the process of completing the desired journey, e.g. changing from an automobile to a train at railway station and *vice versa*.

Channels of Movement: *(T)* Include physical facilities involved in the movement of people and goods and include railways, waterways, highways, roads, as well as related facilities such as terminals, parking, and loading and unloading bays.

***Chawl*:** *(H)* In Hindi, a multi-storeyed residential unit with small one-room dwelling units constructed for accommodating industrial workers in Maharashtra and Gujarat having a poor quality of life due to low rents and lack of maintenance.

Check dam: *(P)* Small temporary or permanent dam constructed across a swale or drainage channel for the purpose of reducing the runoff speed and erosion, or storage and recharge of ground water.

Checklist: *(TQ)* (a) A method, where a list of tasks and steps to be taken to accomplish them is prepared to serve as a guide while taking the action, (b) In surveying, a precise and exhaustive listing of the information needed, along with the nature, unit, and source of each set of information.

Chequer Board Plan: *(P)* see *Grid-iron Pattern*.

Child Mortality Rate: *(D)* Number of deaths of children between birth and age of 5 years per 1000 live births.

Child Mortality: *(D)* The probability of a child dying between birth and age of 5 years, also *Under-five Mortality.*

Chimney: *(E)* A structure with an opening or out let from or through which any air pollutant may be emitted.

***Chungi*:** *(P)* In Hindi, a place near the entry to a settlement where octroi is collected.

Church: *(P)* A premises serving the Christian community as a place of worship.

Cinema: *(P)* A building with facilities for projection of movies, hall for seating of the audience including public conveniences and parking, see also *Drive-in-cinema.*

City Centre: *(P)* The central area of an city characterised by convergence of transportation and communication networks, concentration of socio-economic, cultural and administrative activities and very high land value, also *Town Centre, Downtown.*

City Challenge Fund: *(P)* A fund created by the Government of India to meet the transitional and transaction costs of restructuring the urban services with a view to improving service quality and efficiency and also bringing down losses, raising adequate revenues and making projects viable and bankable.

City-level Density: *(P)* see *Overall Density.*

City Park: *(P)* A large, above 100 hectare or more, open space serving an entire city as a place for active recreation and leisure and may include botanical garden, amphitheatre, play grounds, water sports, theme parks, food court, aquarium, and related infrastructure including parking.

City Planning: *(P)* see *Physical Planning.*

City Region: *(P)* The urban and rural areas located contiguously around a city that are under the influence of the developmental impulse emanated by it and comprise the regional core (the city and its fringe area) and the periphery (rest of the area in the region further divided into sub-regions having similar structure i.e. sub-regional core and sub-regional periphery), also *Urban Region.*

City: *(P)* (a) Administratively, a place governed by a municipal corporation and having a population of more than 100,000, (b)

Physically, a phenomenon in space, a product of a variety of activities taking place over the time, and the perception of people who live there, see also *Classification of Urban Centres.*

Civil Society: *(P)* The people living and working in an area.

Classes of Society: *(P)* Different sections of society classified by (i) social characteristics, e.g. cast / tribe, and classified as scheduled casts or scheduled tribes, (ii) income, e.g. high, middle and low income and classifies as high income group, medium income group, and low income group, and (iii) poverty and classified as economically weaker section.

Classification of Industries: *(P)* (a) By scale of operation – large industries, medium industries and small industries, (b) By nature of industrial product – manufacturing industries, service industries, (c) By location in the city – formal industries, household industries, (d) By level of pollution – (i) polluting industries or red industries, (ii) polluting under acceptable norms termed as orange industries, (iii) non-polluting industries or green industries, (e) By legal status – conforming industries or permissible industries and non-conforming or prohibited industries.

Classification of Urban Centres: *(TQ)* A system of grouping of urban centres into classes (a) By type of their central functions such as administration (capital cities, district headquarters), cultural (pilgrimage centres, temple towns, university towns), production (industrial towns), extraction (mining towns, fishing towns) commerce and trade (market towns, mandi towns), recreation (holiday resorts, tourist towns), defense (cantonment, naval base), transport (railway junction towns, port towns), (b) By their population size such as the classes defined by the Census of India that are:

Class-VI	-less than 5,000 population,
Class-V	-5,000- 9,999,
Class-IV	-10,000-19,999,
Class-III	-20,000-49,000,
Class-II	-50,000-99,999 and
Class-I	-100,000 and above.

India is a large country by population size and therefore the class – I has further been divided as:

M-1	-less than 200,000,
M-2	-200,000 to 299,999,

M-3	-300,000 to 499,999,
M-4	-500,000 to 999,999, and
M-5	-1,000,000 and above.

Census of India has further divided this M-5 into:

M-5(i)	-1,000,000 to 1,999,999,
M-5(ii)	-2,000,000 to 4,999,999 and
M-5(iii)	-5,000,000 and above.

Clearance Area: *(P)* Under urban renewal programmes, a dilapidated area not fit for human habitation to be cleared by demolition of buildings and rebuilt a fresh as per the redevelopment plan.

Client: *(P)* A person, organisation or body, which appoints a consultant and to whom the professional services are rendered by a consultant.

Climber: *(LA)* A non-supporting plant which clings to any structure or object as it grows upwards, also *Creeper, vine.*

Clinical Laboratory: *(P)* A building equipped with facilities for carrying out various tests for confirmation of symptoms of a disease.

Closed Cluster: *(H)* A housing cluster with only one common entry into the cluster open space.

Club: *(P)* see *Recreational Club.*

Cluster Court Town House: *(H)* Generally, a self-occupied dwelling in a cluster plot having nearly 100 per cent ground coverage with possibility of vertical expansion limited to one more floor, see also *Cluster Plot.*

Cluster Plot: *(H)* A plot in a group of plots arranged in a cluster.

Cluster: *(H)* A group of generally up to maximum 20 plots or dwelling units arranged around a group open space, see also *Back-to-back Cluster, Closed Cluster, Cul-de-sac Cluster, Group Open Space, Independent Cluster, Interlocking Cluster, Open Cluster.*

CMDA: *(P)* Chennai Metropolitan Development Authority.

Coach: *(ET)* A person who instructs, demonstrates, directs and prompts learners, also *Trainer.*

Coaching: *(ET)* An approach to training the participants through instructions, demonstrations, hands-on-exercises, group discussions, group assignments, and *Field Visits.*

Coastal Regulation Zone - 1: *(E)* A zone where no new construction activity shall be permitted, and includes (i) the areas located within 500 m. of high tide line on the landward side, that are ecologically sensitive and important, such as: national parks / marine parks, sanctuaries, reserve forests, wild life habitats, mangroves, corals/coral reef, areas close to breeding and spawning grounds of fish and other marine life, areas of outstanding natural beauty, areas of historical / heritage significance, areas rich in genetic diversity, areas likely to be inundated due to rise in sea level consequent upon global warming, and such other areas declared by the Central Government, and (ii) areas between the low tide line and the high tide line.

Coastal Regulation Zone - 2: *(E)* Areas located within 500 m. of high tide line on the landward side that have already been developed (substantially built-up and provided with approach roads, water supply, drainage and sewerage system) up to or close to the shore-line and form part of a municipality or other legally designated urban area where buildings shall be permitted only on the landward side of an existing road / existing authorised structures provided such new buildings follow the relevant zoning and subdivision regulations and building bye-laws.

Coastal Regulation Zone - 3: *(E)* Areas located within 500 m. of high tide line on the landward side that are undisturbed and those which do not belong to either CRZ-1 or CRZ-2 category where, (i) the area up to 200m. from the high tide line shall be no-development zone and no construction shall be permitted there while repairs to existing structures, if any, shall be permitted provided that there is no change in area, density and FAR, and (ii) in the area between 200m and 500m, of the high tide line, development and construction of hotels / beach resorts for temporary occupation by tourists shall be permitted.

Coastal Zone: *(P)* An area of land situated along a sea or estuary.

Cold-Storage: *(P)* A building where perishable commodities are stored using mechanical or electrical devices to maintain the temperature required.

Collateral: *(F)* Any marketable property (movable or immovable) that can be pledged by a borrower as a security for mortgage or loan.

Collective Housing: *(H)* Multi-family housing where a group of households live and share some communal facilities and services, also *Communal Housing*.

Collector Road: *(T)* A road having 20-30 m. right-of-way, for collecting and distributing traffic from and to local streets and also providing access to arterial and sub-arterial roads, with no restriction to frontage access but no parked vehicles but very high cross traffic at intersections spaced at least 150 m. apart, also *Collector Street*.

Collector Street: *(T)* see *Collector Road*.

College: *(P)* An institution located in a building or a campus of several buildings with or without hostel accommodation, managed by public or private institution, for offering education on a variety of courses including professional courses and providing play facilities to students at graduate (bachelors degree) and post-graduate (masters degree) levels generally affiliated to an university for award of degrees.

Colloquium: *(ET)* A meeting of a group of like-minded persons for discussion on a specific subject or issue, see also *Conference, Symposium, Workshop-(b)*.

Columnar: *(LA)* A slender, upright plant form.

Combined System of Drainage: *(S)* A system in which both the foul water (sewage) and surface water are conveyed by the same sewers or drains.

Commercial Land Use: *(P)* A parcel of land, shown on a development or layout plan, where retail or wholesale commercial and related activities are being carried out (existing land use) or will be permitted in future (proposed land use).

Commercial Office: *(P)* A built space in a commercial building used for office of an individual, group or organisation.

Commercial Plot: *(P)* A plot designated in a layout plan for commercial activities.

Commercial Presence: *(M)* In the context of the World Trade Organisation's General Agreement on Trade in Services, a form of service provision, where the service-supplier of one member country establishes office, in owned or leased premises, in another member country and provides the services, e.g. opening of branch office by a planning, architecture or engineering firm in another country to deliver the services, also *Mode-3.*

Commercial Projects: *(F)* see *Remunerative Projects.*

Commercial Value: *(EC)* The market value of a real estate on the date of its sale or purchase or acquisition.

Committee: *(A)* A group of 3,5,7, ...n (odd number only) persons appointed by a competent body, to perform a specified task through discussions and evolve solutions, considered opinion or recommendations as required by the task where the members can be specialists or personnel from the concerned organisations or both as per requirement of the task.

Communal Facilities: *(H)* In a collective housing, facilities that are shared by a group of households and include kitchen, bath rooms, toilets, common room, lifts, and central heating / cooling.

Communal Housing: *(H)* see *Collective Housing.*

Communal Latrines: *(H)* Toilets used by several households or public, also *Public Toilets, Public Latrines.*

Communal Tap: *(H)* Water faucet serving several households or the public, also *Public Tap.*

Community Center: *(P)* (a) At city level, a commercial center serving a population of 100,000 and comprising shops (retail, service, and informal), offices, cinema, hotel, nursing home, service industries, post office, electric sub station and conveniences, (b) At residential area level, an enclosed space used for various social and cultural activities of a neighbourhood of 15,000 population, also *Community Hall.*

Community Development: *(P)* A participatory process where the people living in a locality, identify problems and initiate action for improvement of the area or quality of life of a section of the community such as women, children or the elderly, through mobilising physical, social, human and financial resources, also *Community Planning.*

Community Hall: *(P) see Community Centre (b)*

Community Park: *(P)* A park about 5 hectares in size, serving a population of about 100,000 as a place for active recreation and leisure and may include play fields, children's play area, food court, and related infrastructure including parking.

Community Participation: *(P)* Active involvement of the local community in the decision-making process and implementation of developmental programmes beneficial to the entire group.

Community Planning: *(P)* see *Community Development.*

Community Toilets: *(P)* see *Public Toilet.*

Community: *(P)* (a) A self-conscious social unit having common identity and interests, (b) An identifiable group of people living, studying or working in close proximity, (c) A planning unit, in a large city or metropolis, serving a population of 100,000 with a community centre as its core.

Commute Trips: *(T)* Work-trips made on a daily or regular basis.

Commute: *(T)* To travel daily between places of residence to place of work located in another settlement.

Commuter: *(T)* The person who commutes, see also *Commute.*

Commuting: *(T)* An urban phenomenon, where people commute, for employment, from far away places to large cities, see also *Commute.*

Company Housing: *(H)* Housing developed or procured on rent by a corporate body for the benefit of its employees.

Company Town: *(P)* A town developed by a company for locating its business operations as well as providing housing and other facilities and services to its employees and service personnel with a view to achieve optimum out put from workers by ensuring them a better quality of life through good housing, e.g. Modinagar, Tata Nagar.

Compatible Uses: *(P)* Two or more uses that are located together in accordance with each other and do not cause any pollution.

Compensation: *(F)* (a) A suitable payment of money to make up for any loss or damage to the affected person or party, (b) In case of land acquisition, a fair payment of money paid, for acquiring a parcel of land or property for public purpose, to the owner of such land or property.

Competency: *(ET)* The ability of a person to perform with skills needed for a task and show positive results.

Competition: *(P)* (a) The act of competing for a prize or profit, (b) A processes for testing the skill or ability of consultants for award of a project, (c) The simultaneous demand by two or more activities/ land uses/ projects for the same limited resources, such as land or finance.

Competitive Bidding: *(F)* Bids submitted by several contractors or consultants in response to a public notice or advertisement for an intended action which could be preparation or implementation of a project, professional or technical service, procurement of materials or any other work.

Completion Certificate: *(L)* A written document issued by a competent local authority indicating that the project / building is complete and meets all requirements building bye-laws.

Component Building: *(H)* see *Prefabricated Building.*

Comprehensive Plan: *(P)* Based upon analysis of existing conditions and future projections, a plan, formulated in a comprehensive manner, indicating, defining and providing for (i) areas designated for development of housing, commerce, industries, transportation, and utilities, facilities and services, (ii) zoning regulations and development controls, (iii) phasing of development and financial implications in each stage.

Comprehensive Planning: *(P)* (a) The processes of preparation of a comprehensive plan of an area, also see *Comprehensive Plan*, (b) In US, a processes of planning that (i) creates a master plan to guide deliberations of specialist planners, (ii) evaluates the schemes prepared by the specialists in the light of the master plan and (iii) coordinates the planning efforts of the specialists agencies with a view to ensuring implementation of master plan and interest of the public.

Compressed Workweek: *(T)* A work scheduling technique to reduce traffic in office areas that allows extended weekends or an extra holiday in between workdays, through reduction in number of workdays from the usual 6 or 5 in a week and increasing work hours per day.

Computer-aided Design and Drafting: *(TQ)* An design process that is assisted by computer software for producing drawings and graphics.

Computer-assisted Learning: *(ET)* see *Alternative Learning Methods.*

Concentration: *(P)* In urban planning, a process of grouping of economic, socio-cultural, political and administrative activities in a city centre or CBD, (b) In regional planning, a phenomenon where economic, socio-cultural, political and administrative activities tend to polarise in a city or metro-regional core due to locational advantages and agglomeration economies.

Conceptual Design: *(P)* see *Conceptual Plan.*

Conceptual Plan: *(P)* A preliminary plan / design giving the schedule of requirements, general approach, and alternative concepts / solutions for the consideration of the client and his comments, suggestions, and choice of a preferred alternative for further detailing, also, *Conceptual Design, Inception Plan, Planning Concept, Preliminary Plan, Schematic Design, Schematic Plan.*

Conciliation: *(L)* see *Reconciliation.*

Condemned Building: *(P)* A building legally declared unfit for use or occupancy due to unsafe structure or any other requirement of building bye-laws.

Condominium: *(H)* A multi-family dwelling where each unit is individually owned but the land and common spaces and facilities are jointly owned by all owners and maintained by them on prorated share basis.

Conference: *(ET)* A congregation of experts and other persons for discussion on a specific issue or subject with a view to achieving a wider understanding and support on the issue and getting directions for further actions, see also *Colloquium, Symposium, Workshop-(b).*

Confiscation: *(L)* Seizure of a private property by government without paying any compensation to the owner to halt abuse or misuse connected with land use or any other provision of law.

Conflicting Uses: *(P)* Two or more uses that are located together that are not in accordance with each other and cause pollution.

Conforming Use: *(P)* A use that is in accordance with an approved master plan, zonal plan or layout plan.

Congestion Management System: *(T)* A system of traffic congestion management that identifies the location, analyses the problems, monitors changes and recommends alternative solutions.

Congestion Pricing: *(T)* A system of management of traffic especially during peak-periods by charging for the use of road based upon the traffic congestion. Charges increase with increase in congestion during the morning and evening peak-periods.

Congestion: *(M)* (a) In transportation, overcrowding of vehicles hindering the free flow of traffic, causing delays, accidents and air pollution, (b) In planning, overcrowding of people in a residential area causing overloading of services and threatening health and safety.

Conifer: *(LA)* A pine, or a fir tree that produces cones.

Conservancy: *(S)* Collection of night soil.

Conservation Area: *(P)* An area of natural, historical, socio-cultural or architectural significance designated for conservation in a development plan or under a relevant Act.

Conservation of Monuments: *(P)* Judicious and planned use and management of monuments and their respective immediate environs in such a manner that their architectural, historical, socio-cultural glory is maintained.

Conservation of Resources: *(P)* Judicious and sustainable use and management of natural or manmade resources in such a manner that their natural, ecological, and economic significance, as applicable, is maintained,

Conservation Plan: *(P)* (a) A plan for sustained management of built-heritage resources of an area with a view to restore their past glory and includes proposals for accessibility, planning, landscaping, assigning compatible uses in and around the monuments, restoration of various buildings, cost estimation, and organisational setup for management and maintenance, (b) A plan for sustained management of natural resources in a region.

Conservation: *(P)* Judicious and sustainable use and management of natural or manmade resources in such a manner that their natural, ecological, architectural, historical, socio-cultural significance, as applicable, is maintained.

Construction Industry: *(M)* The system of production, marketing and maintenance of buildings, structures, roads, railways, bridges and tunnels, that enjoys, in some countries the benefits granted to the industrial sector, also *Building Industry.*

Construction Management: *(H)* A process of efficient, time oriented, and cost effective co-ordination of building construction activity right from tendering for the project to project completion ensuring high level of professional responsibility in quality of construction as per design and specifications, also *Site Management.*

Construction Safety: *(H)* Measures taken for the safety of workers on the construction site, safety of temporary structures like scaffoldings, and safety of adjoining buildings and structures.

Construction Sector: *(H)* The sector of economy contributing to development and employment generation comprising construction, marketing and maintenance of buildings and structures, and manufacturing of building material and building equipments.

Construction Site: *(H)* The plot of land where the construction activity takes place.

Construction: *(H)* A process of creation, renovation or repair of structures including all on-site work (excavation, erection, assembly of equipments and finishing), and management of supply of materials, manpower and money.

Consultant: *(P)* An out side expert engaged by a client (public agency or private body or individual) to provide specialised service or technical advice as per agreement.

Consumption Abroad: *(M)* In the context of the World Trade Organisation's General Agreement on Trade in Services, a form of service provision, where a service-consumer moves to the member country to obtain the desired services, e.g. consumers traveling for tourism, medical treatment, professional education from one country to another, also *Mode-2.*

Contact List: *(P)* A list of names of team / committee members or key players along with their office / home address phone / mobile phone numbers etc. to serve as a handy information when need arises to contact them during or after office hours or on holidays.

Container: *(M)* (a) In transport, a large portable device in which goods are packed for transportation by sea followed by rail or road before it reaches the destination, (b) In environmental management, a portable device in which waste (including hazardous waste) is stored, transported, treated, disposed off, or otherwise handled.

Contiguous Development: *(P)* The development of areas immediately adjacent to one another.

Contingency Amount: *(F)* An amount up to 10 per cent of the estimated cost of a project, charged from the client, for meeting unforeseen expenses encountered during period of the project.

Contingency Plan: *(M)* A plan that specifies ways, means and procedures to be followed in case of specific failure of system or disruption of operations that may occur by chance or under unforeseen circumstances.

Contingency Planning: *(M)* A process of identifying the nature and extent of various events that may occur by chance or under unforeseen circumstances and specifying in advance the ways, means and procedures when the event or similar event occurs.

Contour Interval: *(P)* A vertical distance measured between two contour lines.

Contour Line: *(P)* A line drawn on survey map joining points of the same ground elevation above the mean sea level or an assumed datum line.

Contour: *(P)* A line that depicts the existing or proposed form of the land.

Contract: *(L)* An agreement, for doing something, between two parties that is enforceable by law and it defines the respective obligations, functions and duties of both the parties.

Contractor: *(M)* A person engaged by a client to perform some functions, such as construction of building and supply of goods and services, as per agreement.

Control Tools for Plan Implementation: *(P)* Tools that control location, nature, and extent of development as per provisions of a master plan and include zoning, sub-division regulations, and spatial standards, see also *Zoning, Sub-division Regulations, Standards.*

Controlled Intersections: *(T)* Road intersections where traffic is managed with automatic traffic lights or other traffic control devices.

Controlled Market: *(EC)* A market where government intervention regulates it with a view to create stable conditions and control inflation.

Controlling Function: *(A)* An act that deals with performance appraisal and ensures that the performance of the personnel is according to the plans and programmes, see also *Management.*

Conurbation: *(P)* Spatial merging of two or more settlements located along a transportation route; the term was originally coined in reference to urban growth in Britain.

Convenience Goods: *(P)* Items that are usually needed on a regular basis e.g. milk, bread, eggs, vegetables and meat.

Convenience Shopping Centre: *(P)* A place, located in residential area having about 2,000 to 5,000 population (this number may vary with size of settlement), where a group of shops (not exceeding 50 in number or 1 per 100 persons) sell convenience goods and services, see also *Convenience Goods.*

Convenience Shops: *(P)* shops selling convenience goods and located within walking distance, also *Corner Shops.*

Conventional Housing: *(H)* Housing constructed according to local traditions, design, methods of construction and use of building materials.

Conventional Source of Energy: *(S)* Energy generated by use of fuels such as wood, coal, natural gas and petroleum.

Cooperative Society: *(M)* A group or association of people registered under Cooperative Societies Act, or any other Act for performing a declared function in a manner as given in its Articles of Association.

Coordinate: *(TQ)* In GIS, a set of numbers that define location in a given reference system, such as x, y in a planar coordinate system or an x, y, z in a three-dimensional coordinate system.

Coordination: *(P)* A processes of bringing together the various agencies engaged or needed for formulation and implementation of a plan, project, or activity in a manner that attracts their participation and yield positive results.

Copy Right: *(L)* The right of authors, professionals, artists, researchers, or others who produce original work, to protect their work from copying, reproducing, storing in a retrieval system, transmitting in any form or by any means by others, and also, to permit such actions, on written request, also *Intellectual Property Rights.*

Core Area: *(P)* see *Inner City Centre.*

Core Dwelling: *(H)* A dwelling unit comprising the basic structure such as floor and roof or a habitable room which forms the core of the house around and above which further improvements / expansions can be done by the owner depending upon needs and resources.

Core Housing: *(H)* Housing development comprising core dwellings, also *Progressive Housing, Shell Housing,* see also *Core Dwelling.*

Corner Plot: *(P)* A plot / site located at the junction of and fronting on two or more intersecting roads, also *Corner Site.*

Corner Shops: *(P)* see *Convenience Shops.*

Corner Site: *(P)* see *Corner Plot.*

Corporate Office: *(P)* A building used for performing the functions and activities related to a corporate body.

Correlation Analysis: *(TQ)* Statistical methods for measuring the degree of relationships among different variables.

Corridor: *(P)* A linear pattern of spatial development along a highway evolved by the accessibility and locational advantages provided by such roads, also *Development Corridor, Highway Corridor..*

Cost Effectiveness: *(F)* Net gain in the outcome of an intervention in relation to the cost.

Cost Matching: *(F)* A system of financing a project on 50-50 sharing basis between two governments or the government and private group of beneficiaries.

Cost of Capital: *(F)* The rate of interest paid on the capital employed in development projects or business.

Cost Overrun: *(F)* The amount of money spent over and above the budgeted sum for any item of the project such as land, labour or interest on loan.

Cost Planning: *(P)* A process of planning where a pre-determined cost of the project guides plan.

Cost Sharing: *(F)* A system of financing a project by sharing the cost, in an agreed proportion, between two or more agencies that can be government bodies, development authorities, or private organisations.

Cost-benefit Analysis: *(TQ)* An analytical technique that follows the procedure of systematic comparison between the costs incurred and benefits accrued in implementation of a plan or a policy with view to evaluate its performance. A plan or policy is good if the benefits exceed the costs. This technique can also be used to evaluate various alternative plans or policies and selection of one that has greater benefits than costs and not necessarily least cost.

Cost-effectiveness Analysis: *(TQ)* A method of analysing the cost of various plans / projects for finding the one that has net gains in the outcome, see also *Cost Effectiveness.*

Cottage Industry: *(P)* A system of production of traditional products and goods depicting art and culture, utlising specific local skills, raw materials and resources, and include handloom, hand-knitted, cane, bamboo, gold, silver, ceramic, clay products and toys.

Council: *(P)* A body of persons, generally elected, to exercise certain specified powers and functions.

Counterpart Funds: *(F)* Funds set up by a country receiving assistance from another country to match the assistance as per terms of agreement.

Counterpart Personnel: *(A)* Local experts of a country attached to a technical assistance project, that have the same role as, and complement the work of, the international experts.

Country Belt: *(P)* see *Rural Belt.*

Country Planning: *(P)* A spatio-economic planning process that addresses to the issues of rural areas.

Countryside: *(P)* Rural areas including primary conservation areas such as forests, wetlands, floodplains, steep slopes, prominent vistas and natural habitats and secondary conservation areas including active agriculture, heritage sites, and national and regional parks.

Course Outline: *(ET)* A summary of organisation of a training course including its objectives, target groups, list of subjects classified by modules, group-work, field visits, and expected results.

Course Schedule: *(ET)* see *Programme-(c).*

Course Syllabus: *(ET)* A short and precise description of the major components of each subject forming part of a course.

Courseware: *(ET)* The training materials needed to conduct a course (e.g., course syllabus, schedule and outline, questionnaires, case studies and role plays).

Court Yard: *(H)* An space open to sky, enclosed by buildings, boundary walls or railings that may be on the ground floor or on any other level within a building or adjacent to it.

Courts: *(P)* A premises used for the office of the judiciary and several rooms for hearing cases along with necessary facilities and services including offices of lawyers.

Coverage: *(TQ)* In GIS, (a) A digital version of a map, which forms the basic unit of vector data storage in ArcInfo: (b) A set of thematically (such as soils, streams, roads, or land use) associated data considered as a unit.

Covered Area: *(P)* The area of a plot, expressed as percentage of the total plot area, that is permitted to be covered and built upon and includes the ground area covered by the building immediately above the plinth level and does not include (i) garden, well, pool, open to air swimming pool, open to sky unenclosed platform, fountain, (ii) compound wall, gate, un-storeyed portico, uncovered stair case, ramps, *chajja*, (iii) pump house, watchman's booth, utility structures meant for serving the building, and (iv) covered or open drainage, also *ground coverage.*

CPA: *(TQ)* see *Critical Path Analysis.*

CPM: *(TQ)* see *Critical Path Method.*

Crèche: *(P)* An educational or custodial facility, managed by an individual or an institution on commercial or non-commercial basis, for infants and pre-school children during day time when both parents are out to work, also *Day Care Centre, Day Nursery.*

Creditworthiness: *(F)* Ability and standing of a potential borrower to repay loan, as assessed by the lender.

Creeper: (LA) see *Climber.*

Cremation Ground: *(P)* A premises with facilities for consignment the dead bodies into flames.

Crisis Management: *(P)* An agreed procedure of effective, timely cooperation and coordination of various agencies involved in minimising losses due to a disaster.

Critical Functions: *(P)* In disaster management, functions that can not be interrupted without significant losses, e.g. saving of life is topmost priority and any function that supports this operation is critical function.

Critical Habitat: *(E)* An area where endangered species are found and is in need of protection for their survival and recovery.

Critical Infrastructure: *(P)* Systems that are important to economic security of an organisation, community, nation, and their destruction will severely affect them and include power plants, communication systems, drinking water, bridges etc.

Critical Path Analysis: *(TQ)* see *Critical Path Method.*

Critical Path Method: *(TQ)* A network analytical technique for organising and controlling activities pertaining to a project and highlighting those activities that are critical and must be undertaken at the earliest time possible to maintain the project schedule and avoid delay and losses, also *Critical Path Analysis.*

Critical Records: *(P)* Documents such as land records that, if damaged or destroyed, would cause considerable inconvenience and/or require replacement at considerable expense.

Cross Boarder Trade: *(M)* In the context of World Trade Organisation's General Agreement on Trade in Services, a normal form of trade in goods between two countries, where the final product or a service flows from one member country to another crossing the national frontiers, e.g. design and report or an architectural, landscaping, planning, urban design service transmitted by post or e-mail from one country to another, also *Mode-1.*

Cross Subsidy: *(F)* A system of raising funds for providing affordable housing for economically weaker sections of population where a portion of the cost of such housing development is recovered by increasing the cost of dwelling units in middle and high income group housing programmes, (b) A system of raising funds for providing affordable housing for economically weaker sections of population where those sections of society who can pay, subsidise for those who cannot pay.

Crude Birth Rate: *(D)* see *Birth Rate.*

Crude Death Rate: *(D)* Number of deaths in a year per 1000 population in a given year.

CRZ-1: *(E)* see *Coastal Regulation Zone – 1.*

CRZ-2: *(E)* see *Coastal Regulation Zone – 2.*

CRZ-3: *(E)* see *Coastal Regulation Zone – 3.*

Cul-de-sac Cluster: *(H)* A cluster where the plots or dwelling units are grouped around a cul-de-sac serving as road as well as cluster open space.

Cul-de-sac: *(T)* A dead end street with appropriately designed area at the end for turn around.

Cultivated Area: *(AG)* Is the sum of the net cropped area, area sown more than once, and fellow lands area.

Cultivation: *(AG)* The processes of ploughing, sowing, and production of cereals and millet crops (such as *wheat, paddy, jowar, bajra, ragi*, etc.), pluses, raw jute and kindred fiber crops, cotton, etc. and includes supervision or direction of cultivation but does not include growing of fruits and vegetables, keeping orchard or groves or working in plantations like tea, coffee, rubber, cinchona and medicinal plants.

Cultivator: *(AG)* A person engaged as employer, single worker or family worker in cultivation of crops on land.

Culturable area: *(AG)* Is the sum of the net cropped area, area sown more than once, fellow lands area, and other uncultivated area excluding fellow land.

Culturable Waste: *(AG)* It includes lands available for cultivation but has not been taken up for cultivation being covered with scrubs and jungles, or abandoned up to five years in succession after a few years of cultivation for one reason or the other.

Cultural and Information Centre: *(P)* A building managed by institutions, central or state government, and foreign missions to serve as a centre for dissemination of information to the people as per objectives of the institution / government / mission.

Cultural Heritage Protection: *(P)* Measures taken to secure and / or protect invasion of culture and deterioration of monuments, buildings and sites.

Cultural Resource: *(P)* (a) Physically, all the monuments, structures, objects, and sites of historical, architectural and cultural significance, (b) All music, dance, drama, and paintings, (c)

Socially, all customs, traditions, fairs, festivals, way of living, dressing and behaving.

Culture: *(P)* Social heritage of a society including material artifacts, aesthetic perceptions, values, beliefs, and behavioural pattern transmitted from one generation to the other.

Cumulative Effects: *(P)* The combined effect of separate, individual actions on environment, economy or society that, collectively, becomes significant over time.

Curb: *(T)* see *Kerb.*

Curb-stone: *(T)* see *Kerb-stone.*

Current: *(P)* The present time.

Curriculum Vitae: *(M)* A description of one's personal details, qualifications, experience, and interests.

Curriculum: *(ET)* (a) A list of all courses offered by a teaching institution, (b) For a course of study, a scheme of distribution of all subjects, practical / studio programmes, and tutorials, offered in semesters of an academic year, giving time allocated in hours and total marks for each of them.

Custom: *(P)* A frequent repetition of the same act by different members of a society that, with passage of time, becomes acceptable to all as a custom.

Cutcha House: *(P)* see *Kachcha House.*

Cycle Lane: *(T)* A portion of a road right-of-way reserved for use by bicycles exclusively: also *Bike Lane, Bicycle Lane.*

Cycle Rickshaw: *(T)* A three-wheeled vehicle driven manually with the help of a cycle and serving a city as a para-transit.

Cycle Track: *(T)* A path, physically separated from automobile and pedestrian traffic by an open strip or barrier, reserved for exclusive use by cycles and may or may not be part of the road right-of-way, also *Bike Path, Bike Way, Bicycle Path, Bicycle Track.*

Cycle-rickshaw Stand: *(T)* A place designated as such for parking of cycle rickshaws for hiring.

Cyclic Process of Planning: *(P)* A processes that includes (i) identification of goals and objectives, (ii) assessment of problems, potential and priorities, (iii) preparation of alternative conceptual plans and their evaluation to select most appropriate concept, (iv) preparation of the plan based upon selected concept and its approval, (v) implementation, (vi) feedback and (vii) review of the plan and then, depending upon the results of review repeat implementation (step –v) or revise / refine the action at steps (ii) or (iii) or in worst case, abandon the plan and start a fresh at step (i) and continue the cycle.

D

Daily-wage Worker: *(EC)* An unskilled worker hired and paid by the day, also *Day Worker.*

Dairy Farm: *(P)* A premises having facilities for rearing of cattles and processing of dairy products.

Dam: *(AG)* A system of retaining wall and sluice gates constructed across a water body to divert its flow or to raise water level for the purpose of irrigation and generation of hydro-electricity.

Damage Assessment: *(TQ)* The process of assessing nature and extent of damage to life and property, following a disaster, to serve as a basis for actions pertaining to rescue, relief, reconstruction, and rehabilitation.

Data Backups: *(TQ)* A system of generating copies of data regularly and storing the same on-site and or off-site to be used to restore corrupted or lost data or to recover entire systems and databases in the event of a disaster.

Data Recovery: *(TQ)* The restoration of data from the data backup system to the state that existed at the time of the last backup saved.

Databank: *(TQ)* A system of collection, classification, storage and retrieval of information on a variety of related themes using predetermined indicators and computers.

Database: *(TQ)* Information stored on a computer system that can be updated, modified and retrieved by authorised persons for further analysis and presentation.

Date of Completion: *(P)* The last date, as mentioned in an agreement or contract document, or a mutually agreed subsequent date on which all work on the project is completed.

Datum: *(TQ)* In GIS, a set of parameters and control points used to accurately define the three-dimensional shape of the Earth.

Day Care Centre: *(P)* see *Crèche.*

Day Nursery: *(P)* see *Crèche.*

Day Worker: *(EC)* see *Daily-wage Worker.*

Dead-end Street: *(T)* see *Cul-de-sac.*

Deadheading: *(T)* The segment of a trip made by a public transport from the bus depot to the starting point in the morning or the end point to the bus depot in the evening that does not generate any revenue.

Debenture: *(F)* An unsecured bond backed by the assets and credits of the issuing organisation and not by a specific property.

Decentralisation: *(M)* (a) In planning, the processes of shifting of selected existing activities of a large city to its fringe areas, or in selected towns located in its area of influence, as a result of market forces or planned interventions, (b) In administration, delegation of decision-making powers from higher to lower administrative levels, also *Delegation,* see also *Industrial Decentralisation.*

Decentralised Planning: *(M)* A process of planning where the decisions are made at lower administrative levels.

Decibel 'A' Weighted (dBA): *(E)* A measure of intensity of sound levels in average decibels usually over a 24-hour period calculated using a logarithmic average

Decision Theory: *(P)* Logical decision is made, by the decision-maker, by choosing the most appropriate alternative under given situations and is based upon his analysis of various alternative choices that are available or alternative effects that will be caused by the decision, see also *Decision-making.*

Decision-making: *(P)* A processes of making judgment regarding course of action to be taken in certain situations after due consideration of some alternative choices and the approaches to decision-making include: (i) quantitative approaches such as systematic approach, thinking approach, and normative approach, (ii) qualitative approaches such as intuitive approach, feeling approach and, descriptive approach, and (iii) planned approach, see also *Descriptive Approach, Feeling Approach, Intuitive Approach, Normative Approach, Planned Approach, Systematic Approach,* and *Thinking Approach.*

Deconcentration: *(P)* The processes of geographical spread of new residential, commercial and or industrial activities in the fringe areas of a large city, or in selected towns located in the city-region, as a result of market forces or planned interventions.

Decree: *(L)* (a) A judgment passed by a court of law, (b) An order given by an authority having the force of law.

Deferred Payment: *(F)* A monitory system that allows the payment of interest and principal amount postponed to a mutually agreed future date.

Degree of Urbanisation: *(P)* see *Level of Urbanisation.*

Delay: *(T)* In transportation, the time difference in the actual travel time between two points on a congested road and the travel time taken for the same distance during free-flow conditions.

Delegation: *(P)* see *Decentrialisation-(b).*

Delphi Method: *(TQ)* A method of finding solutions to problems by (i) asking in a brain-storming session, the views of experts, administrators, politicians as representatives of the people, and other informed persons, (ii) collating their ideas, on each problem, (iii) resolving conflicting views if any, (iv) evolving a solution of each problem by majority consent, and also (iv) noting major areas of disagreements that could not be resolved, to assist further decisions.

Demand Estimation and Demand Forecasting: *(T)* Procedures for determining the desire for travel by potential users of the transportation system, including the number of travelers, the time of day, and the travel routes.

Demand Modeling: *(T)* The development of computer models to represent the relationships between land use and the transportation system to serve as a tools for demand estimation, see also *Demand.*

Demand: *(P)* The quantity of goods or services required as per accepted norms and standards or need of the people, see also *Need.*

Demand-responsive Transit Services: *(T)* A transit service using vehicles like taxies, vans, and mini-buses that are dispatched and operated only in response to specific request from passengers, also *Dial-a-ride.*

Demarcation: *(P)* Transferring the layout plan on the site by marking the boundaries of land subdivisions.

Demography: *(D)* The scientific study of characteristics of human population

Demonstration: *(ET)* An interactive learning technique where the trainer actually shows a skill or activity and simultaneously explains the steps and sequence required to perform the same.

Density: *(P)* (a) In case of spatial distribution, number of persons or things per unit area (i.e. hectare, acre, sq. mile, or sq. km.) (b) In case of population served, number of things or facilities per unit of population (i.e. 100, 1000, 10,000 etc. persons) where depending upon need, the things may include telephone, cell phone, doctors, schools etc., see also *Overall Density, City Level Density, Gross Residential Density, Net Residential Density, Population Density.*

Dependent Population: *(D)* The non-working portion of population including young, the elderly, the disabled and unemployed who must be supported by others.

Dependent: *(D)* A person being supported by another who has an obligation to provide such support, see also *Dependent Population.*

Depopulation: *(P)* Reduction in number of inhabitants in an area as a result of economic, social or environmental policy of the government.

Depot: *(P)* A premises where specialised goods such as petroleum products, oil and gas are stored, see also *Bus Depot.*

Depreciation: *(F)* Loss of market value of a real property resulting from age, use, physical deterioration, functional or economic obsolescence or any other cause.

Depressed Area: *(P)* see *Depressed Region.*

Depressed Region: *(P)* An area where quality of life is far below the national average due to cultural and economic backwardness or isolation from the rest of the nation, also *Depressed Area.*

Derelict Land: *(P)* Land that is rendered incapable of beneficial use due to damage by mining operations, industrial pollution, or other factors and requires special treatment before its reuse.

Desalinisation: *(S)* The process of treating sea water for removal of salt and other chemicals for use of human beings, industry or agriculture.

Descriptive Approach: *(A)* In decision-making, a processes that incorporates, (i) identification of action goals which, in the perception of the decision-maker, should be achieved, (ii) identification of alternatives based upon the loosely defined rules of approximation, and (iii) search for a satisfactory alternative which fulfills the action goals.

Descriptive Model: *(TQ)* A model that provides descriptive analysis, in words and graphics, of the structure and change of urban and regional system and it ignores time and hence is generally static in nature.

Desert Resort: *(P)* see *Resort.*

Design: *(P)* Conceptualisation of a thought and its planning, architectural and / or engineering details, through plans, elevations, sections and other graphic presentation, as required for its implementation.

Designated Facility: *(M)* A facility which has received permit from the relevant regulatory authority.

Desire: *(EC)* see *Want.*

Destination: *(T)* The end point of a trip, which may be a place, area or zone.

Detached Housing: *(H)* A plotted housing development where each dwelling unit is located on a plot with setbacks on all its four sides.

Detailed Plan: *(P)* A plan supported by drawings and written report that provides the implementation details of a project and includes (i) land use, (ii) subdivision of land with all dimensions, (iii) infrastructure plans with all engineering details and dimensions, (iv) estimated cost of each component and the total cost, (v) sources of finances and cost recovery.

Deterministic Model: *(TQ)* A model that provides a fixed relationship between the variables.

Developed Area: *(P)* see *Developed Land.*

Developed Countries: *(P)* Countries having a high level of industrialisation and economic well-being.

Developed Land: *(P)* A land area in an urban centre that has been equipped with basic network of infrastructure such as roads, water supply, sewerage, drainage, electricity and roadside plantation, also *Developed Area,* see also *Land Development.*

Developer: *(P)* A person, company, association or body, agency, national or international who has an appropriate license to be engaged in the process of real estate development including land assembly, mobilisation of resources, site development, construction of buildings, and share / sale of developed plots or built space as per conditions laid in the license: also *Promoter.*

Developing Country: *(P)* Countries that are generally dependent upon agriculture economy and are in the process of further economic development and improvement in quality of life of their people through industrialisation and other approaches.

Development Aid: *(F)* Aid given by one country to another for support or furtherance of development and includes financial grants, technical advice, and capacity building measures.

Development Assistance: *(F)* Assistance given by a country to a developing country for long-term development purposes.

Development Bank: *(F)* A financial institution set up specifically for mobilising and chanelising medium and long-term capital into the private sector of a country's economy and development.

Development Charges: *(F)* Charges levied to recover the cost of providing new services and infrastructure in an area.

Development Corridor: *(P)* see *Corridor.*

Development Impact Exaction: *(F)* In USA, a widely used system of mobilisation of funds for financing augmentation of city level facilities and services as a result of new development where the developer of such new development pays and recovers the amount as a part of the sale price.

Development Mission: *(P)* A task to accomplish a defined vision, goal or function, by a group or organisation, also *Mission.*

Development Plan: *(P)* (a) As per planning reforms, a medium-term – 5 years – plan, conceived within the framework of the approved perspective plan, providing the comprehensive proposals for socio-economic and spatial development of a nation / state / region / district / city as the case may be, indicating the manner in which the use of land and development therein shall be carried out by the development authorities and other agencies (b) A master plan of an area prepared under an Act, see *Master Plan.*

Development Vision: *(P)* A perception of the future pattern of development based upon anticipated changes, dreams and aspirations that inspires further planning interventions, also *Goals, Vision.*

Development: *(M)* (a) Spatially, a process of change in physical conditions and quality of life of people in an area, initiated by spatial planning interventions (b) Economically, a product of planned investment in various sectors of economy and the resultant economic welfare of the people, (c) Socially, a process of change in the society caused by impact of socio-economic and physical changes on the behavior, attitudes and beliefs of the people.

Developmental Impulse: *(P)* The force of development emanated by a metropolis.

Devolution of Power: *(A)* Transfer of administrative, planning and implementation-related powers from state government to panchayats and municipalities.

Dhaba: *(P)* In Hindi, a way side eating place.

Dhallao: *(S)* In Hindi, an enclosed space, covered or open to sky, for collection of garbage from houses before its onward transportation to the sanitary land-fill site.

Dharamshala: *(H)* In Hindi, a building, normally located near religious places or hospitals where rooms are let out for short duration on no-profit basis.

Dhobi Ghat: *(P)* in Hindi, a place equipped with facilities for cleaning and drying of clothes by washer men.

Diagramming: *(TQ)* A participatory technique to find perception of the respondents pertaining to an issue or a problem expressed in the form of sketches and maps prepared by them independently without any assistance following a given colour code, very simple symbols, and notations.

Dial-a-ride: *(T)* see *Demand-responsive Transit Service.*

Dialogue: *(TQ)* A technique of survey through the processes of semi-structured interview with the respondents where a precise record of discussion is maintained in written and or electronically recorded audio-visual form.

Digitise: *(TQ)* In GIS, (a) To encode geographic features in digital form as x, y coordinates, (b) The process of using a digitiser to encode the locations of geographic features by converting their map positions to a series of x, y coordinates stored in computer files.

Dilapidated Buildings: *(H)* see *Dilapidated Housing.*

Dilapidated Housing: *(H)* Dwellings that are unsafe for occupancy due to decay caused by age, neglect or misuse, also *Dilapidated Buildings.*

Directing Function: *(A)* An act that deals with stimulation and motivation of the personnel to perform the desired actions in accordance with the predetermined objectives, plans and procedures, also see *Management.*

Disabled: *(M)* A person having physical impairment or defect that reduces ability to lead a fruitful daily life and may cause temporary or permanent incapacity for work, also *Handicapped.*

Disadvantaged: *(M)* A person or group that is underprivileged, due to social or economic reason, to have a desirable quality of life.

Disaggregation: *(M)* (a) Break up of data into sub sets, (b) Functional separation of the vertically integrated establishment into smaller, divisions, and units having their own vertical hierarchy with divisional / unit heads.

Disaster Mitigation: *(P)* In case of disaster, the precautionary, legal, administrative, and planning measures taken to minimise the loss of lives and properties, also *Pre-disaster Planning.*

Disaster Preparedness: *(P)* State of readiness, in a coordinated, timely, and effective manner, to cope with disaster by educating people and relief groups, and allocating funds where disaster occurs frequently.

Disaster Relief: *(P)* An organised system of provision of assistance to victims of a disaster after its occurrence and includes supply of food, medicine, tents and information.

Disaster: *(P)* Any natural or man-made event such as earth quake, drought, flood, fire, hurricane, tornado, tidal wave, explosion, and epidemic, causing misery, suffering, distress, and / or loss to life and property.

Disaster-prone Area: *(P)* Areas susceptible to disasters such as high density areas, slums, heavily settled flood plains, hazardous industries, and storage areas of hazardous substances.

Disbursement: *(F)* Payment made to settle debts or account payable.

Discharge: *(E)* The accidental or intentional spilling, leaking, pumping, pouring, emitting, or dumping of hazardous waste into or on any land or water.

Disclaimer: *(P)* The rejection, refusal, or renunciation of a claim, power or property.

Disincentive: *(T)* The programs, policies, and measures that are aimed at discouraging a specific type of action or activity.

Dispensary: *(P)* A health-care facility providing medical advice and medicines to patients suffering from illness, disease or injury and managed generally by a public body or charitable institution on non-commercial basis.

Dispersal: *(P)* (a) In regional planning, a process of geographical spread of existing and new activities from regional-core of a large city into the existing or new settlements located in its regional-periphery or in another region depending upon their potential and propensity, (b) In urban planning, a process of geographical spread of existing economic, administrative and / or social activities located in a large city into its periphery / fringe areas because of market forces or by planned intervention.

Dispersed Settlements: *(P)* A pattern of habitat development that is in isolated patches and such pattern may be evolved naturally in hill areas or villages, or may be as a result of a planned intervention, also *Fragmented Development.*

Disposal Facility: *(E)* A facility on land, underground, or under water, as the requirement may be, where waste (including hazardous waste) is intentionally placed after taking all safety precautions and where it will remain after closure.

Dissertation: *(ET)* A guided research and discussion, generally by an individual student, conducted during the final phase of a course of study, and submitted, in the form written report, for the award of a degree from an university, see also *Thesis, Terminal Project.*

Dissolve: *(TQ)* In GIS, the process of removing boundaries between adjacent polygons that have the same values for a specified attribute.

Distance Learning: *(ET)* A system of learning, away from the traditional face-to-face, chalk-and-talk or teacher-led format, where a candidate registered with an 'open university', staying at home, uses a self-study format with assistance of study materials sent by post by the university in the form of books and computer floppies or CD and instructions given through internet and special television programmes, also *Open Learning.*

Distribution System: *(P)* The system of delivery of a commodity, product or service to the retail customer's home or business.

District Park: *(P)* A park having 25 to 40 ha. area serving the active recreational needs of about 3 to 5 lakh population and may include theme park, children play area, play ground, water park, food court and related infrastructure including parking.

District Shopping Centre: *(P)* In a metropolis, a second tier commercial centre serving a population of 300,000 to 500,000 accommodating retail commercial, offices, hotels, restaurants, cinema, banquet halls, socio cultural centre, police station, fire station, electric sub-station, telephone exchange, post office, petrol stations, bus terminal and related infrastructure including multi-level parking.

District: *(M)* (a) An administrative division of a state managed by a District Collector, (b) A planning unit in a large city or metropolis serving a population of 300,000 to 500,000 with a district centre serving as its core and further divided into 3 to 5 communities (see *Community – c*), (c) An area where there is a large concentration of a specific type of activity such as business district having concentration of commercial activities, recreational district, airport district etc., (d) In urban design, districts are residential, commercial, or socio-cultural zones of a city that are immediately identifiable, with local names, by the inhabitants and provide the mental picture of the city the moment their name is pronounced e.g. Karol Bagh (commercial district) – reminds of Delhi, Bhindi Bazar (commercial) – Mumbai, Soho (commercial) – London, Harlem (residential) – New York.

Domain: *(TQ)* In GIS or any other database, the set of allowed values for a table column, for example all positive integers.

Domestic Help: *(P)* see *Domestic Servant.*

Domestic Servant: *(P)* A person engaged in house work such as cleaning, washing utensils and clothes, cooking and others. also *Domestic Help.*

Domicile: *(P)* The place of one's home or permanent residence.

Donor: *(F)* A person, body or country, that makes a gift or provides fund as a grant to another.

Dormitory Town: *(P)* A sub-urban residential area, with necessary facilities and services, located on the fringe of a large city where a majority of residents commute to the city for work.

Double-frontage Plot: *(P)* A plot / site, other than a corner plot / site, having frontage on and accessible from two roads.

Double-frontage Site: *(P)* see *Double-frontage Plot.*

Doubling Time: *(D)* The number of years required for the population of an area to double its present size at the current rate of growth.

Down Payment: *(F)* Part payment made at the time of purchase of a property or any other commodity.

Down Zoning: *(P)* In USA, a popular term for an action that results in less-intense uses than previously permitted or de-densification of an area.

Downtown: *(P)* see *City Centre.*

Downward Transitional Area: *(P)* An area, which is characterised by essentially rural economy that is stagnating or declining.

Draft: *(P)* A document, report, design, or plan prepared for discussion, comments and suggestions of the client before its finalisation.

Drive-in-cinema: *(P)* A cinema with projection facilities and stalls for parking of cars and viewing the movie from the car including an auditorium for other audience.

Dust Bins: *(P)* A container places at strategic placed for collection of solid wastes.

Dwelling Unit: *(H)* A single self-contained house with independent access designed and constructed as an independent unit of a residential area.

Dwelling: *(H)* see *House*

Dyke: *(P)* Earth embankment constructed to confine water or prevent flooding.

Dynamic Model: *(TQ)* A mathematical model that has variables, which change with respect to time.

E

Earmark: *(F)* see *Allocate.*

Earnest Money: *(M)* A specified sum of money deposited by a contractor along with a tender document, as a security that he will execute the work after it has been awarded to him and in case of his refusal to do so, the amount will be forfeited.

Earning Power: *(F)* The financial capacity of a person to pay for buying an asset, see also *Purchasing Power.*

Earnings: *(F)* Money received from a person, institution, or agency for doing an agreed work or service.

Earthquake: *(G)* A natural phenomenon caused by a sudden rupture inside the earth's crust resulting in shaking or movement of its surface which results in damage to life and property depending upon its intensity measured on a 10 point Richter scale, see also *Quake.*

Earthquake Resistant Construction: *(TQ)* A construction based upon structural design that withstands the effect of earthquakes and provides safety to the people and the property.

Easement Right: *(L)* A right of an individual or public authority to make limited use of property of another person to gain access to his own property or to gain access to install or repair a utility.

Eco-city: *(P)* A city where socio-economic activities have been planned in harmony with environment and where the resultant spatial development is environmentally sustainable, economically vibrant, and aesthetically pleasing.

Eco-development: *(P)* A socio-economic and physical development, which is environmentally sustainable, also *Environment-friendly Development, Eco-friendly Development.*

Eco-friendly Development: *(P)* see *Eco-development.*

Eco-industrial Estate: *(P)* A designated industrial area, developed and managed in an eco-friendly manner where the industries share resources, effluent is treated in a common treatment plant, wastes are recycled and common facilities are jointly looked after, also *Industrial Park.*

Ecological Approach: *(P)* An approach to planning of an area where the conflict between environment and development is minimised.

Ecological Footprints of a City: *(E)* An accounting tool to measure the environmental sustainability of the growth of a city that assesses the amount of biologically productive land and water required to produce the nature's resources consumed by the city in a year and to assimilate the wastes generated using prevailing technology.

Ecology: *(E)* The study of complex relationship among the living organisms including human beings and their natural environment.

Eco-mark: *(E)* A recognised label for marking on a product, under notification of the Ministry of Environment and Forest (or any other authorised body), that provides it accreditation of being eco-friendly and meeting all the prescribed environmental criteria for that product.

Economic Activity: *(EC)* Generation and distribution of goods and services through activities of the primary (agriculture), secondary (manufacturing) , and tertiary (commerce and services) sectors of economy.

Economic Base: *(EC)* (a) In regional context, economic activity in a region that meets the requirements of other regions and contributes to state and national economy. (b) The goods and services produced in a region and exported to other regions form its economic base, (c) In the context of a city, goods and services produced in a city that meet the demands of other settlements, and contribute to state and national economy, form its economic base.

Economic Conditions: *(P)* (a) Economic status of an area identified through analysis of representative indicators indicating growth, recession, and equilibrium, (b) In regional context, economic status of different parts of a region identified through analysis of representative indicators presenting a comparative spatial pattern of growth, recession, and equilibrium in the region.

Economic Cooperation: *(P)* Cooperation between two or among many countries in matters pertaining the banking, industrial, trade, and commerce sectors.

Economic Growth: *(EC)* Pattern of growth of production and services in an area, region, or country.

Economic Indicators: *(TQ)* Factors used for analysis of spatial and temporal patterns of growth of economy of an area and include wages, price, profits, investment, unemployment and others.

Economic Planning: *(EC)* The process of directing the development of a region, state or country through implementation of fiscal policies and programmes and planned investment in all sectors of economy with a view to improve the quality of life of people, see also *Sectors of Economy.*

Economic Rent: *(H)* Rent of a property justified on the principle that the owner should not be at a loss and is calculated having regard to the cost of land, building, utilities and services, fittings and fixtures, loan repayment if any, repairs and maintenance, and depreciation.

Economies of Location: *(EC)* The attractiveness of a area or region to serve as a preferred location for industries, markets, and business establishments and includes factors like good access by different modes of transportation, access to market, raw materials, and support services, availability of skilled labour, cheap power, land, conducive tax regime and administrative procedure, and no law and order problems.

Economies of Scale: *(EC)* The phenomenon that, the average long-run per unit cost of a product decreases with increase in scale of its production, which in turn, increases the sales and also demand of the product, hence, more production and more profit.

Eco-region: *(P)* An area that is endowed with different landscape-zones with varying spatial patterns of ecosystems, see also *Ecosystem.*

Ecosystem: *(E)* An arrangement of living (plants and animals) and non-living (mountains and minerals) things and the forces (climate and wildfire) that influence them.

Ecosystem Management: *(E)* An approach to natural resource management that ensures productive and healthy ecosystems while addressing to social, economic, physical, and biological needs and values.

ECS: *(T)* see *Equivalent Car Space.*

Edge: *(LA)* In landscaping, the margin where two or more vegetation patches meet.

Edge Matching: *(TQ)* In GIS, an editing procedure to ensure that all features that cross the adjacent map sheets have the same edge locations.

Edges: *(UD)* In urban design, the linear elements of a city, both natural and man-made, including features such as sea or lake shoreline. river front, a major road, and a railway line that guide the pattern of a city and add to positive (good) or negative (bad) urban perception by the people depending upon their characteristics and individual experiences.

Effect of Plan: *(L)* The legal impact of an approved plan upon the property rights, investment decisions, and land value, also *Legal Force of a Plan.*

Effective Date: *(L)* The specific date on which an agreement becomes operative.

Efficiency: *(A)* (a) A quality of doing things right and on time, (b) Providing the desired results with the minimum of resources, (c) The ratio of output to input which should be more than one.

Egress: *(T)* A way out or exit.

Electric Crematorium: *(P)* A premises with facilities for consignment of the dead bodies into flames using an electric furnace.

Electricity Grid: *(S)* A high voltage grid of transmission lines connecting power stations in a country to sub-stations and finally to local networks serving consumers, also *National Grid.*

Emergency operations center: *(P)* A site or building from where the persons in charge of disaster management exercise direction and control in an emergency.

Emergency Procedures: *(P)* A plan of step by step actions to be taken by various agencies in pre, during and post disaster operations to commence immediately to prevent the loss of life and minimise injury and damage to property.

Eminent Domain: *(L)* The power to acquire any private property for a public purpose on payment of compensation to the owner as per Act.

Emission: *(E)* Any solid, liquid, or gaseous substance coming out of any chimney, duct, or fluc or any other outlet.

Enabling Legislation: *(L)* A law that empowers an authority, undertaking, or agency to perform certain assigned functions or take defined actions.

Encroachment: *(L)* Unauthorised occupation of someone's land or building by another person or group of persons.

Endangered Species: *(E)* A plant or animal that is in danger of extinction and, if not protected, will be lost forever.

Endogenous: *(TQ)* Appertaining to that which happens within a system or a model or a region, see also *Exogenous*.

Energy: *(S)* The power to work available in the form of mechanical, radiant, chemical, electrical, or muscular force.

Energy Conservation: *(P)* Measures to conserve energy consumption and include – use of public transport, energy efficient design of buildings, and such others.

Energy Efficiency: *(P)* Consumption of less energy/electricity to perform the same function.

Energy Efficient Design: *(P)* The design of buildings and appliances that use lesser energy in performing the desired functions without loss of efficiency.

Energy Efficient Technology: *(TQ)* The technology that uses energy-efficient principles and practices.

Enforcement: *(A)* The function of administration that ensures execution of the various rules and regulations relating to planning and development.

Entropy: *(TQ)* The state of balance of probability within a system.

Environment: *(E)* (a) Ambiance created by three elements - air, water and land and the interrelationship that exists among and between these three elements and human beings, other living creatures, plants, microorganisms and property, also *Natural Environment*, (b) The surroundings of the planet earth comprising air, water, land and things imbibed or embedded in the land, (c) The part of ambiance created by man-made buildings, structures, rendering of open spaces and other actions, also *Man-made Environment, Built Environment.*

Environmental Analysis: *(TQ)* An analysis of predictable long and short-term environmental effects of an action, development or policy on an area having regard to physical, biological, social, and economic factors.

Environmental Audit: *(E)* A systematic, documented, periodic, and objective evaluation of performance of environmental organisation, management system and equipments of an industry.

Environmental Impact Assessment (EIA): *(E)* An assessment of environmental effects of a proposed action or project with a view to according environmental clearance as required by Law, *also Environmental Statement, Environmental Impact Statement.*

Environmental Impact Statement: *(E)* see *Environmental Impact Assessment.*

Environmental Pollutant: *(E)* Any solid, liquid, or gaseous substance present, due to any process of substances, in such a concentration as may be, or tend to be, injurious to environment.

Environmental Pollution: *(E)* Presence of any environmental pollutant in the environment, see also *Environmental Pollutant.*

Environmental Statement: *(E)* see *Environmental Impact Assessment.*

Environment-friendly Development: *(E)* see *Eco-development.*

Equilisation: *(E)* The process of bringing about conformity to a common standard.

Equity: *(P)* (a) The principal of fair justice to all, (b) Provision of equal opportunity to all irrespective of their social or economic classes.

Equity Capital: *(F)* The money owned by the holders of ordinary shares of a company and is equal to the residual value of a company after deducting all outside (other than to shareholders) liabilities.

Equivalent Car Space: *(T)* A unit used to specify parking norms / requirements where one equivalent car space (ECS) is equivalent to one standard car and the other modes are converted into this unit depending upon their size and parking space requirements.

accordingly the ECS of a two-wheeler, bicycle, and a truck is 0.25, 0.10, and 3.00 respectively, also *ECS*.

Erosion: *(P)* The wearing away of the land surface by blowing wind or running water or ice.

Estuary: *(G)* The point where a river meets a sea and the mixing of fresh and seawater creates unique ecological conditions such as marshes and lagoons along with their rich bio-diversity.

Ethnic Group: *(H)* A group of persons of same race, cultural background and a sense of identity, which lives in a larger society as a sub-group.

Evacuees: *(H)* Group of persons displaced from a dangerous or disaster-prone area for safety or protection.

Evaluation: *(TQ)* (a) The study and analysis of the advantages and disadvantages of different alternatives of a policy, programme, project, plan, course of action, or land uses with a view to choosing the one that fulfils most of the physical, social and economic objectives, also *Project Appraisal, Project Evaluation, Evaluation of Plan, Evaluation of Land Uses* (b) The analysis of the performance of students or a training course.

Evaluation of Land Uses: *(TQ)* see *Evaluation.*

Evaluation of Plan: *(TQ)* see *Evaluation.*

Evergreen: *(LA)* A tree that remains green for most of the time of the year and sheds leaves slowly throughout the year.

Evict: *(L)* To remove a tenant from a property he occupies.

EWS: *(M)* economically weaker section (of society).

Exercise: *(ET)* A training activity aimed at improving performance of the participants.

Exogenous: *(TQ)* Relating to things outside a system or model or a region, see also *Endogenous.*

Exotic: *(LA)* A plant that is not native to the area where it is planted.

Expectation of Life at Birth: *(D)* The average number of years a child is expected to live at the time of birth if current mortality trends were to continue.

Expendable House: *(H)* A house designed in such a way that it can be expended further horizontally on the same floor or vertically on the roof top when such need arises due to increase in household size or income or both.

Expenditure: *(F)* Payment made or disbursed for buying goods and services.

Expert: *(P)* A person having special knowledge, skill and experience in a field who can form an opinion or render expert advice on matters he is invited or appointed to address.

Express Bus Service: *(T)* High-speed public transport service with a limited number of stops.

Expropriation: *(L)* (a) The compulsory transfer of land-ownership rights from private hands to public ownership, with or without compensation, (b) Confiscation of foreign property.

Extension of Building: *(H)* see *Alternations.*

Extension Services: *(ET)* Dissemination of information and technical training provided to the general public through special programmes organised by an institution.

Extensive Industry: *(P)* An industrial unit employing up to 50 to 500 (this figure may change depending upon local rules) workers.

Extensively Built-up Area: *(P)* A site where more than 50 per cent of its area is covered with buildings.

Extractive Industry: *(P)* Quarrying and crushing of stone or extracting sub-soil materials.

Extreme Poverty: *(EC)* A condition where the people live on earnings less than US $1 per capita per day (World Bank).

F

Façade: *(UD)* Generally the front face of a building with main entrance.

Façade Control: *(UD)* Regulations governing the design, colour scheme, display panels, and other characteristics of façade of buildings facing a street.

Facilitator: *(P)* In planning, an organisation or agency that makes it easier for people and private sector to participate and invest in the development process.

Facility: *(M)* (a) In environmental management, any location where the processes incidental to waste generation, collection, reception, treatment, storage and disposal are carried out e.g. sewage treatment facility, (b) Any location where safe storage of hazardous substances is provided, (c) In urban planning, a premises where health care, educational, socio-cultural and recreational activities take place.

Fair Grounds: *(P)* A multipurpose, centrally located, facility for a variety of short-duration socio-cultural, economic, and political functions.

Fair Market Value: *(EC)* A price at which a commodity can be sold, at the present time, between two unrelated persons not under any obligation to buy or sell.

Fallow Lands (Current): *(AG)* These are lands which have been sown previously but are not being sown at the time of reporting and such lands are taken as good as cultivated and therefore, included in the estimation of cultivated area.

Fallow Lands (other than Current): *(AG)* Lands which were taken up for cultivation but are out of cultivation (for reasons such as poverty of former, lack of water, unfavourable climate, or unremunerative returns from farming) for a period not less than one year and not more than five years.

Family: *(H)* A basic kinship unit comprising husband, wife and their children.

Family Cycle: *(H)* A cycle beginning with emergence of the family at marriage, increase in family size due to birth of children, departure from home of female children because of marriage and beginning of new family cycle at the new home, marriage of male children and beginning of new family cycle, old age of parents and death, and cycle continues. Housing needs increase or decrease with successive stages of the family cycle.

Family Income: *(EC)* The gross income from all sources of all the earning members.

FAO: *(M)* see *Food and Agriculture Organisation.*

FAR: *(P)* see *Floor Area Ratio.*

Fare: *(T)* The money to be paid by a passenger to travel by a public transit.

Farm House: *(P)* A farm, located in the green belt around a city, used generally for agriculture and allied activities where a dwelling unit of a specified size (e.g. 100 to 150 sq. m.) is also permitted.

Farming: *(AG)* An activity related to production of field and tree crops, raising of livestock, fishery, and growing of flowers.

Farmland: *(AG)* Land exclusively used for farming activity, see also *Farming.*

Fast Moving Traffic: *(T)* Refers to motor-propelled vehicles such as private cars, taxies, trucks, buses, auto-rickshaws, and motor cycles.

Fauna: *(E)* The animal life of an area.

Feasibility Study: *(P)* A study conducted to assess the financial, economic, technical and physical viability and environmental sustainability of a project or course of action before its actual implementation, also *Pre-investment Survey, Pre-investment Study.*

Feature Class: *(TQ)* In GIS, a classification describing the format of geographic features, such as point, arc, node, route-system, route, section, polygon and region, and the supporting data in a coverage.

Fee: *(M)* An amount of money paid by a client to a consultant for the services rendered by him, also *Remuneration.*

Feedback: *(M)* Communication of the response or reaction to a project or event back to its initiator for evaluation with a view to guiode the subsequent course of action.

Feeder Service: *(T)* The type of transportation connecting an activity area to the mass transportation system and includes walking, bicycling, motor bike/scooter, three-wheeler auto or cycle rickshaw, and automobile, also *Access Mode.*

Feeling Approach: *(A)* In decision-making, an approach where the decisions are based on highly personal considerations and feelings of the decision-maker about the problems and their solutions.

Fence: *(LA)* A barrier to set off the boundary of an area and to restrict visual or physical passage in or out of it, also *Screen.*

Fencing: *(LA)* Plant or construction materials used for provision of fences around an area.

Field Work: *(P)* On site, first-hand study, investigation or research of actual situation, conditions and views of the respondents.

Final Plot: *(P)* see *Land Pooling.*

Financial Affordability: *(M)* (a) Ability of a person to pay for acquiring a commodity, (b) In housing, it is expressed as the income of a person needed to pay the house rent or to pay installments of loan for buying a minimum dwelling unit.

Financial Institution: *(F)* Any organisation, authorised by a competent authority, to conduct business relating to finance and includes banks, trusts, building and loan associations, saving and loan companies and credit unions, also *Housing Finance Institutions.*

Financial Rate of Return: *(F)* In case of investment in properties, it is the ratio of annual net income or profit after deducting depreciation, to invested capital.

Financial Statement: *(F)* (a) A statement made in writing that provides summary of financial state of an organisation and includes assets, liabilities, and net worth, (b) A balance sheet and profit and loss statement of an organisation.

Financial Year: *(F)* A period of 12 months commencing from 1 April and ending on 31 March.

Financing: *(F)* Measures adopted to raise capital resources for implementation of a plan or project.

Finger Plan: *(P)* A pattern, generally of a large city, where development spreads along transportation routes radiating from the city core area, like fingers of a hand, with green areas developed in-between like wedges.

Finished Grade: *(LA)* The grade accomplished after landscape features are installed and completed as shown on plan as proposed contours.

Fire Regime: *(E)* The characteristics of fire in a given ecosystem, such as its frequency, predictability, intensity, and seasonality.

Fire Station: *(P)* A premises with all facilities and equipments including parking for fire-tenders and residential accommodation to essential staff.

Fire Wood: *(S)* Wood used for burning and generating heat energy, also *Fuel Wood.*

Five-year Plan: *(P)* see *National Plan.*

Fixed Guide-way Transit System: *(T)* A public transit system where the vehicles ply on a permanently fixed guide-way and include heavy rail, light rail, tram, monorail, sky car and others.

Fixed Rate Financing: *(F)* see *Fixed Rate Mortgage.*

Fixed Rate Mortgage: *(F)* A long-term mortgage loan with fixed term, fixed interest rate, and fixed monthly installment to be paid, also *Fixed Rate Financing.*

Fixed Route Transit: *(T)* A transit service that operates on a predetermined set route and time schedule.

Flat: (H) A complete dwelling unit, with independent entrance, for one household within a group housing complex containing similar such units, also *Apartment, Residential Flat.*

Flatted Factory: *(P)* A premises with multi-storeyed buildings comprising independently accessible rooms accommodating several factories and common services, generally producing non-hazardous products using non-polluting processes.

Fleet: *(T)* The group of vehicles belonging to a public transit system.

Flexible Work Hours: *(T)* A policy initiative to reduce congestion on road that allows employees the option of varying their starting and stopping times each workday without altering the total daily work-hours as per rules.

Floating FAR: *(P)* An additional FAR over and above the permissible limit, that can be permitted through a processes of public auction or any other method as publicly specified by the development authority/ local body, to any building located in a specified area where the infrastructure has been augmented and has a scope for permitting such additional built-up space.

Floating Zone: *(P)* In US, a zone that is flexible in terms of permissible densities, intensities and land uses and overall development design opportunities.

Flood Area: *(P)* see *Flood Zone.*

Flood Control: *(P)* Measures taken to prevent the damage to human life and property due to floods and include dredging, maintaining vegetation as groundcover, and construction of dams.

Flood Plain: *(P)* Area on either side of a river that is covered with water during periodic floods and gets fresh deposits of alluvial soil carried by rivers when flood water recedes.

Flood Zone: *(P)* Area inundated during floods, also *Flood Area.*

Floor Area Ratio: *(P)* The ratio of the gross floor area on all floors of a building to the area of the plot on which it is located and multiplied by 100, e.g. an FAR of 250 means that the gross floor area on all floors of a building can be 250 per cent of the area of the plot on which it is located, also *FAR* see also *Floor Space Index.*

Floor Space Index: *(P)* The ratio of the gross floor area on all floors of a building to the area of the plot on which it is located (and NOT multiplied by 100 as in case of FAR) e.g. a FSI of 2.5 means that the gross floor area on all floors of a building can be 2.5 times the area of the plot on which it is located, also *FSI,* see also *Floor Area Ratio.*

Flora: *(E)* The plant life of an area.

Flow Chart: *(TQ)* (a) A sequential diagrammatic representation of the interrelation of a series of processes, (b) A graphic presentation of an operational sequence.

Flush Toilet: *(S)* Sanitary facility with a device for its cleaning with water.

Flying Club: *(P)* A club with additional facility of training in flying a small aircraft / gliders and joy-riding on such flying machines. see also *Recreational Club.*

Focal Point: *(M)* (a) In urban design, a structure or an element of design serving as a point of attraction in an area and providing it a unique identity. (b) In planning, a point of concentration of socio-cultural and economic activities in a city, (c) In administration, a key person or organisation serving as a link between international and national or regional institutions.

Foliage: *(LA)* The collective leaves of a plant or group of plants.

Food and Agriculture Organisation: *(M)* A specialised agency, joined to the UN through special agreement, which works to improve agricultural productivity and food security, and to better the living standards of rural populations.

Footpath: *(T)* Paved or unpaved way for movement of pedestrians. also *Footway, Path, Pathway, Pedestrian Path, Sidewalk,. Walkway.*

Footway: *(T)* see *Footpath.*

Forecasting: *(TQ)* The technique of estimating the future conditions related to demographic and socio-economic characteristics, demand and supply of infrastructure, traffic volume etc.

Foreclosure: *(H)* Forfeiture of the property of a mortgagee on failing to meet the mortgage terms.

Foreground: *(LA)* The part of a scene or landscape that is nearest to the viewer's eye.

Foreign Aid: *(F)* Financial and technical assistance given by a donor country to a recipient country.

Foreign Mission: *(P)* A premises for office, housing, and other uses of a foreign mission / embassy / high commission as per regulations in this regard.

Forest Based Industries: *(P)* Industries, which depend upon the forests as the source of raw materials for production of goods such as lumber, veneer, plywood and paper.

Formal Organisation: *(A)* an organisation where the basic relationships like responsibility, authority and accountability, are predetermined by an Act establishing the organisation or the service rules or decisions of the management board and defined as: functions (for responsibility), powers (for authority), and expected results (for accountability).

Forum: *(M)* An assembly of people for discussion on a subject of common interest of the participants.

FPS: *(M)* The foot, pound and seconds system of weights and measures.

Fragmented Development: *(P)* see *Dispersed Settlements.*

Free Market: *(EC)* A market in which the forces of supply and demand are allowed to operate free of government regulation or other interference.

Freehold: *(H)* A property held by an owner free of any duty or ground rent with right to transfer it to one's heirs or sell.

Freeway: *(T)* A high speed divided highway intended to serve through traffic and long distance trips where there is full access control and grade separation at selected roads junctions.

Freight Complex: *(P)* see *Integrated Freight Complex.*

Freight Transport: *(T)* Movement of goods by means of common carriers.

Frequency of Service: *(T)* The number of vehicles on a route plying in the same direction and is expressed as the number of vehicles per hour passing a certain point on the route.

Fringe: *(P)* see *Urban Fringe.*

Fringe Area: *(P)* see *Urban Fringe.*

Fringe Parking: *(T)* A parking facility located adjacent to a major activity centre, generally a commercial area or city centre, supported by a transit service and pedestrian system, with a view to expanding the number of parking spaces and reducing congestion in the core of the activity centre.

Frozen Capital: *(F)* Capital invested in a project that has not yet started producing expected returns on the investment and is tied up so that transactions are restricted or impossible.

FSI: *(P)* see *Floor Space Index.*

Fun park: *(P)* A park designed and landscaped with all necessary infrastructure for entertainment in a variety of ways covering both indoor and outdoor activities.

Functional Assistance: *(F)* Assistance given by a donor country to a recipient country for a specific project under a specific programme or from specified fund.

Functional Association: *(P)* A functional relationship between two settlements that can be measured by the flow of people, commodities, and information between them.

Functional Plan: *(P)* A plan supported by written text and prepared with a focus on a specific function or component such as traffic and transportation, water supply, sanitation, redevelopment, education, health, tourism, trade and commerce, industries, or population assignment (in regional context).

Funding Gap: *(F)* Shortfall of funds to complete a project.

Fuzzy Tolerance: *(TQ)* In GIS, it is an extremely small distance used to resolve inexact intersection locations due to limited arithmetic precision of computers.

G

Gaming: *(TQ)* A method of simulation involving decisions and actions by people.

Gaon: *(P)* In Hindi, a village.

Gap Analysis: *(TQ)* A process of evaluation of the difference between the demand and supply of an activity at a given point of time, or between the current and future state of an activity, with a view to identify the action needed and resources required to bridge the gap, if any.

Garage: *(H)* A building or a portion thereof designed or used for parking or servicing / repairing or hiring and selling of vehicles, see also *Motor Garage and Workshop, Private Garage, Public Garage, Service Garage.*

Garbage Dump: *(S)* A designated site used for disposal of municipal solid waste.

Garbage: *(S)* Organic waste generated in handling, preparation, cooking and consumption of food.

Garden City: *(P)* (a) According to the original concept evolved by Ebenezer Howard: a small new town designed around a park in semi-circular pattern, surrounded by rural belt, for healthy living and industry, where the entire land is owned by the local body and is held in trust of the community. It was a total concept of integrated development, management and revenue generation to the local body to enable it to perform its functions efficiently. (b) As per later variations, a well planned and self-contained place of living and working having good accessibility and large open spaces where good qualities of both, urban and rural areas are available.

Garden House: *(H)* A summer house located at a place full of trees, water bodies and landscaped areas.

Garden Suburb: *(P)* A town located in outskirts of a city having a well-planned open layout and it may or may not have industries, also *Garden Village*.

Garden Village: *(P)* see *Garden Suburb*.

Garden: *(LA)* (a) An open space landscaped with trees, plants, flowers, water bodies, and other manmade elements of landscape for outdoor relaxation and pleasure, (b) A place for growing flowers, fruit trees, and vegetables, see also *Botanical Garden, Hanging Garden, Kitchen Garden, Ornamental Garden, Terrace Garden.*

Gas Gowdown: *(S)* A premises where cylinders of cooking-gas and other types of gases are stored taking appropriate safety precautions as required by regulations.

Gas Station: *(P)* (a) In USA, a petrol pump, (b) In India, a premises having facility for supply of CNG for vehicles.

Gas Supply System: *(S)* The entire system of transmitting gas through distribution network of pipelines from the source to storage facility and then to the consumers.

Gazette: *(P)* The official publication of the government containing public notices and events.

GDP: *(EC)* see *Gross Domestic Product.*

General Fertility Rate: *(D)* Number of live births per 1000 women in the reproductive age group (15- 49 years) in a given year.

General-purpose Lanes: *(T)* The lanes on a freeway that are open to all motor vehicles.

Geocode: *(TQ)* In GIS, the process of identifying the coordinates of a location given its address.

Geographic Information System: *(TQ)* A system for collecting, inputting, checking, processing, integrating, analysing, modeling, reporting and displaying all forms of geographically referenced information.

Geomorphic Processes: *(G)* Processes such as volcanic activity, running water, and glacial action that change the form of the earth.

Geomorphology: *(G)* The study of the relief features of the earth's surface.

GIS: *(TQ)* see *Geographic Information System.*

Global Positioning System (GPS): *(TQ)* A system comprising a constellation of 24 satellites orbiting the Earth that makes it possible, with the help of a GPS receiver held by a person, to calculate his geographic position.

Global Program or Activity: *(M)* A specialised and focused global program or activity like humanitarian assistance, economic growth, or poverty alleviation etc., that takes place across various countries and is initiated by a world body like the UN, the World Bank, the World Health Organisation or such others, which extends financial support for their implementation.

Global Warming: *(E)* Warming of the planet earth by trapping of its heat, due to rapid accumulation of Carbon-di-oxide and other greenhouse gases in the atmosphere.

Glossary: *(M)* A partial dictionary of terms used for a specific purpose.

GNP: *(EC)* see *Gross National Product.*

Goal-achievement matrix: *(TQ)* A technique of evaluation in which performance or cost-benefit of a plan, policy, or project is assessed in the context of accomplishment of its goals and objectives.

Goals: *(P)* Broad and general statements, that highlight the vision and development approach which direct further planning and implementation efforts, see also *Development Vision, Vision.*

Golf Course: *(P)* A premise developed as a place for playing golf and may have a club building and related infrastructure including parking.

Government: *(A)* The system that has authority to govern a country and comprises three arms: the legislature – to make laws, the administration – responsible for implementation of the laws, and the judiciary – to protect the laws and ensure justice.

Gowdown: *(S)* see *Warehouse.*

Grace Period: *(P)* An extended period of time during which a consultant / contractor or any other person or body may complete the agreed task or pay an overdue premium without causing any breach of agreement / contract or penalty.

Grade Separation: *(T)* The vertical separation of an intersecting transportation route (road, railway, waterway) to prevent conflicts, delays, and accidents.

Grade: *(P)* see *Slope.*

Gradient: *(M)* The degree of slope of land, pipe invert or road as compared with horizontal.

Grading: *(LA)* Movement of earth to accomplish the form of contours as per landscape design.

***Gram Sabha*:** *(P)* In Hindi, the general body comprising all persons of voting age living in a village.

Gram: *(P)* In Hindi, a village.

Grant: *(F)* A financial assistance, given by a country or government body to another, in the form of money to carry out an approved project or activity.

Graph Theory: *(P)* According to the theory, a hierarchy of cities may be reduced to an abstract network of points and lines where points represent cities and lines indicate functional association among them.

Grasses: *(LA)* Plants that characteristically have joint stems, sheaths and narrow blades.

Grassroots: *(P)* (a) The common people as the originators of political feelings, national character, cultural forms or citizen participation, (b) In the national or regional context, the local area, village or town.

Grassroots-up Procedure: *(P)* A procedure where, following a set of guidelines, basic plans are prepared at the grassroots-level (local areas, villages, and towns) and are aggregated step by step at the next higher levels (district, state, nation) to form the plans at the respective levels (district plan, state plan, national plan), also *Bottoms-up Procedure.*

Gray Scale: *(TQ)* A monochromatic strip of shades ranging from white to black with intermediate shades of gray.

Green Area: *(LA)* see *Open Spaces.*

Green Belt: *(P)* An area of land predominantly agriculture in use, located around the proposed urbanisable limit of an urban area with a view to controlling its growth, preserving neighbouring towns from merging into one another or to preserve special character of a town, also *Green Girdle, Park Belt.*

Green Building: *(E)* Buildings designed and constructed having environmental considerations in mind especially energy and water efficiency, elimination of the use of harmful building materials, minimisation of construction waste, and reduction of operation and maintenance costs.

Green Corridor: *(LA)* A network of large undisturbed natural or landscaped land areas connected by designated pathways for the movement of pedestrians and may allow cycles.

Green Girdle: *(LA)* see *Green Belt.*

Green Industry: *(E)* An industry that uses processes or produces effluents, which are non-polluting and are not included in the red or orange industrial category, see also *Classification of Industries-(d).*

Green Wedge: *(P)* An area of land, predominantly agriculture in use, designed as a wedge, penetrating the city to serve the built up area on its either sides as a planned open space.

Greening of Wastelands Programme: *(P)* A programme under 10th Five Year Plan with basic thrust on distribution of government waste land to communities or landless rural poor and provide the allottees financial assistance for its improvement and growing of tree crops suitable to agro-economical zones, medicinal plants, bamboo, bio-fuel and other plants varieties that suit food and nutrition requirements.

Greenways: *(LA)* Areas of protected open spaces provided for recreation, transportation and conservation purposes, that follow natural and manmade linear features and link ecological, cultural heritage and recreational amenities with pedestrian paths.

Grid Plan: *(P)* see *Grid-iron Pattern.*

Grid: *(TQ)* In GIS, a geographic data model representing information as an array of equally sized square cells, referenced by their respective geographic x, y locations, and arranged in rows and columns.

Grid-iron Pattern: *(P)* An urban pattern where every street crosses another at right angles, also *Grid Plan, Chequer Board Plan, Rectangular Plan.*

Gross Domestic Product: *(EC)* The market value of total output of final goods and services produced within a country, during a financial year, regardless of the ownership of the factors of production involved, i.e., local or foreign. It does not include earnings from capital invested abroad (mostly interest and dividend receipts), but includes earnings on capital, owned by foreigners, located in the country, also *GDP.*

Gross National Product: *(EC)* The market value of total output of final goods and services produced by a nation's factors of production, regardless of location of those factors, i.e., in the country or abroad, during a financial year. It includes earnings from capital owned by nationals but located abroad (mostly interest and dividend receipts), but excludes earnings in the country by factors owned by foreigners, also *GNP.*

Gross Residential Density: *(P)* The number of persons per unit area (hectare or acre) of a residential sector including area devoted to the sector-level facilities, services, commercial activity, parks, open spaces, and roads and this is generally double the overall density as about 50 per cent area of a settlement is devoted to non- residential uses, see also *Overall Density.*

Ground Control Points: *(TQ)* Reference points on ground, obtained through ground survey, to control and correct distortion of remote sensing images.

Ground Cover: *(LA)* Planting material that forms a carpet of low height.

Ground Coverage: *(P)* see *Covered Area.*

Ground Fire: *(E)* A forest-fire that burns along its floor and does not affect trees with thick bark or high crowns.

Ground Lease: *(L)* Legal document for rental of land over a specified number of years generally 33 to 99 years.

Ground Pollution: *(E)* Contamination of soils as a result of air pollution (excess sulphur), disposal of industrial effluents, excessive use of pesticides, insecticides, and herbicides, also *Soil Pollution.*

Ground Rent: *(H)* The rent paid for the long-term lease of land.

Ground Resolution: *(TQ)* Size of the smallest object, in metre, that can be seen or detected by the sensors on a remote sensing satellite.

Ground Survey: *(TQ)* A survey made by ground methods as distinguished from an aerial survey.

Ground Water: *(S)* The water under the earth's surface in an aquifer or in the soil, water of a spring or a shallow well.

Groundwater Recharge: *(S)* A system of augmentation of groundwater through the natural processes or a man-made system.

Group Discussion: *(ET)* An interactive learning technique where the participants, under the guidance of the trainer or moderator, develop most of the ideas, thoughts, questions and answers through discussion among them.

Group Housing: *(H)* A housing developed by a group of individuals, forming a cooperative society under the Societies Act, where the dwelling units are individually owned and the land and common spaces are jointly owned and managed on a pro rata basis.

Group Open Space: *(H)* An open space, around which the plots or dwelling units are grouped in a housing cluster, that is common to all and each dwelling has a right of its use and responsibility to maintain it.

Growth Centre: *(P)* see *Growth Pole.*

Growth Point: *(P)* see *Growth Pole.*

Growth Pole: *(P)* (a) As per original concept by Perroux, growth poles are centres or foci in abstract economic space from which centrifugal forces emanate and to which centripetal forces are attracted, (b) In regional planning, growth poles are centres located in geographical space where, depending upon its propensity and potential, a variety of socio-economic activities concentrate providing market for farm produce and employment and emit developmental impulse that supports further development of its influence area and in practice, a hierarchy of such centres, in descending order, is termed as *Growth Pole, Growth Centre, and Growth Point.*

Growth Rate: *(P)* Statistical estimate of the percentage increase or decrease in size of an entity or population of an areas in a given year.

Growth: *(P)* (a) A process of positive change, (b) Quantitative increase or expansion in size.

Guest House: *(H)* A building having suits of rooms for housing the staff of government, semi-government, public undertaking or private companies for a short duration.

Guidelines: *(P)* A statement issued by a government agency having authority or expertise in a given area specifying principles, procedures, practical suggestions for application in planning and development activities by the concerned departments, agencies, and individuals.

H

Habitable Room: *(H)* (a) Considering its function, a room occupied or designed for occupancy for the purpose of living, sleeping, eating, or studying and includes kitchen, if used as a living room, but. excludes bathroom, water-closet compartments, laundries, serving and storage pantries, corridors, cellars, attics and all other spaces not used frequently, (b) Considering health and safety aspects. a room for living having at least 9 sq. m. area and reasonable light and ventilation.

Habitat: *(M)* (a) A human settlement, (b) Any natural environment where plants and animals live and grow, see also *Human Settlement.*

Hamlet: *(P)* A physically identifiable part of a dispersed village comprising a few households, see also *Dispersed Settlement.*

Handicapped: *(H)* see *Disabled.*

Handicraft Industry: *(P)* Production of goods, using manual technology, by the family members generally working within the house they live in.

Hanging Garden: *(LA)* A garden formed on terraces or over the other structures, also *Terrace Garden.*

Harbour: *(T)* A place with sufficiently deep water serving as a shelter for ships.

Hard Landscape: *(LA)* Inanimate components of landscape planning and design and include pavements, walls, benches, sculptures and the like.

Hardy Plant: *(LA)* Plant that can withstand harsh temperature variation, pollution, dust, extreme soil conditions, and has minimal water requirements.

Haveli: *(H)* In Hindi, a palatial traditional house.

Hawker: *(P)* A trader moving from place to place to sell small mercantile, also *Street Vender.*

Hazardous Building: *(E)* Any building or part thereof, where hazardous substances are manufactured, processed, stored, handled, or used.

Hazardous Chemical: *(E)* Any chemical which is liable to cause harm to human beings, and other living creatures, plants, microorganism, property or the environment.

Hazardous Site: *(E)* Any location where hazardous substances are manufactured, processed, stored, handled, used, disposed off and include the whole of the area under control of the occupier and includes piers, jetty or similar structure whether floating or not.

Hazardous Substance: *(E)* any substance or preparation that, by reason of its chemical or physico-chemical properties or handling, is liable to cause harm to human beings, and other living creatures, plants, microorganism, property or the environment.

Hazardous Waste Site: *(E)* A place, duly authorised by a competent authority, for collection, reception, treatment, storage, and disposal of hazardous wastes.

Hazardous Waste: *(E)* Any refuse generated from any source that has hazardous substance(s) categories of which are generally specified in the schedules of Hazardous Waste Management and Handling Act or Rules.

Head Post Office: *(P)* A building with related facilities used for administrative offices of the postal department as well as service area and collection and distribution of post from various post offices under its jurisdiction.

Health Care Establishment: *(E)* Any hospital, nursing home, clinic, diagnostic centre, clinical laboratory, irrespective of its size or bed strength.

Health Care Facilities: *(P)* The premises where health care service are located e.g. hospitals, clinics, nursing homes, pharmacies, and training centres for health workers.

Health Centre: *(P)* A building, having up to 30 (this number may vary) beds with all necessary facilities and services, providing general health-care and family welfare facilities including observation, care, treatment to indoor patients and consultation to outdoor patients suffering from illness, disease or injury and managed by a public body or private institution on non-commercial basis.

Health Resort: *(P)* see *Resort.*

Hearing Disabilities: *(P)* Deafness or hearing deficiency in individuals making them insecure in public places.

Hedge: *(LA)* A row of shrubs or small trees planted closely together that can be pruned to various shapes or allowed to grow to assume its natural shape, also *screen.*

Heir: *(L)* A person entitled by law to inherit part or all of the estate of an ancestor who died without leaving a valid will.

Herb: *(LA)* Annual plants that have high medicinal value.

Herbal Garden: *(LA)* An area landscaped using herbal plant material.

Heritage Zone: *(P)* An area where a group of two or more properties having historical, architectural, archeological, or cultural value are located and, which is designated as such in a development plan or layout plan for conservation.

Heterogeneous Town: *(P)* A large town with complex structure and multiple nuclei, performing a variety of functions and having diverse socio-economic classes.

Heuristic: *(TQ)* A procedure to deal with a complex situation based upon intuition and appropriate experience.

Hierarchy of Open Spaces: *(P)* In a descending order, the hierarchy of open spaces include national park, regional park, district park, neighbourhood park, local park and tot-lot see also *National Park, Regional Park, District Park, Neighbourhood Park, Local Park and Tot-lot.*

Hierarchy of Settlements: *(P)*, Ranking of human settlements in a region classified by population size, functions, and socio-economic importance ranging from megalopolis, metropolis, city, town, central village, and village or regional centre, sub-regional centre, service centre, central village, village.

HIG: *(P)* high income group.

High-density Zone: *(P)* A zone designated for development with intensive land use, high density of population, higher FAR and heavy investment.

High-occupancy Toll Lane: *(T)* On a toll-road, a lane designated for exclusive use by high-occupancy vehicles where a lesser toll rates will be charged. It is a concept of using congestion or priority pricing on a toll facility by charging variable toll rates depending on the number of people in a vehicle and the time of day.

High-occupancy Vehicle Facility: *(T)* Any traffic management measure that gives priority to buses, vanpools, and carpools, including provision of HOV lanes, and park-and-ride.

High-occupancy Vehicle Lane: *(T)* A lane, on a freeway, highway, arterial street, or in a separate right-of-way, designated for exclusive use by high-occupancy vehicles for all or a portion of the day indicating with road signs such as 2+ (two or more passengers per vehicle), or 3+ (three or more), also *HOV-lane*.

High-occupancy Vehicle Network: *(T)* An incremental and coordinated planning, designing, implementing, and operating the network of HOV-lanes, park-and-ride facilities, transit services and facilities, see also *HOV-lane*.

High-occupancy Vehicle: *(T)* (a) A passenger vehicle carrying more than one person and allowed to ply on HOV-lanes, also *HOV*, see also *HOV-lane*.

High-rise Housing: *(H)* see *Multi-storey Housing*.

High-risk Areas: *(P)* Areas in a city that are vulnerable to disasters because of high concentration of population and / or economic activities, key communication installations, bridges, major transportation bottlenecks, and major defense installations.

Hill Resort: *(P)* see *Resort*.

Hinterland: *(P)* (a) Outlying areas or the region surrounding a city and supplying raw materials, manpower, and farm produce, (b) The area surrounding a sea port from where goods are sent for export or to which the imported goods are distributed.

Hire Purchase: *(H)* see *Lease Purchase*.

Historic Building: *(P)* A building having historical, architectural, archeological, or cultural value.

Historic Preservation: *(P)* Restoration of sites, monuments or buildings of historical, architectural, archeological, or cultural significance with a view to protect their past glory.

Historic Resources: *(P)* Sites, buildings, structures and/or objects, located in a city or region, having historical, architectural, archeological, or cultural value.

Historic Site: *(P)* An area having historical, architectural, archeological, or cultural value that is protected by Archeological Survey of India or needs to be protected by the local community or state government.

Historical Monument: *(P)* A place along with its structures that has historical significance.

Holding Capacity: *(P)* The maximum development potential of a site taking into account the land use and zoning regulations, existing and proposed infrastructure, and environment.

Home for Aged: *(H)* A facility providing lodging, boarding, custodial care, recreation, and limited medical care for elderly.

Home Ownership: *(H)* Ownership of one's place of residence.

Home: *(H)* An abode to which a person or family has a feeling of belonging, warmth and protection.

Home-based Trip: *(T)* trip generated from or destined to the traveler's home.

Homeless: *(H)* A person or household having no permanent shelter of any kind, also *Pavement Dweller.*

Homogeneous Town: *(P)* (a) A town that has a simple unified pattern of development which may be planned or unplanned indicating a natural growth, (b) A small town with one central area as its nucleus, or (c) A company town with one large place of work and simple unified pattern of development where a majority of people have the same occupation, see also *Company Town, Heterogeneous Town.*

Horizontal Exit: *(H)* A protected opening through or around a fire wall or a bridge connecting two buildings.

Horizontal Mixing of Land Uses: *(P)* On a single plot, a pattern of mixing where the different portions of the ground floor may have different uses e.g. shop in the front and residential use in the rear, see also *Mixed-use Zoning.*

Hospital: *(P)* A building complex, having more than 30 (this number may vary) beds with all necessary facilities and services, providing general or specialised health-care facilities including observation, care, treatment to indoor patients and medical advice to outdoor patients suffering from illness, disease or injury and managed by a public body or private institution.

Hostel: *(H)* A building having several rooms with independent access and attached or common toilet/bath as well as other facilities like dining and indoor recreational spaces for letting out a on long-term basis to students or other persons belonging to an institution or otherwise.

HOT Lane: *(T)* see *High-occupancy Toll Lane.*

Hotel: *(P)* A building having several rooms with independent access and attached or common toilet/bath with or without dining and other facilities and accommodating more than 15 (this figure may be changes depending upon the local rules) persons for short duration, on payment of room charges.

House Connection: *(S)* Connection of a residential property to the water, electricity and gas supply network as well as telephone service.

House Drain Combined: *(S)* see *Building Drain.*

House Drain Sanitary: *(S)* see *Building Drain.*

House Drain Storm: *(S)* see *Building Drain.*

House Drain: *(S)* see *Building Drain.*

House Improvement: *(H)* Rehabilitation of dwelling unit including additions and alterations.

House Maintenance: *(H)* Upkeep of dwelling unit to prevent progressive deterioration of the property.

House Rent Allowance: *(H)* A cash allotment given to workers by the government or private organisation as assistance in meeting their expenses towards payment of house rent.

House Sewer: *(S)* see *Building Sewer.*

House Sub-drain: *(S)* see *Building Sub-drain.*

House Trap: *(S)* see *Building Trap.*

House: *(H)* A self-contained building with independent access, intended exclusively for residential purposes for a single family or household, also *Dwelling*.

Household Industry: *(P)* A small-scale industry, operated from a house by one or more members of the household for production or for servicing and repairs of goods.

Household: *(H)* A group of persons, related or otherwise, living in the same dwelling and sharing meals and expenses related to housekeeping, see also *Institutional Household*.

Housing Allowance: *(H)* A cash allotment given to its workers by the government or any other organisation as assistance in meeting their expenses towards housing cost.

Housing Authority: *(H)* A state-level public body established under an Act and empowered to implement public housing policies and programmes especially for economically weaker sections of the society.

Housing Bank: *(F)* A financial institution set up, as per legal procedures, solely for mobilising savings and issuing loans for house building purposes.

Housing Cluster: *(H)* see *Cluster*.

Housing Code: *(H)* see *Building Bye-laws*.

Housing Complex: *(H)* A group of individual dwelling units or block of flats, planned built and managed as a unit by one agency that could be government or private body or cooperative society.

Housing Conditions: *(H)* General state of housing stock as measured by its age, quality, state of repairs and value.

Housing Cooperative: *(H)* A cooperative society or association of people, registered under an Act, that holds the title of land, constructs the dwelling units, gives to its shareholders the occupancy rights to the individual dwelling units and then may cease to exist or may be converted as the resident's welfare society, see also *group housing*.

Housing Economics: *(H)* Analysis of economic efficiency of housing policies, programmes and projects.

Housing Estate: *(H)* see *Housing Complex*.

Housing Finance: *(F)* The methods of mobilising the finances for construction or purchase of housing units.

Housing Management: *(H)* The processes of administering rental property and includes selection of occupants, rent collection, building maintenance, and tenant relations.

Housing Need Assessment: *(H)* The various methods of assessing the current and future housing needs, see also *Housing Need.*

Housing Need: *(H)* The additional housing units required to meet the existing and projected demands.

Housing Obsolescence: *(H)* Reduction in value, usefulness and desirability of houses in an area as a consequence of economic or technological changes (it does not refer to physical deterioration).

Housing Policy: *(H)* A series of financial, land-related and administrative measures undertaken by the government to bridge the gap between the supply and demand of housing stock, ensure access to shelter to all sections of the society especially the economically weaker sections, see also *Housing Programme, Housing Project.*

Housing Programme: *(H)* A specific plan of action to implement a specific component of housing policy, e.g. housing for economically weaker sections as EWS housing programme see also *Housing Policy.*

Housing Project: *(H)* A scheme for implementation of a housing programme at a specified location providing number of houses, location, design, specifications, cost estimates, sources of funds, recovery of funds, beneficiaries, allotment procedure and such other details, see also *Housing Policy.*

Housing Rehabilitation: *(H)* Restoration of housing in a blighted or dilapidated area by partial rebuilding and / or repairs to desirable standards.

Housing Requirement: *(H)* see *Housing Need.*

Housing Shortage: *(H)* The gap between the demand and supply of dwelling units of various types for different sections of the society.

Housing Standards: *(H)* The minimum acceptable level of size and quality of housing taking into account factors such as location (e.g. hills), income of households, local traditional construction methods, climate, health and safety.

Housing Stock: *(H)* The total quantity of housing units, irrespective of condition, legal status, or compliance to norms and standards, existing in a housing market area at a given point of time.

Housing Supply: *(H)* The number of dwelling units of various types available in a given area, at a given point of time, for sale or rent.

Housing Survey: *(H)* Collection of information regarding housing stock such as its quality, size, occupancy, ownership, and rental structure.

Housing Unit: *(H)* see *Apartment.*

Housing: *(H)* The total physical environment within and outside the house where families and households live and includes houses and all necessary utilities, community facilities, park, playground, and roads. In low income group housing accommodating households engaged in same or similar occupation, a common place of work is also included as an integral part of housing.

Housing-finance Institution: *(F)* see *Financial Institution.*

HOV: *(T)* see *High-occupancy Vehicle.*

HUDCO: *(F)* Housing and Urban Development Corporation.

Human Resource: *(P)* A pool of persons, skilled or unskilled, available to fill the labour needs.

Human Settlement: *(P)* A place, rural or urban, where people live, work, raise family and fulfill their physical, spiritual and intellectual needs and where, depending upon its hierarchy in the national or regional system of settlements, a variety of activities, facilities and services are located.

Hut: *(H)* A building principally constructed in wood, mud, thatch, or other temporary materials.

Hydrology: *(TQ)* The science dealing with the study of water on the surface of the land, in the soil and underlying rocks, and in the atmosphere.

I

ITS: *(T)* see *Intelligent Transport Systems.*

IAEA: *(M)* see *International Atomic Energy Agency.*

ICAO: *(M)* see *International Civil Aviation Organisation.*

Idle Land: *(P)* A parcel of land not being used for any purpose.

IFAD: *(M)* see *International Fund for Agricultural Development.*

IGP: *(P)* see *Interim General Plan.*

ILFS: *(F) Infrastructure Leasing and Financial Services.*

Illiterate: *(D)* (a) A person who can merely read but cannot write, (b) A person who can neither read nor write, (c) A child of age below seven years.

ILO: *(M)* see *International Labour Organisation.*

Image Enhancement: *(TQ)* The manipulation of image density or image digital data to highlight its certain features so that they can be more easily seen.

Image of a City: *(UD)* The physical structure of a city as visualised by people through the impact of five elements, as given by Kevin Lynch, which include paths, edges, districts, nodes, and landmarks, see also *Paths, Edges, Districts, Nodes, Landmarks.*

Image: *(TQ)* The recorded representation of an object produced by optical, electro-optical, optical mechanical, or electronic means.

IMF: *(M)* see *International Monetary Fund.*

IMO: *(M)* see *International Maritime Organisation.*

Impact Fee: *(F)* see *Development Impact Exaction.*

Implement: *(P)* To execute or carry out the provisions of a policy, plan, programme, project or scheme.

Implementation Objective: *(M)* A set of written statements that specify in quantitative terms the operational targets, within the framework of the operative principles, to achieve the goals or the vision, see also *Planning Objective.*

Implementation: *(P)* The process of execution or carrying out of the provisions of a policy, plan, programme, project or scheme, see also *Policy / Plan / Programme / Project / Scheme Implementation.*

Improvement: *(H)* see *Upgrade*, see also *Alteration.*

Inbound: *(T)* A trip destined towards city centre, CBD, or major activity centre.

Incentive: *(P)* A monitory or other kind of attraction, given by the government or a public or private agency, to incite or stimulate people to act towards achieving the set goals under a policy or programme, e.g. tax incentive to industrialists to set up industries in a specified area or a 20 per cent rebate incentive given by a municipality to those who pay property tax on time.

Inception Plan: *(P)* see *Conceptual Plan.*

Incinerator: *(E)* Any enclosed device for solid waste decomposition by burning using controlled flame combustion that neither meets the criteria for classification as a boiler nor is listed as industrial furnace.

Income Bracket: *(P)* A grouping of people by their income, e.g. high, medium, or low income groups (HIG, MIG, LIG), also *Income Group.*

Income Group: *(P)* see *Income Bracket.*

Income: *(F)* A one-time or recurrent gain, in the form of money or kind, derived from rendering a professional or other service, trade, business or investment.

Incompatible Waste: *(E)* A hazardous waste that is unsuitable for (i) placement in a particular device or facility, because it may cause corrosion or decay of containment material, (ii) mixing with another waste or material under uncontrolled conditions because this processes might produce heat or pressure, fire or explosion, violent reaction, toxic dust, mist, fumes or gases, or flammable fumes or gases.

Incorporation: *(P)* In city planning, combining separate urban areas and villages into one legal entity, e.g. annexation of peripheral villages into municipal limits while extending its urban limits.

Independent Cluster: *(H)* A housing cluster that is surrounded by vehicular roads and/or pedestrian paths on all sides, see also **cluster.**

Indicators: *(TQ)* Tools to diagnose the status of an activity they represent at a given point of time in the past, present or future, which assists in policy formulation, preparation of action plan and setting up of targets as well as their implementation and monitoring.

Indigenous Building Materials: *(H)* Building materials such as clay, bamboo, stone that exist naturally in a given area.

Indigenous Housing: *(H)* A house design, material used and construction method that are native to a given area.

Indigenous Species: *(E)* Any species of wildlife, which is native to a given land or water area by natural occurrence.

Indigenous Technology: *(TQ)* Technology evolved in an area based upon native traditions and natural and human resources.

Indigenous: *(E)* Native to a given land.

Indoor Stadium: *(P)* A place used for indoor games and gymnastics with pavilion and other structures for seating spectators and having parking, public toilets, and changing rooms for players.

Industrial Cluster Development Scheme: *(P)* A scheme of the 10th Five Year Plan to make strategic interventions in existing high growth-potential industrial clusters with a view to (i) convert static local efficiency into dynamic competitiveness through creating conducive climate for development of inter-firm cooperation, (ii) promotion of innovative and collective learning, (iii) creation of infrastructure support and services network, (iv) setting up common facilities, (v) assisting appropriate technology transfer, (vi) information sharing, and (vii) quality improvement.

Industrial Decentralisation: *(P)* Process of shifting industries located in a city from its centre or other congested areas or non-conforming zones to other places in its periphery or its influence region.

Industrial Estate: *(P)* An area designated for location of a variety of different types and sizes of industries and planned accordingly with all necessary infrastructure and developed and managed by a public and / or private agency.

Industrial Land Use: *(P)* The use of a parcel of land, where process of manufacturing and related activities are being carried out (existing industrial land use) or will be permitted in future (proposed industrial land use).

Industrial Park: *(P)* see *Eco-industrial Estate.*

Industrial Plot: *(P)* A plot designated in a layout plan for industrial activities.

Industrial Pole: *(P)* A growth pole (existing or proposed) which has / provides a conducive conditions and attractive location for concentration of industries as the main economic activity.

Industrial Policy: *(P)* A government policy for promotion and regulation of industrial development in the country /state, also *Industrialisation Policy.*

Industrial Pollution: *(E)* Release into any environmental medium – air, water or land – from any industrial process, which are capable of causing harm to man or any other living organism supported by environment.

Industrial Sector: *(EC)* The sector of economy contributing to development and employment generation comprising manufacturing of products, machines and consumer goods.

Industrial Waste: *(E)* Residue or by-products of an industrial process that may contain in-organic, non-biodegradable and polluting substances such as metals, plastics, liquids, gases, and chemicals.

Industrialisation Policy: *(P)* see *Industrial Policy.*

Industry: *(P)* Carrying out of any manufacturing process.

Infant Mortality Rate: *(D)* Ratio of the number of infant deaths (deaths of children below one year) per 1000 live births during that year.

Infill Development: *(P)* Further development, in an already developed area having access to urban services, covering vacant or underutilised plots as per bye-laws.

Infiltration: *(S)* see *Percolation.*

Informal carpool: *(T)* A composition of passengers in a carpool that is random and varies each time a trip commences. also *Casual Carpool, Instant Carpool.*

Informal Housing: *(H)* see *Jhuggi-jhopri.*

Informal Organisations: *(A)* Unofficial organisations formed, within an organisation, as a consequence of social interaction and informal relationships among the people working in the office, because of their desire to socialise, effort to minimise the psychological fatigue of routine job in the office, or desire to escape from the work environment when their capabilities exceed those needed by the job.

Informal Sector: *(EC)* The sector of economy where the labour force is self-employed with family support, in economic activities such as trading and street vending that do not have any formal structure and designated areas, and is characterised by small scale, labour-intensive operation, also *Parallel Economy,* see also *Marginal Economic Sector.*

Informal Shop: *(P)* A shop generally without roof, stationary or mobile, located along road sides, legally under *tehbazari* system or illegally, and selling goods in retail and services see also *Tehbazari.*

Informal Training: *(ET)* Training that occurs on the job and often is accomplished through personal instruction, general guidance from a supervisor or even observing coworkers.

Infrastructure: *(P)* The basic components of a human settlement that make it functional and improve its quality of life and include network of water supply, sewerage, drainage, electricity, communication, transportation, and facilities and services, see also *Facilities, Services.*

Ingress: *(T)* A way in or entry.

Inhabitant: *(P)* (a) A person who is a domicile of the place by birth, (b) A person who has a permanent house at the place for living.

Inland Transport: *(T)* Mode of transport, such as container trolleys, trucks and goods train, dedicated to goods arriving by sea for inland distribution.

Inland: *(P)* see *Land Ward.*

Inner City: *(P)* The central part of a city generally characterised by old age of buildings with congestion, poverty and deteriorating environmental conditions.

Inner Liner: *(E)* A continuous layer of material placed inside a tank or container that protects the construction material of the tank from the contained waste or reagents used to treat the waste.

Innovation: *(TQ)* New ideas introduced, as a result of research, observation, discovery or invention, in the existing conditions, systems, technology, processes, or products as the case may be, also *Technological Innovation.*

Input: *(M)* Goods, services or information fed, into a system that could be industrial production, planning, policy-making or computing, with a view to achieving a desired output.

Input-output Analysis: *(TQ)* A method of deriving knowledge of relationships among various regions through transactions among them as physical outputs and inputs, output of one being the input to the other.

In-service Training: *(ET)* A training programme aimed at capacity building of the already employed workers with a view to improving their job performance.

In-situ Upgradation: *(P)* Provision of basic infrastructure in an unauthorised informal housing located on a project site with a view to recover the remaining portion of the site for implementation of the project and save on relocation cost and delays due to litigations.

Installment: *(F)* The part of payment of money for buying something, spread over a period of time as per conditions of loan or purchase document.

Instant Carpool: *(T)* see *Informal Carpool.*

Institution: *(P)* A society or organisation established, through law, or otherwise, for a specific purpose.

Institutional Framework: *(A)* A framework of interrelated institutions, organisation and agencies engaged in planning, development, and implementation of policies, plans, programmes, and projects in a particular field.

Institutional Households: *(D)* A group of persons, unrelated to each other, who commonly live together and take food from a common kitchen and include boarding houses, hostels, messes, rescue homes, orphanages, jails etc.

Institutional Plot: *(P)* A plot designated in a layout plan for activities performed by socio-cultural and non-profit institutions.

Integrated Freight Complex: *(P)* A strategically located premises. with access from both railway and a highway, comprising wholesale market, warehousing, truck terminal, railway station and other related uses and infrastructure with a view to facilitate integrated movement of goods by rail as well as road.

Integrated Plan: *(P)* (a) A plan that fits into the framework provided by governmental plans and programmes of different sectors and levels, (b) A plan that integrates the spatial development and investment initiatives having regard to environmental considerations, (c) A plan that is in concurrence with national and sectoral plans on the one hand and on the other, the local plans fit into its framework, (d) A regional plan that integrates the rural and urban development needs of an area.

Integrated Resource Planning: *(P)* A planning process and framework within which the costs and benefits of both demand- and supply of resources are evaluated to develop the least-total-cost mix of utility resource options.

Integrated Rural Development: *(P)* A process that integrates all rural development needs including agriculture and allied activities, roads, housing, schools, health care, infrastructure, employment, social justice, and environmental management in a coordinated manner.

Integrated School: *(P)* An institution located in a building or a campus of several buildings with or without hostel accommodation, managed by public or private institution, for offering education and play facilities for children in the age group of 6 to 17 years and having both primary and secondary level education from I to XII class / standard.

Intellectual Property Right: *(L)* see *Copy Right.*

Intellectual Property: A product of the intellect that has commercial value like computer software, research and consultancy results, books, paintings, and such others.

Intelligent Transport System: *(T)* A system that effectively utilises the advance technologies such as electronic identification, electronic positioning, and satellite based communication, navigation. and electronic information dissemination in operation, maintenance and safety of transport system including traffic monitoring and control, traffic information broadcasting, fleet management, dynamic route guidance, and automatic vehicle detection, classification, location, and navigation.

Intended Mixed Land Use: *(P)* An anticipated pattern of mixed land use, in a residential area, guided by a layout plan that specifies the location, type and quantum of mixing of various land uses.

Interconnectedness: *(TQ)* Refers to interconnection among settlements measured in terms of specific rate of flow of people, commodities, money, and information where higher flow indicates strong connection.

Interdisciplinary Expertise: *(P)* An expert who has knowledge, experience, or specialised skill in more than one area of pursuit.

Interdisciplinary: *(P)* Requiring contribution from more than one branch of knowledge, see also *Multidisciplinary.*

Interest-free Loan: *(F)* A loan where only the principal amount is payable.

Interim General Plan: *(P)* see *Outline Development Plan.*

Interior Plot: *(P)* see *Interior Site.*

Interior Site: *(P)* A site / plot having access by a narrow street / path which may or may not form part of the site / plot, also *Interior Plot.*

Interlocking Cluster: *(H)* Housing clusters joined at the back and on sides with at least one side of the cluster common and having some dwellings opening onto or having access from the adjacent cluster, see also *Cluster.*

Intermediate City: *(P)* Depending upon the size and function, it is a second or third order settlement in the system of urban centres in a region.

International Atomic Energy Agency: *(M)* An autonomous intergovernmental organisation under the ages of the UN, that works for the safe and peaceful use of atomic energy.

International Civil Aviation Organisation: *(M)* A specialised agency, joined to the UN through special agreement, for setting international standards for safety, security and efficiency of air transport, and serves as the coordinator for international co-operation in all areas of civil aviation.

International Conference Centre: *(P)* Complex of buildings designed and maintained with international standards and provided with all necessary facilities and services for conducting conference, meetings, seminars, symposium where the participants are from various countries.

International Fund for Agricultural Development: *(M)* A specialised agency, joined to the UN through special agreement, which mobilises financial resources to raise food production and nutrition levels among the poor in developing countries.

International Labour Organisation: *(M)* A specialised agency older than the UN itself, joined to the world body through special agreement, for formulating policies and programmes to improve working conditions and employment opportunities, and set labour standards used by countries around the world.

International Maritime Organisation: *(M)* A specialised agency, joined to the UN through special agreement, which works to improve international shipping procedures, raise standards and foster cooperation on copyrights, trademarks, industrial design and patents.

International Monetary Fund: *(M)* A specialised agency, joined to the UN through special agreement, which facilitates international monetary cooperation and financial stability and provides a permanent forum for consultation, advice and assistance on financial issues.

International Organisation: *(P)* An organisation in which the membership is open to the relevant bodies of all countries in the World.

International Telecommunication Union: *(M)* A specialised agency, joined to the UN through special agreement, which fosters international cooperation to improve telecommunications of all kinds, coordinates usage of radio and TV frequencies, promotes safety measures and conducts research.

Inter-regional Migration: *(P)* A pattern of migration where the movement of people is between two regions, see also *Migration*.

Inter-urban Transport: *(T)* Transport system that operates among different urban centres.

Interval Scale: *(P)* One of the two types of cardinal scale which provides graduated intervals without a fixed zero point e.g.

temperature scale here a temperature of 2 degree centigrade is not twice warmer than 1 degree, see also *Cardinal Scale, Rational Scale.*

Intra-regional Migration: *(P)* A pattern of migration where the movement of people is from within the region, see also *Migration.*

Intra-urban Transport: *(T)* Transport system that operates within an urban centre.

Intuitive Approach: *(A)* In decision-making, a processes that avoids rigorous analysis and evaluation and heavily depends upon the accumulated experience of the decision-maker and his intuition at the time of taking decision.

Inventory: *(M)* A detailed item-wise list of things.

Investment: *(F)* Use of capital in a project, business or shares with the expectation that it will yield profit or return of income.

Invitation Bid: *(P)* An advertisement, published in news papers, inviting bids for a particular project, or for supply of goods, or services, or sale of property by one who intends to receive such bids.

Irregular Pattern: *(P)* A settlement pattern where the streets are haphazard with varying width and direction having no dominant route or focal point.

Irreversible: *(P)* A process that cannot be reversed or a resource that is non-renewable such as minerals and archaeological sites.

ITU: *(M)* see *International Telecommunication Union.*

J

Jai Prakash *Rozgar* Guarantee *Yojana*: *(P)* A new pragmatic initiative of the 10th Five Year plan for providing both wage and self-help employment guarantee to unemployed in most distressed districts of India.

Jail: *(P)* A secured, enclosure with necessary buildings and facilities for detention, confinement and reform of prisoners under the law.

Jam: *(T)* A blockage of traffic flow due to overcrowding, encroachment or obstruction.

***Janta* Flat:** *(H)* A self-contained dwelling unit with independent entrance, for one poor-income or EWS household within a group housing complex containing similar units.

Jeep: *(T)* A light vehicle with high maneuverability in different terrains (derived from G.P. meaning for general purpose).

Jetty: *(T)* A pier used for embarking and disembarking passengers and / or loading and unloading of goods from boats /ships.

JFM: *(P)* see *Joint Forest Management.*

***Jhuggi-jhopri*:** *(H)* In Hindi, generally an unaûthorised informal dwelling unit constructed with temporary makeshift materials providing a very poor quality of life, see also *JJ Colony, Slum.*

***Jhuggy*-cluster:** *(H)* see *JJ Colony.*

Jitney: *(T)* A privately owned vehicle, which carries passengers and operates commercially on a fixed or semi-fixed schedule.

JJ Cluster: *(H)* see *JJ Colony* see also *JJ.*

JJ Colony: *(H)* A group of unauthorised *jhuggi-jhopris* located, on a site with or without basic services like drinking water, toilet, drainage and access roads, also *jhuggi cluster, JJ cluster,* see also *JJ, Jhuggi-jhopri, Slum.*

JJ: *(H)* see *Jhuggi-jhopari.*

Jobless: *(EC)* A person who is capable and seeking job actively but is currently unemployed.

Job-oriented Training: *(ET)* Training designed to improve the knowledge, skills and ability of a person to perform efficiently on the specific job he is engaged or likely to be engaged.

Joint Development: *(P)* A process where projects are implemented jointly through public-public or public-private partnership.

Joint Forest Management : *(P)* The 10th Five Year Plan initiative of forest management based on the principle of partnership and equity share.

Joint Ownership: *(H)* Common ownership of a property held jointly by two or more persons, each with equal interest and equal right with right of survivorship.

Joint Planning: *(P)* A process where the plan is prepared by a planning agency with active, transparent and open consultation with another relevant and interested public, private, national or international agency.

Joint Project: *(P)* A project involving two or more relevant and interested public, private, national or international agencies.

Joint Venture: *(P)* An grouping of two or more persons, firms or agencies, exclusively for the purpose of improving their combined financial and technical strength for undertaking a specific project and this association may cease to exist on completion of the project.

Journey: *(T)* Any travel from one point to another using any mode of transport.

JPRGY: *(P)* see *Jai Prakash Rozgar Guarantee Yojana.*

Judgment: *(L)* (a) The written order of a court of law, on a case, after hearing the arguments of all concerned parties and considering evidences presented, (b) A decision taken after due analysis of facts.

Judicial: *(L)* (a) Pertaining to a court of law, (b) Established by statute.

Judiciary: *(L)* A system of courts.

Judicious Consideration: *(P)* An action taken that is based on sound judgment.

***Jugar*:** *(A)* In Hindi, informal, unconventional but practical and effective way of handling a problem.

Junction: *(T)* A place, serving as an interchange point, where two or more roads or railway lines meet.

Jungle: *(E)* A dense tropical forest.

Junk Yard: *(P)* An area where storage, sale and purchase of waste goods, commodities and materials takes place in covered, semi-covered structures or in the open.

Jurisdiction: *(P)* The area, defined by a clear boundary (such as the municipal area, district, or state) within which the authority and powers of a legally constituted body extends and ceases beyond it.

Jury: *(ET)* A committee of examiners.

Justification: *(P)* A verbal or written statement giving sufficient reasons for doing some thing or taking some action.

K

***Kabari Bazaar*:** *(P)* In Hindi, a place for buying and selling junk and second hand goods

***Kabari*:** *(P)* In Hindi, a person engaged in buying and selling second-hand household and recyclable material from municipal solid waste.

***Kachcha* House:** *(H)* A house with walls and roof made of mud or other temporary or makeshift materials; also *Kacha House, Cutcha House.*

***Kar*:** *(F)* In Hindi, a general term for tax and with appropriate prefix, it becomes a term for specific tax e.g. *aaya kar* for income tax, *jal kar* for water tax, *path kar* for road tax or *bhawan kar* for house tax; also *Shulka.*

Kasba: *(P)* In Persian, a subdivisional town, next in hierarchy to a district headquarter

Kerb: *(T)* A concrete or stone edging along a pathway or road, also *curb.*

Kerb-Stone: *(T)* A single monolithic unit of kerb, also *Curb-stone,* see also *Kerb.*

Key Industry: *(EC)* An industry that is essential to national economic welfare e.g. oil industry for oil producing countries.

Key Personnel: *(P)* (a) In an organisation, those persons who are authorised to take major decisions. (b) In a project, the principal coordinator, investigator or researcher or any other individual who contributes substantially to the conception, planning and implementation of the project.

Key Sector: *(EC)* A sector of economy such as agriculture, industry, trade, commerce, or infrastructure, which has significantly contributed to or is most essential for economic development of a region, state or country.

***Kharif*:** *(AG)* The crops sown before rainy season that ripens in autumn.

***Khasra* Map:** *(P)* Official map of a village record indicating boundaries of all properties, dimensions, property number, ownership and other details.

***Khasra** Number:* *(P)* The property number, as recorded on the official *khasra* map, normally used in land acquisition notification to identify the property and its other details.

***Khokha*:** *(P)* In Hindi, a small shop, made of temporary or permanent materials, generally located on roadsides and other places for selling soft drinks, fruits, eatables, cigarette, *pan* etc.

Kilo: *(P)* A prefix denoting 1000 times the unit to which it is attached, e.g. kilometer, kilolitre, kilowatt-hour

Kilogramme: *(P)* The mass of the platinum-iridium cylinder kept in the International Bureau of Weights and Measures near Paris (1000 gram)

Kilowatt-hour: *(P)* The commercial unit of electrical energy – 1000 watts an hour

Kin: *(H)* (a) Persons of the same family, (b) Relatives, see also *Kith and Kin, Next of Kin.*

Kinder Garden: *(P)* see *Nursery School.*

Kiss-and-ride Facility: *(T)* see *Kiss-and-ride Lots.*

Kiss-and-ride Lots: *(T)* Located near transit stations or park-and-ride lots, these are short-term parking spaces that are used for picking-up or dropping-off commuters traveling by the mass transit system; also *Kiss-and-ride Facility.*

Kitchen Garden: *(P)* A place, generally attached to a house, for growing vegetables for use by the household and not for sale.

Kitchen Stuff: *(E)* Kitchen refuse or garbage.

Kitchen Unit: *(H)* A kitchen along with all fittings and fixtures.

Kitchen: *(H)* A place used for cooking of food.

Kith and kin: *(H)* Friends and relatives.

L

LAA: *(L)* Land Acquisition Act.

Labour Force: *(D)* see *Work Force.*

Labourer: *(P)* An unskilled worker generally employed on per day basis.

Lagan: *(F)* In Hindi, tax paid on agriculture land.

Lagoon: *(G)* A shallow lake near sea or connected with sea or river.

Lake District: *(P)* An area characterised by picturesque lakes and has potential for water supply and development of water-sports or leisure activities that attract tourists.

Lake: *(G)* A large body of water within land and can be natural or man-made.

***Lal Dora*:** *(P)* In Hindi, a red line drawn on a *khasra* map indicating the boundary of the territory of a village settlement within which, if located in municipal area, the building by-laws and subdivision regulations are not applicable unless specified otherwise, see also *Khasra Map.*

LAN: *(TQ)* Local Area Network.

Land Acquisition: *(L)* Compulsory acquisition of land for public purposes as per provisions of Land Acquisition Act 1894 as amended from time to time, see also *Pre-emption.*

Land Assembly by Negotiated Settlement: *(P)* A processes of assembly of land, for development purposes, at a mutually agreeable price arrived at through discussion among the land owners and buyers who could be a government or non-government body.

Land Assembly: *(L)* The innovative procedures of acquiring land for development purposes by way of negotiated settlement, accommodation reservation, or transferable development rights, see also *Accommodation Reservation, Land Assembly by Negotiated Settlement, or Transferable Development Rights.*

Land Bank: *(M)* (a) In planning, a pool of acquired and assembled land in urban areas held in reserve, by the public agency, until needed for a public purpose, (b) In finance, a bank established for financing real estate transactions and development, also *Land Reserve.*

Land Consolidation: *(P)* see *Land Pooling.*

Land Development Rights: *(P)* see *Transferable Development Rights (TDR).*

Land Development: *(P)* A process of provision of basic network of infrastructure such as access road, water supply, sewerage, drainage, electricity in an area designated as residential, industrial, commercial, and public and semi-public, see also *Developed Land.*

Land Disposal: *(P)* The procedure of sale or lease of land, acquired by a planning and development authority or local body for public purposes, according to the rules made in this respect.

Land Grabber: *(P)* A person who seizes upon land in an unfair manner.

Land Grant: *(P)* Gift of public land by government to an individual, organisation, institution, or sub-ordinate department for a public purpose.

Land Information System: *(TQ)* A system of collection, storage, maintenance, processing, analysis, and dissemination of land related data including maps and records for land registration, land assessment and evaluation used for strategic and operational management of land.

Land Locked Country: *(P)* A country that is surrounded by land on all sides and does not have direct access to a sea and is, therefore, deprived of low-cost water transport by ship and also exploitation of marine resources.

Land Management: *(A)* The processes of judicious use of land resources with an objective of ensuring sufficient supply of serviced land at affordable cost, at right place and time, for development through public sector interventions and land market operations.

Land Policy: *(P)* A statement of intention of the government in respect of development of urban and rural land including land use control, land acquisition, land disposition, and land-related taxation and reforms.

Land Pooling: *(P)* A system of land assembly where a number of individual owners of land willingly pool their plots (termed as *original plots*) for the purpose of planning, as a single composite site, by a planning agency as per sub-division regulations incorporating roads, shops, open spaces, community facilities and services as per norms (termed as common areas) and then readjust the plots. The readjusted plots (termed as *final plots*) are then redistributed to the landowners in proportion to the original plots and the common areas are transferred to the local authority on payment of the land cost by the authority. It is followed by a systematic valuation exercise where cost of land under common areas, cost of each original plot, cost of each final plot as well as the amount to be received or paid by a landowner is calculated. On settlement of the amount, the land in the form of the final plot is transferred to the landowner. In this process the area gets planned development with all facilities and services, also *Land Readjustment, Land Consolidation* and *Land Sharing.*

Land Readjustment: *(P)* see *Land Pooling.*

Land Reclamation: *(P)* A processes, employing landfill or land management techniques, for recovery of land, that is unserviceable due to flooding, pollution, over-utlisation, or desertification, to a condition in which it can be used for development of settlement, open space, or agriculture.

Land Reforms: *(P)* Changes in land matters for the benefit of the common people and include, pattern of ownership and land use, distribution of land and modification of the land laws.

Land Register: *(P)* see *Cadastre.*

Land Reserve: *(P)* see *Land Bank.*

Land Sharing: *(P)* see *Land Pooling.*

Land Speculation: *(P)* Sale or purchase of property exclusively for the purpose of making profit and no intention of its development or improvement, also *Speculation.*

Land Sub-division: *(P)* Division of land into plots for various activities in accordance with sub-division regulations, for the purpose of sale by the owner of the property who could be a public agency or private body or individual, also *Parceling-out of Land, Sub-division.*

Land Survey: *(TQ)* The art, process and technique of surveying the characteristics of land including features, use, area and tenure.

Land Tax: *(F)* Tax on real estate including property tax, vacant land tax.

Land Tenure: *(L)* Regulations governing the right of holding, using, or disposing off a parcel of land by individuals or groups.

Land Title: *(L)* A legal document that provides the ownership details of a parcel of land.

Land Use Control: *(M)* The legal or planning or fiscal measures to ensure planned use of land employing tools such as zoning and sub-division regulations, land use plan, taxation and tax incentives.

Land Use Plan (existing): *(P)* A plan that gives the existing (in a given year) land use of all parcels of land in the planning area of a settlement and is supported by quantitative an qualitative analysis of each land use.

Land Use Plan (proposed): *(P)* A plan that gives the proposed land use of the area of a settlement that is likely to be developed during the plan period (5 years, or 20-25 years as the case may be) for various purposes and activities having regard to socio-economic development needs as well as physical, environmental and accessibility considerations. Such plans serves as a guide to planned development of the settlement, land acquisition for public purposes, and future capital budgeting, see also *Master Plan.*

Land Use Planning: *(P)* see *Physical Planning.*

Land Use: *(P)* (a) The manner in which land is used at a given point of time to accommodate various human needs, (b) The activity that can be legally performed on a parcel of land and includes, in the context of urban settlements, residential, commercial, manufacturing, public and semi-public, recreation including open spaces, transport and communication, agriculture and other special areas, which are further subdivided into sub-categories, also *Use of Land.*

Land Valuation: *(P)* The process of determining the value, for the purpose of taxation, mortgage, or expropriation, of urban or rural land depending upon its location, accessibility, use and future potential.

Land Value Increment Tax: *(F)* A cess widely collected along with property tax, in countries like Australia, Canada, Israel, Italy, Malaysia, and New Zealand, on increase in land value as a result of development in the city as well as due to economic phenomenon of rise in general price, see also *Land Value Increment.*

Land Value Increment: *(F)* The increment in the value of parcel of land as a result of development on and/or around it, executed by a public agency or private body, or general development of the settlement.

Land Value: *(P)* (a) The value of parcel of land apart from the structure or crops standing on it, (b) The value at which a person is ready to buy or sell a plot of land, (c) The value at which sale or purchase of a plot of land has been recently registered.

Land Ward: *(P)* At a seashore, the area lying towards the land, also **inland.**

Land: *(M)* (a) Ground, soil or earth, (b) A site for location of human activities and development initiatives, (c) A property with definite tenure.

Landed Property: *(P)* see *Real Estate.*

Landfill Cells: *(E)* Trenches or pits dug on land in a waste disposal facility that provide isolation of hazardous wastes from adjacent cell or wastes.

Landfill: *(E)* A designated disposal facility or part thereof, generally located on the out skirts of a city or away from residential zone, where municipal wastes are placed in or on land

Landholder: *(P)* A tenant holding land from a landlord.

Landlady: *(P)* see *Landlord.*

Landless: *(P)* A person, living in rural areas, having no landed agricultural property.

Landlord: *(P)* A person who owns a property comprising plot of land and/or building who lets it out to one or more tenants, also *Landlady, Landowner,* see also *Absentee Landlord.*

Land-man Ratio: *(P)* The area of land per person in a region, state or country.

Landmark: *(M)* (a) In landscape, an element that dominates the landscape of an area, (b) In urban design, a physical element that dominates the composition of buildings and open spaces in an area giving it an identity and serving as a reference point in locating the area, (c) A distinctive building or feature which can be entered or passed through and which stands out as being easily identifiable and easily retained image, forming part of the mental picture of a city and just a mention of its name reminds the city e.g. Qutab Minar - Delhi, Eiffel Tower – Paris, or Big Ben – London, (d) In history, an event that marks a period or turning point.

Landowner: *(P)* see *Landlord.*

Landslide: *(E)* Downwards movement of mass of earth or rocks generally caused by seepage of rainwater into the soil.

Lane Capacity: *(T)* The maximum number of vehicles passing over a given section of a lane during a given period under a specified speed or level of service.

Lane: *(T)* (a) A portion of a road surface, usually indicated by road markings, that is intended for movement of one row of vehicles, (b) A narrow road between houses

Large Industries: *(P)* Industries that have fixed assets without depreciation, or project cost of more than Rs. 5 crore.

Law: *(M)* (a) The rules of a community or state – the statute, (b) in research, the theoretical principles deduced from practice or observations.

Lawful: *(L)* Allowed by law, also *Rightful.*

Lawn: *(LA)* see *Park.*

Layout Plan: *(P)* A plan of an area showing its sub-divisions, land use, infrastructure services, prepared within the framework of the Master Plan, and/or zoning and sub-division regulations, also *Site Plan, Site Layout.*

Leaching: *(E)* The processes of percolation of liquid through or drained from hazardous or other wastes.

Leadership: *(A)* The ability of a person to think, take decision and motivate others to follow the decision, see also *Traditional Leadership, Participatory Leadership.*

Learner: *(ET)* see *Trainee.*

Learning: *(ET)* A life-long process of acquiring new awareness, knowledge, attitudes and skills.

Lease Purchase: *(H)* A system of lease with an option to purchase the property at a later time, with rental payment applied to the purchase price, also *Hire Purchase.*

Lease: *(L)* A contractual agreement between a tenant and a landlord whereby the landlord permits a tenant to use his property for a specified period and use on payment of a specified rent and compliance of other mutually agreed conditions, see also *Hire Purchase, Lease Purchase, Leasehold Tenure, Leasing, Lessee, Lessor, Long-term Lease.*

Lease Hold Tenure: *(H)* A property held by a tenant for a specific period on payment of rent to the landlord with restrictions on its transfer or sale as specified under the lease deed.

Leasing: *(H)* An arrangement whereby a private firm temporarily takes over the operation and maintenance of a public service at a commercial risk.

Ledger: *(F)* The principal book of accounts.

Legal Appraisal of Agency: *(F)* Appraisal of the legal eligibility of an agency for borrowing or raising loan and includes examination of relevant Act, memorandum of association, sectoral and functional jurisdiction.

Legal Force of a Plan: *(L)* see *Effect of Plan.*

Legal: *(L)* (a) Pertaining to or according to law, (b) Something that is lawful, (c) Something created by law.

Leisure Time: *(P)* The time that is not committed to established routine work or duty and can be used by the individual for recreation and other personal activities.

Lend: *(F)* (a) To allow the use of property on payment of rent, (b) To give money on loan.

Lessee: *(H)* A tenant, who is a party in the lease document to use a property of a landlord, on payment of rent.

Lessor: *(H)* A landlord, who enters into a lease with a tenant, permits him the use of property and receives rent payments.

Let Out: *(H)* To put a property for hire and collect rent thereon.

Letter of Intent: *(L)* An expression, in writing, of intention to do something without legal obligation to do so unless entered into agreement, e.g. intention to sell or purchase a house.

Level of Service (LOS): *(T)* A set of operating conditions that describe the ability of a road network to handle traffic and it is classified from Level A to F where Level A specifies the best traffic conditions and F represents traffic congestion.

Level of Urbanisation: *(P)* The percentage of urban population to the total population in a country, state or region, also *Degree of Urbanisation.*

Lexicon: *(P)* A wordbook or dictionary or a glossary.

Liability: *(F)* A financial obligation, debt, claim, or potential loss.

Licensce fee: *(F)* A fee charged by a competent authority, from an applicant, for granting permission to perform an activity as requested.

License: *(P)* A document giving official permission to do something.

Life Expectancy at Birth: *(D)* Average number of years a new born child is expected to live under the current mortality levels.

Life Expectancy: *(D)* The average number of years an individual is expected to live determined statistically using factors like age, sex, occupation and physical condition.

LIG: *(P)* see *Low Income Group.*

Light Industry: *(P)* An industrial unit producing non-hazardous products using non-polluting processes employing up to 50 (this figure may change depending upon local rules) workers.

Light Rail Transit: *(T)* A mode of urban transit that operates on steel rails and obtains its power from overhead electrical wires and may operate in single or multiple cars on separate rights-of-way or in mixed traffic.

Linear City: *(P)* A narrow and axial city-form where the development is concentrated as a strip on both sides along a major road or river providing water-transport, see also *Transport Corridor-(b).*

Linear Programme: *(TQ)* A mathematical procedure for optimising a liner relationship within the bounds of a set of other relationships represented by the liner equations. it is being used, *inter alia*, for allocation of resources among competing uses.

Linear: *(E)* A continuous layer of natural or man-made materials, beneath or on the sides of a surface impoundment or landfill or landfill-cells to restrict the downward or lateral escape of hazardous wastes and its constituents.

Line-haul: *(T)* That portion of a trip that is express or nonstop between two points.

Lintel: *(H)* A timber or stone or RCC structure over a door or window to support the opening.

Liquid Assets: *(F)* (a) Assets that can be immediately converted into cash at predictable price, (b) Accounts that are receivable, (c) Cash in hand or bank.

LIS: *(TQ)* see *Land Information System.*

Literacy Rate: *(D)* The percentage of literates in the age group of seven years and above.

Literate: *(D)* A person who can read and write in any language and may or may not have received any formal education or passed any minimum educational standard.

Literature Search: *(ET)* The process of consulting the writings on a specific theme with a view to gaining a deeper insight on the subject of research study or project.

Literature: *(ET)* (a) The art of composition in prose or poetry (b) The whole body of compositions or writings on a particular subject.

Litre: *(P)* The metric unit of measurement of volume of liquids where one litre is the volume of one kilogram of water at 4 degree centigrade temperature under standard atmospheric pressure.

Litter: *(E)* Solid waste.

Littoral: *(G)* A coastal area along the shore of an ocean or a sea.

Livestock: *(AG)* Domestic animals such as cattle and sheep, fish, insects (silk worm) and bees (honey bea), raised for personal use or for profit.

Load Bearing Capacity: *(H)* (a) In case of a wall, the amount of load or weight that a load-bearing wall can support, (b) In case of sub-soil, the amount of load or weight of structure that the ground can support.

Loan: *(F)* A sum of money lent to be returned with or without interest and the period of loan may be short-term or long-term and it may be secured through mortgage etc. or unsecured, *Loan Agreement:* an agreement between the lender and the borrower specifying the amount, the period, the interest rate, mode of payment and other details, *Loan Recovery:* the process of getting back from a borrower, a part of the principal amount of loan and interest due as per loan agreement.

Local Authority: *(A)* A municipality, or any other body or agency empowered by the relevant law, to administer developmental activities at local levels.

Local Bus Service: *(T)* An intra-city bus service that usually links residential areas and major activity centers using the local street system.

Local Government Office: *(P)* A building or group of several buildings used for performing the functions and activities related to local government.

Local Government: *(A)* An elected body, authorised as per relevant laws, to make policies, collect taxes, and discharge administrative and developmental functions at various levels such as *panchayat* at village level, *nagar panchayat* in transitional areas, and municipality in urban settlements.

Local Road: *(T)* A way having 10 to 20 m. right-of-way, for access to residence, business or other abutting property, having necessary parking and pedestrian movement space, also *Local Street.*

Local Shopping Centre: *(P)* A place, located in residential area with 15,000 population, where a group of shops (not exceeding 75 in number or 1 per 200 persons) sell goods and services as well as accommodate commercial offices, community hall, and local library.

Local Street: *(T)* see *Local Road.*

Local: *(P)* Someone or something belonging to a place e.g. an inhabitant, a municipality, a bus service.

Localise: *(P)* To assign or limit to a place.

Locality: *(P)* A distinct place locally recognised by its unique name, where people live, also *Mohalla*.

Locate: *(P)* (a) To designate or to find a place for an activity in an area, (b) To search a place having certain characteristics on a map or in an area.

Location Map: *(P)* A map showing the location of the project site in relation to neighbouring areas, settlements, transportation routes and other prominent features with a view to provide a clear comprehension of the locational characteristics of the site, see also *Map*.

Location of Industries: *(P)* The process of selecting site for location of industries considering access to raw materials, market, and availability of labour, land, resources, development control rules etc.

Lodging House: *(H)* A premises where rooms are let out to any one as a temporary accommodation, it may not have dining facility (in some master plans there are restrictions on the number of guest).

Lone Migrant: *(P)* A person who, himself and not along with his family members, moves from his usual place of residence to another place for gainful employment or any other purpose.

Long-term Financing: *(F)* A mechanism that allows to get loan to be returned with interest in installments spread over a longer period of time generally more than 10 years.

Long-term Lease: *(H)* A contractual agreement between a landlord and a tenant where the specified period to allow the use the property is more than 25 years (in lease of residential plots it is generally 99 years but may vary from place to place depending upon local government policy).

Loop-line: *(T)* A branch of railway that returns back to the main line.

Loop-street: *(T)* A branch of a road that returns back and joins the same road.

Lot: *(H)* see *Plot*.

Low Density Zone: *(H)* A zone characterised by low-density of population and low FAR

Low-cost Housing: *(H)* (a) A housing developed through low-cost loan or grant by a public agency and made available to specified low-income group families, (b) Housing constructed with low-cost technology and made available to specified low-income group families at subsidised rent, (c) Shelter build partially or entirely by the occupant himself using cheap building material and unconventional construction technologies sometimes facilitated by government through favourable policies regarding land tenure, building materials and financial assistance.

Low-income Group: *(H)* A group of persons falling in the category of those earning less than Rs. 1,000 per month (this amount may change from state to state or agency to agency), also *LIG.*

Low-income Housing: *(H)* Housing built for families belonging to low-income group in the society, see alas *Low-income Group.*

Low-interest Loan: *(F)* A loan offered for a specified purpose such as housing for the poor, to public agency or non-profit organisation or cooperative institution at an interest rate that is below the market rate of interest.

Low-rise Development: *(P)* A development where the height of buildings does not exceed 4 storeys.

Low-rise High-density Development: *(P)* A development where the gross residential density is 1000 persons per hectare or more and the height of buildings is up to 4 storeys

Low-technology Transport: *(T)* A non-motorised form of transport such as animal driven cart or cycle rickshaw.

LRT: *(T)* see *Light Rail Transit.*

Lump Sum: *(F)* A single amount of money in lieu of several components of the same work.

Lung-space: *(LA)* The system of open spaces in a city that helps in improving the air quality and hence serves as lungs to the city.

Lux: *(P)* A unit of illumination and is equal to one lumen per square metre.

M

Macro Models: *(TQ)* Models that deal with generalised characteristics of larger areas, systems or groups.

***Mahanagar*:** *(P)* In Hindi, a large city or metropolis.

***Maidan*:** *(P)* In Hindi, see *Multipurpose Open Space.*

Main Lane: *(T)* A general-purpose lane on a highway that is open to all motor vehicles.

Main Worker: *(D)* A person who was engaged in any economically productive activity for 183 days or more, in the year preceding the date of enumeration.

Main-Lane Metering: *(T)* Regulating the flow of vehicles on a general-purpose lanes or highway-to-highway connection through the use of traffic signals that allow vehicles to proceed at a predetermined rate.

Major Attractions: *(P)* Building, sites, monuments, and activities located in a city that have regional, national or international relevance and are expected to draw patrons and participants from places out side the city.

***Makaan*:** *(H)* In Hindi, a house.

Mall: *(M)* (a) In transportation, a wide street in a city with shaded walkways and commercial, socio-cultural and recreational activities located on either sides., also *Mall Road,* (b) In planning, a large retail commercial complex with one large establishment acting as the anchor and several other small shops, owned and managed by different persons, selling a variety of goods and services.

Management: *(P)* (a) An executive process of efficiently utlising and coordinating resources to accomplish the defined objectives, (b) Actions taken at right time to achieve the organisation objectives and includes four functions viz. planning, organising, directing and controlling, see also *Planning Function, Organising Function, Directing Function,* and *Controlling Function.*

***Mandapa*:** *(P)* In Hindi, a pillared hall with roof, which is open from all the sides.

Mandate: *(L)* Authority given to representatives by people, workers, members of an association / union by the process of voting.

***Mandi*:** *(P)* In Hindi, see *Agriculture Market.*

***Mandi* Town:** *(P)* A town where trading of agricultural produce is the main economic activity and forms its economic base.

Man-made Disaster: *(P)* A disaster originating from human activities rather than natural processes, such as fire in a slum area or floods due to blockage of natural drainage system by roads and other developments.

Man-made Environment: *(E)* see *Environment-(c).*

Mansion: *(H)* A grand palatial house.

Manual: *(P)* a written document specifying procedures, step-by-step instructions to follow to perform a specific task or to utlise a specific equipment.

Manufacturing Industries: *(P)* Industries that produce goods by using or processing a variety of raw, semi-processed and / or recycled materials.

Map: *(P)* A representation on paper, of physical features, size, location, use, political and administrative boundaries, and other characteristics on land drawn to scale using cartographic techniques as per requirements, see also *Base Map, Background Map, Cadastral Map, Location Map,* and *Thematic Map.*

Map Extent: *(TQ)* In GIS, (a) The rectangular limits (xmin, ymin and xmax, ymax) of the area of the Earth's surface displayed using ArcInfo, (b) The geographic extent of a geographic data set specified by the minimum-bounding rectangle (i.e., xmin, ymin and xmax, ymax).

Marginal Area: *(P)* (a) Part of a city inhabited by economically weaker sections of the society, (b) An area located in the city centre or on its outskirts, having dilapidated structures and poor accessibility and inadequate services.

Marginal Economic Sector: *(P)* That sector of economy, which does not appear in the official statistics and includes informal commercial and service activities, see *Informal Sector.*

Marginal Farmer: *(AG)* A farmer holding 1 ha non-irrigated or 0.5 ha irrigated land, see also *Small Farmer.*

Marginal Land: *(P)* A very poor quality land that is unsuitable for agriculture purposes or urban use without extensive investment in its quality improvement.

Marginal Land Holding: *(AG)* An agriculture land holding up to 1 ha un-irrigated or 0.5 ha irrigated is termed as marginal.

Marginal Population: *(P)* That section of population, which is poor, jobless, and homeless and does not participate in the social life or economy of the area.

Marginal Settlement: *(P)* see *Squatter Settlement.*

Marginal Worker: *(D)* A person who has done some work for less than 183 days in the year preceding the date of enumeration.

Market: *(P)* (a) The actual and potential consumers of a commodity or service, (b) A designated place where sale and purchase of commodities and services takes place, (c) A designated place where sale and purchase of specialised commodities takes place for example vegetable market, paper market, steel market (d) A designated place where sale and purchase of commodities and services takes place on a specific day of a week or time of a day e.g. Sunday market, week-end market, or night market, (e) Socially, a meeting place for socio-cultural interaction..

Market Analysis: *(TQ)* A research technique to identify the needs and characteristic of various groups of consumers pertaining to a product including housing, or service with a view to assist the producers, marketing managers and service providers / builders to plan their respective future course of actions.

Market Economy: *(P)* An economy where high consumption is an important precondition for high production and where forces of supply and demand guide the production choice and methods, as well as distribution and consumption patterns.

Market Garden: *(P)* An area where a variety of farm products such as vegetables, fruits and flowers are grown for sale.

Market Research: *(TQ)* A broad term used for study of the characteristics of markets and the marketing services, using a variety of survey and analytical techniques and approaches depending upon the research objectives.

Market Town: *(P)* A town, with commercial activity as its economic base, serving a wider rural area as the centre for buying and selling farm produce and consumer goods.

Market-based Price: *(F)* The price set by the demand and supply and buyers and sellers in a competitive market.

Mass Rapid Transit System: *(T)* A system of intra-urban mass transportation by rail, serving a large number of riders and may be underground, on surface, or over the ground and includes the entire system ranging from administration, management, to operations and maintenance.

Mass Transit: *(T)* Transportation provided by public or private operators by bus, rail, ferry, or other mode that operates on a regular basis, on predetermined route and serves a large number of riders, also *Mass Transportation, Rapid Transit.*

Mass Transportation: *(T)* see *Mass Transit.*

Master Plan: *(P)* A plan of a settlement for a period of generally about 20 years, prepared and approved after following the relevant legal procedures, that serves as an instrument to guide its socio-cultural, economic and physical development through judicious land use planning, see also *Development Plan, Land Use Plan, Physical Plan.*

Mathematical Model: *(TQ)* A representation of behaviour of a system in the form of mathematical relationships.

Median: *(T)* The central portion of a divided road that separates the opposing directions of traffic.

Medium Industries: *(P)* Industries that have fixed assets, without depreciation, or project cost of more than Rs. 1 crore but less than Rs. 5 Crore.

Megalopolis: *(P)* An agglomeration of cities merged with a metropolis forming a wide-spreading thickly populated mass, accommodating more than 10 million people.

Memorandum of Understanding: *(L)* A written document specifying the details of mutual understanding, between two parties, pertaining to a future activity, action, or commitment, see also *Agreement.*

Metamorphosis: *(G)* The change of form, shape or character of an object or place due to natural and man-made forces.

Methodology: *(TQ)* A set of steps taken to accomplish given objectives or perform different actions.

Metre: *(TQ)* A unit of measuring length in the metric system and is equal to 100 cm.

Metric System: *(P)* The decimal system of weights and measures.

Metro: *(M)* (a) In planning, the short form of the term metropolis, (b) In transportation, a suburban railway that could be underground, on the ground or elevated.

Metro-core: *(P)* The area in a metro-region comprising the metropolis and its fringe areas which may be totally urban or a mix of urban and rural character.

Metro-periphery: *(P)* The rest of the urban and rural area in a metro-region excluding the metro-core and comprising several sub-regions, see also *Metro Core, Sub-region, Sub-regional Core, Sub-regional Periphery.*

Metropolis: *(P)* (a) Demographically, a city having a population of one million and above, (b) Administratively, a city having a population of one million and above and governed by one or more municipal body(ies), (c) Functionally, a city having a population of one million and above serving its influence region as the dominating centre of trade, commerce, art, culture, health care, recreation, education, research, administration and political activity.

Metropolitan Area: *(A)* An area having a population of 10 lakh or more, comprised in one or more districts and consisting of two or more municipalities, or *panchayats* or other contiguous area, specified by the Governor by public notification, see also *Municipality, Panchayat*

Metropolitan City Centre: *(P)* see *Central Business District.*

Metropolitan Planning Committee (MPC): *(A)* A committee constituted, under an Act, by the state government to prepare the draft development plan of the metropolitan area, see also *Metropolitan Area.*

Metropolitan Region: *(P)* The area under the influence of the developmental impulse of a metropolis and comprising the metro-core and the metro-periphery, also *Metro-Region, see* also *Metro-Core, Metro-Periphery.*

Metro-region: *(P)* see *Metropolitan Region.*

Micro Models: *(TQ)* Models that are precise and deal with characteristics of local areas or of a component of a larger system.

Micro-area: *(P)* A well defined sub-division of a micro-regional periphery of a sub-region, comprising micro-area core and micro-area periphery, served by a central village, see also *Micro-Area Core, Micro-Area Periphery, Central Village.*

Micro-area Core: *(P)* The part of a micro-area comprising the central village and its fields and other open spaces, see also *Central Village.*

Micro-area Periphery: *(P)* The rest of the micro-area comprising a group of basic villages and their respective agriculture fields and other open spaces that are served by the central village, see also *Basic Village, Central Village.*

Microclimate: *(P)* The climate of a localised area which may differ from the overall climate of the wider area due to local factors such as tree cover (or the absence of tree cover), or exposure to winds.

Micro-region: *(P)* A well defined sub-division of a sub-regional periphery of a region, comprising micro-regional core and micro-areas, served by a service centre, see also *Service Centre, Micro-regional Core, Micro-areas.*

Micro-Regional Core: *(P)* The area in a micro-region comprising the service centre and its fringe areas which may be totally rural in character, see also *Service Centre.*

Micro-Regional Periphery: *(P)* The rest of the urban and rural area in a micro-region excluding the micro-regional core and comprising several micro-areas, see also *Micro-Regional Core, Micro-Areas.*

MIG: *(M) Middle Income Group.*

Migrant: *(D)* A person who moves from one place to another.

Migration: *(P)* Movement of people from one place to another generally for employment, or other social purposes like education or marriage, also *Population Drift,* see also *Inter-Regional*

Migration, Intra-Regional Migration, Rural-Urban Migration, Seasonal Migration, Urban-Urban Migration.

Mile: *(TQ)* A measure of distance in foot-pound-seconds system and is equal to 1760 yards

Minor Attractions: *(P)* Building, sites, monuments, and activities located in a city that have local relevance and are expected to draw patrons and participants from only certain pockets within a city or region.

Minutes: *(A)* An official record of deliberations made and decisions taken during a meeting of a committee or society or designated body.

Mission: *(P)* see *Development Mission.*

Misuse: *(P)* Wrong use of a designated land use, or premises or provision of rules and regulations.

Mixed Land Use: *(P)* The phenomenon of existence of two or more uses on a site, or plot or in a building, which may or may not be compatible.

Mixed Land Use Zoning: *(P)* A designated area in a development plan that permits a horizontal or vertical mixing of two or more compatible land uses on a site, or plot or in a building, also *Mixed Use Zoning,* see also *Horizontal Mixing of Land Uses, Vertical Mixing of Land Uses.*

Mixed Use Zoning: *(P)* see *Mixed Land Use Zoning.*

Mobile Recovery Van: *(P)* A motorised vehicle equipped with computers, workstations, telephone, electrical power, etc. to serve in post disaster operations.

Mobile Source of Pollution: *(E)* A self-propelled transportation vehicles, such as automobiles, locomotives, boats, ships, and aircrafts that pollute environment from their emissions.

Mode: *(T)* A particular form of travel such as bus, automobile, walking, bicycle, cycle rickshaw, animal driven vehicle, rail, air, and water-borne vessels.

Mode Shift: *(T)* The act of changing from one mode to another like changing from road to rail at the railway station, or road to air at the air port, or from cycle rickshaw to bus at a bus stand.

Mode Split: *(T)* The proportion of total person-trips using the various modes of travel.

Mode-1: *(M)* see *Cross Boarder Trade.*

Mode-2: *(M)* see *Consumption Abroad.*

Mode-3: *(M)* see *Commercial Presence.*

Mode-4: *(M)* see *Movement of Natural Persons.*

Model: *(TQ)* (a) A representation of behaviour of a system by another system such as mathematics or graphics, (b) To the scale, three dimensional representation of an object, building, or physical features of an area using a variety of materials like paper, wood, plastic etc., see also *Model Types.*

Model Types: *(TQ)* (a) Models could be classified as (i) spatial models and (ii) non-spatial models, (b) Spatial could be further divided as supra-national, national, sub-national, conceptual, or mathematical (c) Non-spatial models could be further divided into conceptual, or mathematical, see also *National Model, Non-Spatial Conceptual Model, Non-Spatial Mathematical Model, Non-Spatial Model, Spatial- Conceptual Model, Spatial-Mathematical Model, Spatial Model, Sub-National Model, Supra-National Model* (d) Models could also be classified as macro, micro, static, dynamic, descriptive, behavioural, prescriptive, planning, predictive, deterministic, stochastic, and simulation models, see also *Behavioural Model, Descriptive Model, Deterministic Model, Dynamic Model, Macro Model, Micro Model, Planning Model, Predictive Model, Prescriptive Model, Simulation Model, Static Model, Stochastic Model.*

Modernisation: *(P)* A processes of change from traditional way of life to new ways marked by the impact of industrialisation and mechanisation.

Modular Coordination: *(H)* Planning and designing of housing to accommodate standard dimensions of common building components so as to achieve speed and efficiency in construction, minimisation of waste and scrap, and cost-effectiveness.

Modular Housing: *(H)* A three-dimensional factory-produced modular units of house shipped to a site fully created and placed on a finished foundation.

***Mohalla*:** *(P)* In Hindi, a locality, see *locality.*

Monitoring and Evaluation: *(P)* To inspect, observe or check continuously and keep a record, of an activity or its effect with a view to assessing its progress or impact in the light of the set goals and assisting in charting the next course of action.

Monopoly: *(F)* A market system where only sellers have control over market situation.

Morphology of Towns: *(P)* The study of internal structure of a town as evolved by organisation of land use through planning interventions, transportation network, activity patterns, and organisation of spaces through urban design.

Mortgage: *(F)* Loan made on real estate collateral for construction or purchase of property where the borrower (mortgagee) gives a lien on his property to the lender (mortgagor) as security and has right to use of the property and on full payment of loan, the lien is removed, see also *Mortgage, Mortgagor.*

Mortgage Bank: *(F)* A financial institution engaged in the mortgage business, also *Mortgage Credit Institution.*

Mortgage Credit Institution: *(F)* see *Mortgage Bank.*

Mortgage Financing: *(F)* Money loaned for purchase of real estate.

Mortgage Guarantee: *(F)* A guarantee given by a public institution to insure private lenders against losses on home and project mortgages and property improvement loans.

Mortgage: *(F)* A borrower of money on conveyance of his property, see also *Mortgage*

Mortgagor: *(F)* A lender of money on real estate collateral, see also *Mortgage.*

Mosaic: *(TQ)* An assemblage of overlapping aerial or satellite photographs or images whose edges have been matched to form a continuous pictorial representation of a portion of the earth's surface.

Mosque: *(P)* A building or a complex of building with related infrastructure including parking and serving as an Islamic place of worship.

Motel: *(P)* (a) A motor hotel, (b) A building located generally out side the urban limits of the city but near a highway and providing suits of rooms and parking space for the guests to facilitate traveling motorists.

Motivation: *(P)* The manner of satisfying the personnel so that they perform with best of their ability to mutually accomplish the organisational as well as their personal objectives.

Motor Garage and Workshop: *(P)* see *Garage.*

Mound: *(LA)* A small hill developed as a characteristic feature in landscape.

Movement of Natural Persons: *(M)* In the context of the World Trade Organisation's General Agreement for Trades in Services, a form of service provision, where a professional expert of a member country delivers the services by temporarily entering the territory of another country after obtaining the necessary visa, also *Mode-4, Presence of Natural Person.*

MRTS: *(T)* see *Mass Rapid Transit System.*

MSW: *(S)* see *Municipal Solid Waste.*

***Mufassil* Town:** *(P)* In Arabic, a small town serving as a rural service centre for a group of villages and generally lacking higher order urban facilities and services.

Multi Level Parking: *(T)* A multistoried structure located in a high parking demand area and designed to park vehicles at different levels and may be fully or partially automatic.

Multi-Band System: *(TQ)* A system, usually applied to camera and sensors on satellites, for simultaneously observing the same target with several filtered bands, through which data can be recorded.

Multidiscipiinary: *(M)* A purposeful pattern of interrelation among a discipline and several other related disciplines with a view to utilise their inputs for the performance of the discipline.

Multi-Family Housing: *(H)* Residential structure designed to accommodate more than one family serviced by common passage, staircase, or lift.

Multilateral Assistance: *(F)* Development assistance provided to less or least developed countries (LDC) through multilateral development banks, the United Nations agencies, and other international organisations.

Multimedia: *(ET)* A variety of different media used for education, training and other professional presentations and include audio, video, movies and stills.

Multi-modal: *(T)* More than one mode operating in a corridor or area.

Multiplier Effect: *(EC)* The effect of investment in a basic industry that generates demand in services sectors to catre to its requirements as well as those of its workers with increased purchasing power (e.g. if multiplier-effect of a basic industrial worker is 1.5 workers, it means that or one job in industrial sector supports 1.5 jobs in services sector), also *Spin-off Effect.*

Multipurpose Ground: *(P)* see *Multipurpose Open Space.*

Multipurpose Open Space: *(P)* An open space in a city with parking and other related infrastructure that can be used, with permission of the local authorities, for a variety of purposes such as (i) socio-cultural gathering like marriage celebrations and religious function, (ii) political rallies, (iii) events like entertainment shows, sports, exhibitions, or (iv) open air periodic market, also *Maidan. Multipurpose Park, Multipurpose Ground.*

Multipurpose Park: *(P)* see *Multipurpose Open Space.*

Multi-Spectral Scanning (MSS): *(TQ)* A remote sensing device that is capable of recording data in ultraviolet and visible portion of the spectrum as well as the infrared.

Multi-Storeyed Housing: *(H)* structure, more than five storey high, containing a number of independent dwelling units with individual entrance, also *High-rise Housing.*

Municipal Area: *(A)* The territorial area under the jurisdiction of municipality as notified by the Governor.

Municipal Bond: *(F)* A bond issued by a municipality to raise funds from financial capital market for a specific municipal function.

Municipal Corporation: *(A)* An elected urban local body of self-governance for larger urban areas constituted under the Municipal Act, also *Nagar Nigam.*

Municipal Council: *(A)* An elected urban local body of self-governance for smaller urban areas constituted under the Municipal Act, also *Nagar Palika, Nagar Parishad.*

Municipal Government: *(A)* A municipal council, or corporation or *nagar panchayat,* constituted by election as per relevant municipal Act to make policies, collect taxes, and discharge the specified administrative and developmental functions within their respective area of jurisdiction, see also *Municipal Council, Municipal Corporation, Nagar Panchayat.*

Municipal Services: *(A)* The set of services that a municipality is obliged to provide as per municipal Act.

Municipal Solid Waste: *(S)* All types of solid waste, except hospital waste, generated by different residential and commercial areas located in a municipality.

Municipality: *(A)* The urban local institution of self governance constituted under municipal Act.

N

Nadir: (TQ) The point on the ground vertically beneath the perspective centre of the camera lens or sensor.

***Nagar Nigam*:** (A) In Hindi, a municipal corporation, see *Municipal Corporation.*

Nagar Palika: (A) In Hindi, municipal council, also *Nagar Parishad*, see *Municipal Council.*

***Nagar Panchayat*:** (A) An elected local body of self-governance, constituted under the Municipal Act, for transitional areas that are under transformation from rural to urban in nature and function.

Nagar Parishad: (A) In Hindi, see *Municipal Council.*

Nagar: (P) In Hindi, a city, also *Shahar*.

Naka: (A) In Urdu, a point located on a roads, where modalities are available for monitoring and controlling the movement of vehicles carrying goods and passengers.

***Nakabandi*:** (A) In Urdu, the system of monitoring and controlling the movement of people and vehicles on roads in a town.

***Nala*:** (S) In Hindi, an open main drain carrying storm water and / or sewage in a settlement

Nali: (S) In Hindi, an outlet for domestic waste water.

National Development Planning: (P) A process of planning of national economic and social development incorporating national income and investment in development policies and programmes pertaining to sectors such as agriculture, industrial, trade and commerce, transport, communication, health, education, urban development, environment and infrastructure.

National Goals: *(P)* A set of statements expressing the development vision of the country in improving the quality of life of its people.

National Grid: *(P)* see *Electricity Grid.*

National Memorial: *(P)* A place having a tomb, *samadhi,* or other structures dedicated to the memory of a personality of national importance.

National Model: *(TQ)* A spatial model covering an entire nation that provides spatial variation, generally by states, of an attribute such as level of urbanisation, poverty, literacy etc.

National Park: *(L)* see *Sanctuary.*

National Plan: *(P)* A plan, generally of five years' duration, defining national fiscal and socio-economic issues, goals, priorities, policies, strategies, and investment programmes pertaining to sectors such as agriculture, industrial, trade and commerce, transport, communication, health, education, urban development, environment and infrastructure, also *Five-year Plan.*

National Settlement Policy: *(P)* A policy for evolution of a system of settlements that serve as engines of growth, complement the socio-economic development initiatives, and ensure an efficient rural-urban relationship.

Native Land: *(P)* see *Native Place.*

Native Persons: *(P)* A group of persons belonging to a place / region / country by birth.

Native Place: *(P)* The place of birth of a person, also *Native Land.*

Native Plant: *(LA)* A plant indigenous to a particular locale.

Natural Environment: *(E)* see *Environment (a).*

Natural Grade: *(LA)* Unmodified natural surface of land.

Natural Growth Rate: *(D)* The difference between the crude birth rate and crude death rate.

Natural Growth: *(D)* The surplus of population due to excess of births over deaths and does not include increase due to migration.

Natural Rate of Growth of Population: *(D)* The rate of growth of population by increase in number of births over deaths during a given period and does not include migrant population.

Natural Reserve Area: *(E)* (a) A designated area of ecological significance with diversified flora and fauna kept reserved in their natural state for conservation, study, research and human enjoyment, (b) Designated areas, generally kept reserved in their natural state, that are unsuitable for urban development due to natural constraints and include rivers and their 100-year floodplains, wetlands, steep hill slopes, and the like.

Nature: *(E)* The entire universe including the plants, birds, animals, insects, mountains, water bodies, and forces that control life and weather.

Navigable Waterway: *(T)* A canal or an artificial channel of water that is capable of providing passage to boats and other vessels.

Nazul Land: *(P)* In Persian, the land vested with the government

NDC: *(P)* National Development Council.

Nearside Stop: *(T)* A transit stop located on the approach to or before an intersection.

Need: *(EC)* Utilities, facilities, services, and other socio-economic activities required by people that should be accessible to them through planning and other interventions, see also *Want*

Negative: *(TQ)* A photographic image on film, plate or paper, in which the tone is reversed.

Neglected Area: *(P)* A dilapidated area caused by old age, rent control regime, less economic returns, and absence of maintenance and care.

Negotiated Land Assembly: *(P)* A system of assembly of land at a mutually agreeable price arrived at through a process of discussion between the landowners and purchasers.

Negotiated Settlement: *(L)* A settlement of a dispute arrived at through discussion among the concerned parties on mutually agreeable terms and conditions.

Negotiations: *(L)* The act of arriving at an agreement between two parties through discussion.

Neighborhood Shopping Center: *(P)* A commercial center serving the needs of immediate neighbourhood, see also *Neighbourhood.*

Neighborhood: *(P)* A residential planning unit in a city comprising housing-clusters that can support all necessary facilities and services to serve a population of 3,000 to 6,000 persons.

Neighbourhood Park: *(P)* A park that serves the out door recreational and other needs of the immediate neighbourhood, see also *Neighbourhood.*

Net Area Sown: *(P)* This is the net area of agriculture land that is sown with crops and orchards in a reporting year.

Net Residential Density: *(P)* The number of persons per unit area (hectare or acre) of a residential site and it excludes area devoted to sector level facilities, services, commercial activity, parks, open spaces, and major roads (net residential density is generally double of the gross residential density as about 50 per cent area is occupied by sector level uses).

Network Analysis: *(TQ)* A study, using the PERT and CPM, of different components of a project or activity recorded as a network of sequential and interconnected paths of appropriate length-time, with an objective of achieving efficiency in the planning and control process, see also *PERT* and *CPM.*

Network: *(M)* (a) In transportation, a system that comprises transportation by rail, road, air, waterways, wires and pipe lines, (b) In planning, a system of transport and utility lines including water supply, electricity, gas, communication, roads connecting different areas of a city, (c) In administration, a system of relationship between different institutions, organisations and agencies having similar interests of organisational goals.

New Town: *(P)* A self-contained town having its own economic base, administration and governance, comprehensively planned on a virgin site for accommodating industrial, commercial, and residential activities that are served by necessary utilities, facilities and services, see also *Utilities, Facilities, Services.*

Next of Kin: *(H)* The relatives of a deceased person.

NGO: *(A)* see *Non-governmental Organisation.*

Night Shelter: *(H)* A premises, generally owned and managed by the urban local body or a voluntary agency, for providing accommodation, in the night only, to homeless urban poor on daily payment of a token amount as rent, also *Ran Basera.*

Night Soil: *(H)* Human waste from latrines collected manually generally at night.

No Action Alternative: *(P)* An alternative among several alternatives where it is most desirable not to take any action in the given situation because things are progressing well or more time is needed to get the things settled before a clear solution emerges.

Node: *(M)* (a) In transport, (i) a location, along a corridor, where two or more major roads intersect, that attracts residential-commercial mixed-use development, (ii) a location, along a corridor, where an interchange takes place being a major bus or railway station that attracts residential-commercial mixed-use development, (b) In regional planning, a self contained new town planned at a major intersection or major transit (bus or rail) stop, (c) In urban design, a focal point that is significant due to type of activity or because of being a junction of roads or being a point of reference and represents the image of the city e.g. Times Square – New York, Red Square – Beijing, Piccadilly Circus – London.

Noise Abatement: *(E)* Reduction in intensity of sound using acoustical treatments.

Noise Control: *(E)* Reduction in intensity of sound using regulatory measures or guidelines instituted by the government.

Noise Pollution: *(E)* An undesirable sound produced by any source that has adverse impact on human beings such as annoyance, irritation, and deafness.

Noise: *(E)* Any undesired sound.

Nomad: *(P)* A group of people having no permanent dwelling place and are on the move in search of pasture, food and water.

Nominal Scale: *(P)* A scale which consists of a set of limited qualitative characteristics without a ranking relationship between them, e.g. ecological types: wetlands, forest, grasslands, and dunes it gives a comparative idea of extent of tree-cover and other qualities of the area.

Non-ambulatory Disabilities: *(P)* Impairments that confine individuals to wheelchairs, for all practical purposes and all layouts and building designs should incorporate the needs of such individuals.

Non-basic Activities: *(EC)* Activities located in an area that are generated by and cater to only the local demands e.g. local shops, schools, clinics, see also *Basic Activities, Economic Base.*

Non-commute Trips: *(T)* Trips made for purposes other than work-related reasons, e.g. trips made for shopping, medical treatment, school, and recreation.

Non-conforming Building or Structure: *(L)* Any building or structure that is not in accordance with the building code, or is used for the purpose not permitted in the lease deed.

Non-conforming Use: *(M)* (a) Legally, any land use that is prohibited by or not in accordance with the approved master plan, zonal plan, or layout plan, (b) In planning, any use which would be out of character of an area and if allowed would pollute the environment, see also *Non-conforming Building or Structure, Unauthorised Development.*

Non-conventional Sources of Energy: *(S)* see *Alternative Sources of Energy.*

Non-governmental Organisation: *(A)* An organisation, generally registered under Societies Act and functioning at local, regional, national, or international levels to pursue its declared objectives and often serving as an intermediate link between the people and the government in implementation of projects involving a large section of population.

Non-profit Housing: *(H)* A housing financed by private sector, especially by a non-profit organisation, not for speculation but for the benefit of economically weaker and poor sections of the society.

Non-profit Organisation: *(H)* An institution, trust, association, foundation and such other registered bodies established to serve a declared cause with no profit motive and where no part of the net earnings may be lawfully used for the benefit of its shareholders or members.

Non-property Taxes: *(F)* Land based taxes, other than property tax, levied to regulate land and development and promote urban development objectives that also generate revenue and include vacant developed land tax, land value increment tax, betterment levy, development impact exaction, and development charges, see also *Betterment Levy, Development Charges, Development Impact Exaction, Land Value Increment Tax,* and *Vacant Developed Land Tax.*

Non-renewable Resource: *(S)* A resource, the total quantity of which does not appreciably increase over time, and therefore, its supply diminish with each use and a time will come when it will be extinct.

Non-spatial Conceptual Model: *(TQ)* A model that provides a descriptive analysis of generalised pattern of social, economic or physical change.

Non-spatial Mathematical Model: *(TQ)* Mathematical equations evolved with specified assumptions that calculate the changing value of a pattern of social, economic or physical change having no regard to spatial variations.

Non-spatial Model: *(TQ)* A model where the spatial variables are not considered and do not form its integral part, see also *Model Types-(c), Non-spatial Conceptual Model, Non-spatial Mathematical Model.*

Non-tax Revenue: *(F)* Revenue generated by a local body from sources other than taxes levied under an act and include sources like remunerative and commercial projects, license fee, development charges, and impact fee, see also *Development Charges, Impact Fee, License Fee,* and *Remunerative and Commercial Projects.*

Non-worker: *(D)* A person who has not worked at all in the year preceding the date of enumeration.

Normative Approach: *(P)* In decision-making, a normative framework that describes a traditional situation in which the decision-maker faces a set of known alternatives and selects the preferred course of action by rational selection process.

Notary Public: *(L)* A person authorised to perform function such as certifying copies of documents, attesting signatures and affidavits, and administering an oath.

Notified Area: *(P)* Any land area earmarked on a plan for the purpose of its development and specified by public notification in an official gazette as per legal provisions.

Noxious Industry: *(P)* Any industry or manufacturing process that produces any solid, liquid, or gaseous substance, in such a concentration as may be, or tend to be, injurious to public health and environment.

Nuclear Housing: *(H)* see *Core Housing.*

Nursery School: *(P)* An institution located in a building, managed by public or private institution, for offering education and play facilities for children up to 5 years' age, preparatory to school, with emphasis on 'learn while you play', also *Kinder Garden.*

Nursing Home: *(P)* A health care facility, having up to 30 beds, managed on commercial basis by a doctor or a group of doctors.

O

Oasis: *(P)* A place in desert where there is water, fertile soil and vegetation and hence concentration of population and socio-economic activities.

Oath: *(L)* A solemn affirmation to tell the truth.

Objectives: *(M)* Statements that provide operational means to achieving a set of goals or the development vision, see also *Implementation Objective, Planning Objective.*

Obligation: *(L)* Functions, acts or duties to which an individual or organisation is legally bound to perform.

Obligatory Functions: *(L)* Functions assigned to an agency under law, which must be performed by the agency.

Oblige: *(L)* To bind a person by promise to do something.

Oblique Aerial Photography: *(TQ)* The technique of taking photographs from a camera mounted in an airplane or balloon in an oblique position with respect to the Earth's surface at the time of exposure and is used for general information, sometimes to verify certain attributes, but does not provide accurate measurements for photogrammetric mapping.

Observatory and Weather Office: *(P)* A premises with facilities and equipments to monitor, process and disseminate information related to weather and may include research facilities.

Obsolescence: *(P)* The condition of an area characterised by dilapidation due to non-use, misuse, or going out of use because of factors like inaccessibility, ageing of building, overcrowding, stress on services, falling structures, low rents and hence non-maintenance

Occupancy: *(H)* Number of persons per habitable room in a house, see also *Habitable Room.*

Occupant: *(H)* A person having actual possession of a dwelling unit established by living, sleeping and eating there.

OD Survey: *(T)* see *Origin-Destination Survey.*

ODP: *(P)* see *Outline Development Plan.*

Office: *(P)* A building used for performing the functions and activities related to a government ministry or department, corporate body, private company or an individual, see also *Central Government Office, State Government Office, Local Government Office, Corporate Office, Private Office.*

Off-peak Direction of Travel: *(T)* The direction of travel, in a corridor, experiencing lower demand during a peak commuting period.

Off-peak Period: *(T)* The period of time that is outside the peak commuting period.

Off-site Infrastructure: *(P)* Generally provided by the local body or other agencies, on payment by the users, the main / trunk road, water supply, sewerage, drainage and electricity lines, to which the on-site infrastructure is connected.

Oil Depot: *(P)* An area where storage tanks of petroleum products and other related facilities are located taking into consideration the regulations in this respect.

Old Town: *(P)* (a) Generally the core area of a city that retains buildings and sites of historical, archaeological, cultural and architectural significance and needs conservation, (b) The core area of a city that is dilapidated due to factors like age, uneconomical returns, and poor maintenance, and need rejuvenation and renewal.

One-man Organisation: *(A)* An organisation where the same individual performs all functions related to fulfilment of the organisational-objectives.

On-site Infrastructure: *(P)* Generally provided by a developer, the basic infrastructure such as water supply, sewerage, drainage and electricity lines, roads, roadside plantation and landscaping of open spaces required on a site and serving exclusively the people living there.

On-site Production: *(H)* Construction of building components on the building site itself.

On-site Training: *(ET)* Practical training given to the participants on the construction site, see also *On-the-Job Training.*

On-the-Job Training: *(ET)* One of the alternative learning methods aimed at practical training given to the participants at the work place, see also *Alternative Learning Methods, On-site Training.*

On-time Performance: *(T)* Measure of efficiency, usually expressed as percentage of times that a transit vehicle meets the published schedule arrival timings.

Open Air Theatre: *(P)* A place, open to sky, where live shows of performing arts can be held and viewed by audience.

Open Cluster: *(H)* Housing cluster where the cluster open spaces are linked to form a continuous space.

Open Learning: *(ET)* see *Distance Learning.*

Open Spaces: *(L)* Sites in a settlement, designated and designed as parks, gardens playfields, sports facilities, *maidan,* and outdoor recreation areas, also *Green Areas,* see also *Park, Maidan, Hierarchy of Open Spaces, Botanical Garden, Zoological Park.*

Open Tender: *(M)* A tender received as a result of an advertisement inviting parties for competitive bidding.

Operating Budget: *(F)* Detailed plan of income and expenditure of a public agency or private organisation for current operations excluding capital items.

Operating Cost: *(F)* The ongoing costs associated with administering, operating, enforcing, and maintaining facilities and related services.

Operating Expenses: *(F)* The expenses that are incurred on running a business or operation to implement a project and include salaries, allowances, travel, and all other support costs.

Operating Ratio: *(F)* The ratio of operating expenses to total revenue.

Operation and Maintenance: *(M)* Activities pertaining to actual functioning of a public service and keep it running through necessary repairs and servicing.

Operation Plan: *(M)* (a) In planning, a comprehensive plan, which provides the policies and procedures for administering, operating, enforcing, and maintaining a facility or service, (b) In management, a plan prepared by the lower level management, that focuses on day-to-day and week-to-week operations within the framework of procedures, norms and standards and also provides regular feedback.

Operational Construction: *(P)* Any construction, temporary or permanent, which is necessary for the operation, maintenance, development or execution of any of the following services, namely – railways, national highways, national waterways, major ports, airways and aerodromes, post and telegraph, telephone, wireless, broadcasting, regional grid for electricity and does not include new structures used for residential, commercial, industrial, and warehousing purposes.

Operational Year: *(F)* The current financial year.

Operations Research: *(TQ)* A method of finding optimum solution to a problem related to operation of a system such as transportation, using scientific techniques and systems analysis, for assisting in decision-making process.

Operator: *(M)* A person or agency, body or organisation that performs the actual task in implementing a plan, policy, or facility or service.

Optimise: *(TQ)* To make the action most favourable in given conditions.

Orange Industries: *(P)* Industries that use processes or generate effluents which are moderately polluting and include automobile servicing, hotel, food processing, stone crushing, tyre manufacturing etc.

Orchard: *(P)* An enclosure for growing fruit trees for commercial purposes.

Ordinal Scale: A scale that consists of a set of limited semi-quantitative characteristics of an object or area with a ranking relationship between them, e.g. low, medium, high or good, very good, excellent, here the relationship is not quantitative as very good is not two times better than good, see also *Scale.*

Ordinance: *(L)* A law made by the order of an authority such as the president of a country or governor of a state.

Organic Growth: *(P)* A pattern of growth of an area or settlement that evolves spontaneously without any planned intervention, see also *Spontaneous Settlement, Organic Pattern.*

Organic Pattern: *(P)* An arrangement characterised by irregular, unplanned and spontaneous layout of streets, buildings and open spaces, see also *Organic Growth.*

Organisation: *(A)* All types of departments and agencies in both private and public sectors, whether established / registered by Act, or un registered, to perform certain tasks, also *body,* see also *Formal Organisation, One-man Organisation, Two-level Organisation,* and *Three-level Organisation.*

Organised Development: *(P)* A pattern of development evolved by systematic planning interventions.

Organising Function: *(A)* An act that refers to development of organisational structure, its pattern which could be centralised or decentralised, and assignment of responsibilities, authority as well as accountability, to facilitate the successful accomplishment of plans and programmes, also see *Management.*

Orientation: *(P)* (a) Placing of buildings in a layout plan in such a way that the benefits of the sunlight and wind direction are available in most of the cases, (b) Identification of an element on the ground, which is marked on a map with the help of cardinal points, (c) Aligning a map with the indicated and actual cardinal points so that each element on the map can be identified on the ground.

Origin: *(T)* The starting point or zone of a trip.

Original Plot: *(P)* see *Land Pooling.*

Origin-destination Survey: *(T)* A survey and analysis of the vehicle and trip characteristics by the starting and ending points or zones of the trip.

Ornamental Garden: *(LA)* A richly landscaped garden for visual pleasure and appreciation.

Orphanage: *(P)* A building with facilities for boarding and lodging of children, who are bereaved of parents and it does not include educational facilities.

Orthophotography: *(TQ)* see *Vertical Aerial Photography.*

Oustee: *(P)* A person who has been displaced from his present location due to a major development project (like mining operation, construction of dam or highway) and needs to be compensated, relocated, or rehabilitated in a just and humane way as per rules regulations and guidelines in this respect.

Out House: *(H)* A self contained house, with separate entry, located away from or adjoining the main house.

Outdoor Furniture: *(LA)* Furniture items for use in open areas as part of landscape design

Outdoor Recreation: *(P)* Active recreational activities that are generally performed out side in parks, playfields and other open spaces.

Outdoor Stadium: *(P)* see *Stadium.*

Outgrowth *(P)* Conglomeration of areas such as residential colonies, campuses, commercial centres, and industrial areas, located outside the formal limits of a city but adjoining it having a high degree of interdependence with the city, see also *Overspill.*

Outlay: *(F)* An amount of money earmarked for expenditure during a given period of time on a given programme / project.

Outline Development Plan: *(P)* An interim plan of a settlement to guide development for the period till its comprehensive development plan is prepared and approved for implementation, also *Interim General Plan.*

Outline: *(P)* (a) A general sketch of approach to a project under consideration without details, (b) Expression of an idea, concept or proposal in points without details.

Outlying Areas: *(P)* Areas located at the fringe of a city that is under transformation from rural to urban in function and character, also *Outskirts.*

Output: *(TQ)* (a) The end product of an operation or process, (b) The final result of a study or research, (c) The final product of an industry.

Outside Lane: *(T)* The lane on a highway or road closest to the shoulder or farthest from the median.

Outskirts: *(P)* see *Outlying Areas.*

Outstanding: *(M)* (a) In education and training and also administration, a level of performance of a student / trainee / employee that clearly stands out among others and is rated above 'excellent',

(b) In general, a work, project, or assignment that is still unattained even after expiry of the due date, (c) In finance, a payment that is delayed and needs to be paid.

Overall Density: *(P)* The density of population of a settlement calculated by dividing its total population by the total area covered by all uses, also *City Level Density, Town Density.*

Overcrowding: *(H)* Excessive concentration of activities and people in an area that cannot be supported the existing infrastructure.

Overgrown Settlement: *(P)* A settlement where the population and activities have grown too fast to be sustained by the existing economic opportunities and infrastructure, resulting in chaotic conditions.

Overhead Cost: *(F)* Expenses for management, administration, facilities, services , maintenance, and other indirect costs necessarily incurred to operate a business, which are not directly chargeable to individual unit of production or service.

Overhead Tank: *(S)* A raised structure with large tank and pump used for storage and distribution of water to its service area by gravitation.

Overpass: *(T)* A road over bridge facilitating traffic on one road to cross over another.

Overspill Area: *(P)* The area on the outskirts of a large city that accommodates a part of the expanding city's population.

Overspill: *(P)* The process of overflow of population and activities from a large city to its outskirts or new towns located in the city region, see also *Outgrowth, Overspill Area.*

Owner Occupancy: *(H)* A property where the owner himself lives.

Owner: *(L)* A person or body who has the legal title to hold the property.

Ownership: *(L)* Acquiring the legal title to a property.

Oxidation Pond: *(S)* A water body used for final treatment of partially treated wastewater that, on discharge of such water, allows the growth of algae and bacteria, which in turn decompose the rest of its waste-matter.

P

Panchayat: *(P)* In Hindi, a village level constitutional organisation for grassroots level administration and governance comprising five members elected by the *gram sabha* to serve for a period of five years, see also *Gram Sabha.*

Panchromatic Film: *(TQ)* A photographic films that is sensitive to broad bends or sensitive to all colours.

Panel of Consultants: *(P)* A group of experts identified and listed, through an open and transparent selection processes by an organisation, for a specified period of time, for assigning consultancy work, as and when necessary, to any one or more of them without any further selection process.

Panel of Contractors: *(P)* A group of contractors identified and sometimes classified into categories and listed, through an open and transparent selection processes by an organisation, for a specified task and period of time, for assigning contract work, as and when necessary, to any one or more of them without any further selection process, also *Registered Contractors.*

PAP: *(P)* see *Project Affected Person.*

Parallel Economy: *(EC)* see *Informal Sector.*

Para-transit: *(T)* Transit services, generally privately owned, that sure operate on demand, and include taies and auto rickshaws.

Parceling-out of Land: *(P) see Land Sub-division.*

Parivahan: *(T) In Hindi,* the public transport system in a city

Park: *(P)* An appropriately landscaped place used for outdoor leisure activity and may have fencing, parking space and public toilets, see also *Open Spaces, Green Area.*

Park Belt: *(P)* see *Green Belt.*

Park-and-pool Facility: *(T)* see *Park-and-pool lot.*

Park-and-pool Lot: *(T)* A parking lot where individuals can park their private vehicle and join a carpool or vanpool, also *Park-and-pool Facility.*

Park-and-ride Facility: *(T)* see *Park-and-ride lot.*

Park-and-ride Lot: *(T)* A parking lot where individuals can park their private vehicle for the day and access public transportation, also *park-and-ride facility.*

Parking: *(T)* A place open or covered, owned by a local body, private agency, or an individual, used for parking of vehicles with or without parking charges.

Parking Management: *(T)* Policies, strategies and programmes for managing both the supply of and the demand for parking at employment and major activity centers in a city and may include strategies focusing on space availability and location, parking pricing, and the elimination of free, low-cost, or on-street parking, see also *Parking Pricing.*

Parking Pricing: *(T)* A pricing mechanism to control the demand for parking e.g. charging higher rates for cars with single occupancy and reducing for cars with more riders and eliminating fees for carpools and vanpools, see also *Carpool, Vanpool.*

Partially Separate System of Drainage: *(S)* A system in which part of the surface water is conveyed by the foul (sanitary) sewers and the rest is conveyed through drains.

Participant: *(ET)* see *Trainee.*

Participation Ratio: *(D)* The ratio, expressed in percentage, between the actual workers and the work force at a given point of time, see also *Work Force.*

Participatory Leadership: *(A)* A leadership pattern, which is democratic in nature and has wider acceptability, where a select group thinks together about the problem at hand and decides about the pattern and nature of action which are then followed by the group members under the overall command and supervision of the leader.

Participatory Learning: *(ET)* A method of training that actively involves participants in the learning process.

Passenger Car Unit: *(T)* An adjustment factor to convert a heterogeneous traffic into a homogeneous traffic where each vehicle type is assigned a factor equivalent to a passenger car to convert it to the passenger car unit (PCU) (e.g. car=1PCU, Truck=3PCU), also *PCU.*

Passive Recreation: *(P)* Leisure activities of people that do not require a vigorous movement of limbs such as reading, sitting on a park bench, viewing scenery, watching TV, picnicking, and visiting friends, also *Recreation (passive).*

Pastureland: *(G)* Land reserved for growing grass for grazing cattle and sheep.

Path: *(M)* (a) In transport, see *footpath.* (b) In urban design, channel of movement in a city along which people walk, observe the various buildings and features and form part of the perceived image of the city.

Pathway: *(T)* see *Footpath.*

***Patta*:** *(L)* In Hindi, the legal title to land held by a person.

Pattern of Development: *(P)* The two dimensional shape of a settlement evolved by the land uses and activity patterns, and road network.

Paved Road: *(T)* A road, constructed with durable surface material (cement concrete, asphalt) that can withstand all types of weather and can be used in all weather conditions.

Pavement Dweller: *(H)* see *Homeless.*

Payment Arrear: *(F)* A debt that has not been paid on time and is still unpaid and overdue for payment.

PCU: *(T)* see *Passenger Car Unit.*

PDP: *(P)* see *Project Displaced Person.*

Peak Demand: *(S)* see *Peak Load.*

Peak Direction of Travel: *(T)* The direction of higher travel demand during a peak commuting period.

Peak Hour: *(T)* The hour, generally, in the morning and also in the evening, when there is a maximum flow of traffic on a given transportation facility or corridor.

Peak Load: *(S)* The maximum level of electricity demand in a specified time period, also *Peak Demand.*

Peak Period: *(T)* The time period (covering two or more hours), generally in the morning and also in the evening, when there is heaviest traffic on a given transportation facility or corridor.

Pedestrian: *(T)* A person traveling on foot.

Pedestrian Crossing: *(T)* see *Zebra-crossing.*

Pedestrian Path: *(T)* see *Footpath.*

Pedestrian Walkway: *(T)* see *Zebra-crossing.*

Pedestrian-oriented Plan: (P) A plan where the pedestrian system is designed in such a way that ensures distribution of the activities of daily use within a walking distance from place of residence, and the walk is comfortable and pleasing.

Peer Review: *(TQ)* One of the methods of testing a specific component of a plan wherein persons (other than the owner or author), having appropriate technical or business skill, review it for accuracy and completeness.

Per Capita Income: *(EC)* A ratio obtained by dividing the total income, from all sources, of all inhabitants of an area by the total number of inhabitants.

Percolation: *(S)* Downwards flow of water through soil or rock, also *Infiltration.*

Perennial River: *(E)* A river that flows throughout the year from its source to the end point where it meets sea or another river.

Performance Indicator: *(A)* Tools that depict in quantitative terms (numeric values, percentages, scores and indices) the progress of an activity in the form of actual results as compared with the expected results.

Performance Standard: *(M)* A set of criteria based on accepted practice and approved by a recognised agency for repeated and continued use, see also *Performance Target.*

Performance Target: *(M)* The set of specific benchmarks to be achieved within a given timeframe that forms the basis for assessment of the performance of a person, organisation, a plan, or a project, see also *Performance Standard.*

Peripheral Parking: *(T)* Parking lot or garage located adjacent to the city centre or other major activity area.

Periphery: *(P)* see *Regional Periphery.*

Peri-urban Area: *(P)* see *Urban Fringe.*

Permissible Development: *(P)* see *Permissible Use.*

Permissible Use: *(P)* Use, as specified in the development control rules / master plan, that requires the planning permission and may be permitted on an application to the competent authority, also *Permissible Development, Use Permissible, Activities Permissible.*

Permitted Development: *(P)* see *Permitted Use.*

Permitted Use: *(P)* Use as specified in the development control rules / master plan, that does not require planning permission from the competent authority, also *Permitted Development, Use Permitted, Activities Permitted.*

Person Throughput: *(T)* The number of persons, not vehicles, being carried on by transport facility at a specific point on the road during a predetermined period of time.

Personal Service Shop: *(P)* A premises providing personal services such as tailoring and hair cutting.

Perspective Plan: *(P)* (a) A long-term – 20 to 25 years – plan providing the goals, policies, strategies and programmes of socio-economic and spatial development of a nation / state / region / district / city as the case may be, (b) Socio-economic and spatial development vision of the central / state / local government.

PERT: *(TQ)* see *Programme Evaluation and Review Technique.*

Petrol Pump: *(P)* A premises for sale of petroleum products to consumers and may include a facility for servicing of automobiles.

***Pheriwala*:** *(P)* In Hindi, a hawker, see *Hawker.*

Physical Infrastructure: *(P)* Essential utilities and services like water supply, sewerage, drainage, power supply, and solid waste management.

Physical Plan: *(P)* see *Master Plan.*

Physical Planner: *(P)* see *Town Planner.*

Physical Planning: *(P)* A process of formulation of the plan of a settlement or region, as the case may be, which serves as a tool in guiding the manner in which land will be used for various socio-economic and physical activities and infrastructure provision and development therein shall be carried out by the public or private agencies, also *Land Use Planning, Spatial Planning, Town Planning* see also *Plan-(a) (i), Cyclic Processes of Planning.*

Picnic Hut: *(P)* A premises, located in a recreational or tourist zone and provided with all necessary facilities and services for the use of short-duration stay, outdoor recreation, or leisure activities like picnic.

Pilot Project: *(P)* A project, formulated after incorporating a new idea, concept, technique, policy, or programme, and implemented to test the innovative approach with a view to getting feedback for improvements, if needed, before its finalisation.

Pixel: *(TQ)* (a) In satellite images, an integrated radiance of mapping unit, (b) In GIS, the smallest unit of information in an image or raster map referred to as a cell in an image or grid.

Plan: *(M)* (a) In spatial planning, a two dimensional representation of (i) existing or proposed characteristics of land and arrangement of various land uses and transportation network in an area, or (ii) spatial variations of an attribute, or (iii) distribution of various policy zones in a city or region, (b) In economic planning, a document highlighting the characteristics of different sectors of economy, and proposed policies, programmes along with fiscal allocations for economic development and social justice in an area, (c) In administration, a scheme for accomplishing organisational goals, (d) In design, an arrangement of different components of a building at plinth level, seen from above.

Plan Implementation: *(P)* The process of execution or carrying out of the provisions of a plan, see also *Plan.*

Planetarium: *(P)* A building designed with necessary facilities and equipments for the study of planets.

Planned Approach: *(P)* In decision-making, a process, which recognises that both quantitative and qualitative approaches are needed to take desirable decisions and, therefore, incorporates scientific methods with creativity, intuition, judgment and experience of the decision-maker.

Planning: *(P)* A continuous, time-oriented and cyclic process of identification and achievement of goals, see also *Cyclic Processes of Planning.*

Planning Area: *(P)* An area, declared under Town Planning Act, having well defined boundaries identified by natural or manmade elements, for which the master plan or development plan shall be prepared.

Planning Authority: *(P)* An authority established by a relevant legislation and empowered, among other functions, to declare any area as planning area, prepare its development plan, get it approved from a competent authority and take necessary measures to implement it (some planning authorities do not have the implementation functions which is done by other agencies).

Planning Brief: *(P)* A brief description of the site and intentions, expectations, considerations, constraints, and requirements given by a client (government body or private organisation, individual) to a consultant planner that forms the basis for preparation of development plan of the area.

Planning Concept: *(P)* see *Conceptual Plan.*

Planning Function: *(M)* In management, an act that incorporates setting of goals and priorities, formulation of strategies, policies, procedures, norms and standards, as well as preparation of time bound plans, and programmes of action to be followed to achieve the set goals, also see *Management,* (b) In planning, an act of preparation of physical plan, see also *Planning* and *Physical Planning.*

Planning Model: *(TQ)* A model that deals with selection of an optimum set of alternative actions in managing a situation.

Planning Norms and Standards: *(P)* Criteria, expressed in quantitative terms, that set an expected level of performance.

Planning Objectives: *(M)* A set of written statements that specify the operational planning principals to achieve the goals or the vision, see also *Implementation Objectives.*

Planning Permission: *(P)* On an application on the prescribed form, formal approval given by a competent authority for development requiring such planning permission.

Plant Guard: *(LA)* see *Tree Guard.*

Plant Nursery: *(P)* A premises for growing seedlings of a variety of plants and propagation of plants for sale.

Playfield: *(P)* A premises designated in a layout or any other plan as such and includes open area for sports and outdoor games, and may have parking and public toilets for players and spectators, also *Playground.*

Playground: *(P)* see *Playfield.*

Plot: *(P)* A single unit of subdivision of land, that can be identified and defined in a layout plan, intended for the indicated specific use, also *lot,* see also *Corner Plot / site, Double Frontage Plot / site, Residence-cum-work Plot, Residential Plot in Group Housing, Residential Plot in Plotted Housing, Commercial Plots, Industrial Plots, Institutional Plots.*

Polarisation: *(P)* In spatio-economic development context, concentration of economic, political, administrative, and socio-cultural activities, at a given point of time, in a planned manner in selected cities serving as growth poles, see also *Growth Pole.*

Police Lines: *(P)* A campus with parade ground, necessary facilities, and buildings for providing residential accommodation to police personnel.

Police Post: *(P)* A building accommodating office and residential accommodation of some essential staff of police serving a designated local area having a population of about 50,000 (this figure may change).

Police Station: *(P)* A building accommodating office and residential accommodation of some essential staff of police serving a designated area and having a population of 75,000 to 100,000 (this figure may change).

Policy Implementation: *(P)* The process of execution or carrying out of the provisions of a policy.

Pollutant: *(E)* see *Environmental Pollutant.*

Pollution: *(E)* Release into any environmental medium – air, water or land – from any process or substances which are capable of causing harm to man or any other living organism supported by the environment, see also *Environmental Pollution.*

Pollution Control: *(E)* Precautionary legal, administrative, planning, and monitoring procedures to control various sources of environmental contamination that are capable of causing harm to man or any other living organism supported by environment.

Polygon: *(TQ)* In GIS, a coverage feature class used to represent areas and defined by the arcs that make up its boundary and a point inside its boundary for identification.

Pooled Finance Development Facility: *(F)* A facility of the Government of India to enable smaller urban local bodies, which cannot go individually to financial market borrowing through bonds, to pool their financial requirements and submit to the state level agency (an urban development corporation) that will in turn raise the total required fund form the market and pass down to the urban local bodies. This also includes underwriting of a part of the loan repayment obligation from a Debt Reserve Fund, which will raise the credit rating of participating urban local bodies and help them to get a better terms for market borrowing in future.

Poor and Disadvantaged: *(P)* That section of the society, which by reason of low income suffers from unfavourable social and economic conditions, also *Underprivileged.*

Popular Participation: *(P)* see *Public Participation.*

Population Density: *(P)* Number of persons per unit area (i.e. acre, hectare, sq. mile, sq. km. etc).

Population Displacement: *(P)* Dislocation, permanently or temporarily, of population of an area due to natural disaster or a large project such as dam construction.

Population Distribution: *(P)* In a region, territorial assignment of population to various settlements, existing or proposed new towns, depending upon their respective potential, propensity, and regional development strategy.

Population Drift: *(P)* see *Migration.*

Population Dynamics: *(P)* The study of socio-economic, physical, and other forces that determine growth, decline or stabilisation of population of a settlement.

Population Explosion: *(P)* Sudden and rapid increase in population of an area / settlement due to mass migration.

Population Forecast: *(TQ)* see *Population Projection.*

Population Mobility: *(P)* The alternative choices available to people for inter-regional and intra-regional spatial mobility, for different purposes, during a specified period of time.

Population Planning: *(P)* (a) A process of planned growth of family with a view to achieving population policy goals, (b) The measures adopted to alter or modify existing population trends in the interest of national survival and family welfare.

Population Projection: *(TQ)* The statistical methods of calculation of population size of an area or settlement at a given point of time in future, also *Population Forecast.*

Population Trends: *(TQ)* The temporal pattern of population growth or changes in composition.

Port: *(P)* A harbour for ships and boats with loading and unloading facilities.

Port City: *(P)* A city with a harbour as the main centre of activities.

Post Office: *(P)* A building used for collection, sorting and distribution of articles sent by post to people as well as providing services related to deposit of money as a bank, and money-transfer from one place to another.

Poultry Farm: *(P)* A premises having facilities for rearing of birds and processing and sale of poultry products.

Poverty: *(EC)* (a) A condition characterised by severe deprivation of basic human needs, including food, safe drinking water, sanitation facilities, health, shelter, education and information, (b) A condition where the people live on earnings less than US $2 per capita per day (World Bank) see also *Extreme Poverty, Urban Poverty.*

Power Grid: *(S)* A system of interconnected power lines and power plants to provide uninterrupted supply of electricity to settlements connected to the grid at various points.

Power of Attorney: *(L)* A legal provision through which the right of occupancy, management, and transfer of a property is given by the owner to another person.

Predictive Model: *(TQ)* A model that provides a relationship between the cause and its effect based upon the theory that explains such relationship and through it the effect of change in one variable on the other can always be predicted.

Pre-Disaster Planning: *(P)* see *Disaster Mitigation.*

Pre-emption: *(L)* A legal means of transferring ownership of land from private to public sector through priority right under which the community has the right of first purchase, see also *Land Acquisition.*

Pre-emptive Right: *(L)* A privilege accorded by the government to a settler on a public land to buy the same land at a fixed price, to the exclusion of other applicants.

Prefabricated Building: *(H)* A building constructed with structural components such as columns, beams, trusses, wall panels, and floor panels, manufactured in a factory and delivered at the construction-site for assembly, also *Component Building.*

Pre-investment Study: *(P)* see *Pre-feasibility Study.*

Pre-investment Survey: *(P)* see *Pre-feasibility Study.*

Preliminary Plan: *(P)* see *Conceptual Plan.*

Premises: *(P)* Any building, structure, or land in a settlement used for locating and operating an activity.

Preprocessing: *(TQ)* In GIS, geometric and radiometric correction, making of mosaics, re-sampling, and formatting of image data before information extraction.

Prescribed: *(P)* According to the officially declared manner.

Prescribed Authority: *(P)* A person or body of persons appointed as such by government, by notification in the official Gazette, to perform specified functions.

Prescriptive Model: *(TQ)* A model that behaves normatively i.e. in a standard pattern / behaviour e.g. a linear equation.

Presence of Natural Person: *(M)* see *Movement of Natural Persons.*

Primary School: *(P)* An institution located in a building or a campus of several buildings, managed by public or private institution, for offering education and play facilities for children between 6 to 10 years' age studying in I to V class / standard.

Primary Sector: *(EC)* see *Sectors of Economy.*

Primate City: *(P)* The largest and economically, socially and politically most dominant city in a country / region that is at least twice as large in population as the second largest city in that country / region.

Principal Investigator: *(P)* An individual designated as such who is responsible and accountable for satisfactory completion of a project or activity, also *Programme Director, Project Director.*

Prior Approval: *(P)* A written approval of a competent authority before commencement of the work on site.

Priority Lane: *(T)* Lane providing preferential treatment to buses, carpools, and vanpools.

Priority Lane Pricing: *(T)* Concept of using congestion pricing or priority pricing on a priority lane where cars carrying 1 or 2 passengers may be charged and carpools with 3 or more passengers may be allowed to use the facility for free, also *Priority Pricing.*

Priority Pricing: *(T)* see *Priority Lane Pricing.*

Privacy: *(H)* A desired degree of visual and social seclusion that a dwelling design and housing development need to provide.

Private Aid: *(P)* Development funds received as aid, for a specified project, from private foundations, religious and charitable institutions, voluntary organisations or NGOs.

Private Garage: *(H)* A building or a portion thereof designed or used for parking of private vehicles.

Private Office: *(P)* A building used for performing the functions and activities related to a private company or an individual.

Private Ownership: *(P)* Ownership of a property or goods by a private person with full right to its use, renting out, or disposal.

Private Sector: *(EC)* That sector of economy of a country, region or state, comprising production of goods and provision of services, which is owned and managed, for making reasonable profit, by private persons, firms, institutions, and corporations that are not functioning under the direct control of the government.

Procedure: *(P)* A specified course of action or prescribed steps for achieving a set of specific objectives.

Processing: *(M)* (a) In aerial photography / remote sensing, the operation to produce negatives, slides or prints from exposed film, plate, or papers, (b) Manipulation of digital data by means of a computer, (c) In planning, evaluation, examination, study of documents for approval by the competent authority.

Productivity: *(P)* A measure of overall efficiency guided by inputs and outputs.

Professional: *(P)* A person having specialised knowledge and skill through education, training and practical experience.

Proficiency: *(ET)* The ability to perform a skill or skills efficiently, precisely and with expertise

Programme: *(M)* (a) A proposal that translates the strategies and objectives into a plan of action supported by necessary funds, (b) In planning, a listing of specific tasks to be performed and resources required to accomplish an objective, (c) In education and training, a brief day-by-day listing of the major activities or events to be conducted / organised in a training course / seminar.

Programme Director: *(P)* see *Principal Investigator.*

Programme Evaluation and Review Technique: *(TQ)* A quantitative method of graphically analysing various activities, their interrelationship and sequence they must follow to determine, in advance, the sequence of actions, and minimum time needed to implement a project or activity, also *PERT.*

Programme Implementation: *(P)* The process of execution or carrying out of the provisions of a programme, see also *Programme.*

Progress Report: *(P)* A report giving the quantity of work executed against a set target.

Progressive Housing: *(H)* see *Core Housing.*

Prohibited Development: *(P)* see *Prohibited use.*

Prohibited Industries: *(P)* Industries that are not permitted in certain use zone in a city due to pollution of air, water or land from their process or products, which causes harm to people living in the surrounding areas.

Prohibited Use: *(P)* Use as specified in the development control rules/ master plan, that are not allowed in a particular use zone, also *Activities Prohibited, Prohibited Development, Use Prohibited.*

Project: *(M)* A document related to a building, site, or equipment with all necessary supporting legal, administrative and technical details, estimated cost, sources of finance and cost recovery for submission to a funding agency or an approving body.

Project Affected Person: *(P)* A person who sustains damages due to a project by way of (i) acquisition of land, (ii) loss of movable property in any manner, or (iii) loss of livelihood and it also includes the project displaced persons, also *PAP*, see also *Project Displaced Person.*

Project Appraisal: *(M)* An analysis of the legal, institutional, technical, financial, and environmental soundness of a specific project proposal, keeping in mind its objective, with a view to present specific recommendations to decision-makers regarding its approval for implementation or sanction of loan as the case may be.

Project Budgeting: *(F)* The process of estimation of the total cost of a project including the cost of land, its development, building construction, provision of services, purchase of equipments, professional fee, servicing of loan, contingency charges and other charges if any.

Project Cycle: *(P)* A cycle consisting of seven phases as - identification, formulation, appraisal, negotiations, implementation, supervision, and evaluation, see also *Project Identification, Project Formulation, Project Appraisal, Project Negotiations, Project Implementation, Project Supervision, Project Evaluation.*

Project Director: *(P)* see *Principal Investigator.*

Project Displaced Person: *(P)* A person who is compelled to shift the place of his residence, business or work due to a project, also *PDP.*

Project Evaluation: *(M)* The processes of application of various techniques for assessment of successes and failures of a project during its implementation and / or after its completion to form basis for course correction (if needed) and future policies.

Project Formulation: *(M)* (a) The process of translation of an idea or concept into a specific scheme and plan of action, (b) Preparation of project proposal incorporating the legal, technical and financial details as per guidelines / requirements of the funding agency.

Project Identification: *(M)* The process of selecting various projects within the framework of a policy or programme or development plan, for further detailing and implementation, taking into account the priorities and fiscal resources available, also *Project Selection.*

Project Implementation: *(P)* The process of execution or carrying out of the provisions of a project, see also *Project.*

Project Management: *(M)* The process of actual execution of a project, to achieve the set objectives, through efficient directing, coordinating, and controlling functions.

Project Negotiations: *(P)* A process of agreement on disputes pertaining to a project, through discussion and give-and-take on both sides of the table to ensure the success of the project where the final agreements become legal obligations and form part of the loan / grant / aid document.

Project Prioritisation: *(P)* Arranging the projects in order of priority depending upon felt needs of the people, policies of the government, and resources available.

Project Selection: *(M)* see *Project Identification.*

Project Supervision: *(P)* (a) Form the client's side, the processes to ensure that all necessary inputs and resources are made available, at the right time, for successful implementation of the project as per plans and schedule of operation, (b) From the funding agency's side, to ensure that the proceeds of the loan / grant / aid are used only for the purpose for which it was sanctioned and the progress of the work is in accordance with the guidelines incorporated in the agreement with the client, (c) From planner's side, to ensure that provisions of the plan are being implemented in a satisfactory manner.

Promoter: *(P)* see *Developer.*

Propensity: *(P)* (a) Tendency to move in certain direction, (b) Direction of growth of an area depending upon its physical characteristics, nature of land use, accessibility and other potentials and constraints.

Property: *(P)* Includes real property, equipment, intangible property and debt instruments.

Property Agent: *(P)* A person who buys or sells propertied for others on a commission charged from one party (the seller) or both parties (the seller and the buyer).

Property Deed: *(P)* Legal document that establishes the ownership of a property by an individual or organisation.

Property Market: *(P)* see *Real-Estate Market.*

Property Tax: *(P)* A tax levied by the urban local body on the owners of property (land and / or building), under the provisions of the relevant Municipal Act, with a view to generate resources for carrying out of its functions.

Protected Area: *(P)* An area, building or structure designated as such, by law or otherwise in an approved plan, for protection from its misuse or abuse because of its special characteristics or historical or architectural significance or natural beauty

Public Administration: *(A)* see *Administration-(b).*

Public Affairs: *(A)* All matters pertaining to welfare and service to the people.

Public Awareness: *(P)* The consciousness and knowledge of people regarding their rights and responsibilities including information about developmental activities, policies, programmes and projects applicable to their areas.

Public Conveniences: *(P)* see *Public Toilet.*

Public Facility: *(P)* The facility, which is financed by public funds and available for public use and includes a road, school, a park, or sewage treatment plant.

Public Garage: *(H)* A building or a portion thereof designed or used for parking of public vehicles for hiring and selling of vehicles.

Public Hearing: *(P)* A meeting of people and the representatives of the government, held on a pre-announced date, time and place to hear views, comments and suggestions of interested individuals and groups, on a specific plan, project, or an amendment to an approved plan / project.

Public Housing: (P) A housing owned and build by the government or its agency for low-income and economically weak sections of the society.

Public Involvement: *(P)* see *Public Participation.*

Public Land: *(P)* A parcel of land owned by the government (central, state, or municipal) that holds its title and control.

Public Open Space: *(P)* A parcel of land owned or controlled by central, state or local government or a public agency, which is used or designated in a development or layout plan for the purposes of recreation, ventilation or light and where any member of public has right to access, also *Public Place.*

Public Parking: *(T)* A parking facility for use of any member of public free of charge or on payment of parking fee.

Public Participation: *(P)* The procedure of participation of general public in formulation, implementation, and monitoring process pertaining to a plan, scheme or project, also *Public Involvement, Popular Participation.*

Public Place: *(P)* see *Public Open Space.*

Public Purpose: *(P)* Any purpose that is beneficial to or in the interest of the general public.

Public Sector: *(P)* The part of economic structure that is run by the government or its agencies and financed by public funds.

Public Service: *(P)* (a) The civil service, (b) Services provided for the benefit of the people by the national, state or local government and include supply of water, gas, electricity, education and health care, see also *Facility-(c), Service, Utility.*

Public Tap: *(H)* A common faucet for supply of piped drinking water to a group of households.

Public Toilet: *(S)* A building providing WCs, urinals and wash basins for public use with or without payment of charges, also *Public Conveniences, Community Toilets, Communal Latrines.*

Public Transit: *(T)* see *Mass Transit.*

Public Transportation: *(T)* see *Mass Transit.*

Public Utility: *(S)* see *Utilities.*

Public Works: *(P)* Capital projects such as construction of roads, buildings and provision of infrastructure, financed by the government, for the welfare and convenience of the people.

ublic-private Partnership: *(P)* A system of project implementation where government organisation, bodies or agencies join hands with private enterprises on a mutually agreed terms and conditions for sharing of (i) expenses for assembly and construction, (ii) built spaces, assets and other benefits, and (iii) liabilities, if any.

Pugree: *(P)* In Hindi, a sum of money paid by a person to the occupant of a rental premises, mostly commercial, to gain right of vacant possession of the property and pay rent to the owner as per original agreement.

Purchaser: *(P)* The person, group of persons, or organisation, trust etc. who buys or agrees to buy a real-estate or product.

Purchasing Power: *(F)* see *Earnings.*

Q

Quadrangle: *(UD)* A space designed in the form of a square or rectangle defined by buildings and landscape elements located on three or all the four sides in such a way that a harmonious balance between the building mass and open space is maintained.

Quagmire: *(G)* A marshy area characterised by soft and wet land.

Quaint: *(UD)* Structures or places that are attractive due to their unusual or old fashioned characteristics and ambiance.

Quake: *(G)* The sudden shaking of the earth caused by seismic activity, see also *Earthquake.*

Qualitative Analysis: *(TQ)* A descriptive analysis of characteristics inherent in a situation, processes or phenomenon based upon observations, accumulated experience and logical reasoning.

Quality Control: *(M)* The act of checking performance of an action or event based upon the set goals, norms, standards and procedures.

Quality of Life: *(M)* The socio-economic ambiance of an area evolved by the nature, extent and standard of utilities, facilities and services and design of physical environment.

Quantitative Analysis: *(TQ)* An analysis of characteristics inherent in a situation, processes of phenomenon based upon observations supported by measurable facts and figures and or mathematical models.

Quantity Surveyor: *(M)* A person qualified in the techniques of systematic assessment of the quantity of various types of materials needed for completion of a project and estimation of the project cost.

Quarry: *(P)* A place where mineral resources are being dug out and given primary treatment (like crushing), if needed, before its transportation to other users.

Quasi: *(A)* A prefix to a body or person indicating that it enjoys limited powers.

Quasi-government Body: *(A)* A body or organisation established under a statute to perform certain specified functions of the government and have rights and powers to enforce their obedience, also *Autonomous Body.*

Quasi-official: *(A)* (a) An official of an autonomous body who is empowered under a statute to perform certain specified duties and functions, (b) A document issued by an autonomous body.

Question: *(M)* A sentence that asks a specific information and expects an answer and may be set by (i) an examiner to asses the knowledge gained by the students, or (ii) by a researcher (as research questions) to guide his research work and its outcome, or (iii) a surveyor to assess the responses of the respondents identified for participating in a socio-economic, origin-destination or any other survey, see also *Research Questions.*

Questionnaire: *(TQ)* An instrument for socio-economic, traffic, and other surveys, containing a set of representative questions to be answered by the respondents to assess their response on the subject matter under study.

Queue Jump: *(T)* A short section of road reserved for providing access around a major congestion point exclusively for buses, and sometimes for carpools and vanpools.

Queue: *(M)* A line of vehicles or persons made for a specific purpose.

Quotation Mark: *(ET)* The punctuation marks ('single' or "double" inverted commas) used to enclose the quoted matter to distinguish it from the other written material.

Quotation: *(ET)* A passage or set of words, written by an author, that is quoted by another.

Quote: *(ET)* To repeat, by an author, words written by another author after giving full reference to the source of such quotation.

R

Radial Growth: *(P)* A pattern of growth of a city along roads radiating in all directions from its centre in such a way that the expending areas are contiguous.

Radial Road: *(T)* A road radiating outwards from the centre of a city.

Radial-Concentric Pattern: *(P)* A pattern of growth of a city where a number of roads radiate from the central area are successively cut by a series of concentric circular roads in such a way that the central area serves as the centre for both the radials and the circles.

Radio and Television Station: *(P)* A premises with necessary facilities and services, for recording, broadcasting, and transmission of a variety of information and entertainment programmes and may have transmission-tower and hostel for some artists.

Rag Picker: *(P)* A person informally engaged in collecting re-salable materials from municipal solid waste and selling the same to *Kabari*, see also *Kabari.*

Rail Transit: *(T)* General term used for all types of rail transit systems including light rail transit (LRT), heavy rail, and commuter rail.

Rail Transport: *(T)* The mode of transport of people and goods that runs on fixed rail-tracks and includes sub-urban railways, tramways, and metro-rail.

Railway: *(T)* The entire railway transport system including the network of rail-tracks, rolling stock, stations, workshops, and administrative offices.

Ramp: *(T)* A roadway that allows vehicles to enter and exit a freeway or provides connections between freeways.

Ran Basera: *(H)* In Hindi, a night-shelter, see *Night Shelter.*

Random Sample: *(TQ)* A technique of selecting sample at random for surveying e.g. every fifth house/person, or vehicle for a 20 per cent sample size in a household survey or OD survey respectively.

Range of Goods or Services: *(G)* The maximum distance that people are willing to travel to purchase a product or utilise a service offered at a central place and it depends upon the nature of product or service and the frequency of its need.

Rank Size Rule: *(G)* A rule providing the relationship of population of the largest city and that of the other settlements in an area, and states that if the population of a town is multiplied by its rank size than this will be equal to the population of largest and the highest ranked city in that area.

Rapid Transit: *(T)* see *Mass Transit.*

Rapid Urbanisation: *(P)* Fast increase in urban population of an area generated by rural-urban and urban-urban migration.

Raster: *(TQ)* (a) In GIS, a cellular data structure composed of rows and columns for storing images where groups of cells with the same value represent features, see also *Grid*, (b) In aerial photography / remote sensing – the scanned (illuminated) area.

Rate of Growth: *(M)* The percentage increase or decrease of population/ number of vehicles/ industrial production/ economy/ etc. per year.

Rates: *(F)* Charges levied by a municipal body or any other authorised agency for provision of utilities, facilities or services.

Ratification: *(M)* Confirmation of an agreement between two parties by signature or any other means.

Rational Scale: *(P)* One of the two types of cardinal scale which has a fixed zero point, e.g. in a linear scale 2 inch is twice larger than 1 inch or in a concentration scale, a concentration of 2 ppm is twice as high as 1 ppm, see also *Cardinal Scale. Interval Scale.*

Rationalisation: *(P)* A method of ensuring that the decisions taken at each stage of planning are reasonable and promoting a development which is planned and sustainable.

Real Estate Developer: *(H)* see *Developer.*

Real Estate Investment Market: *(EC)* An investment environment where sale and purchase of properties in principal sectors such as retail, offices, and residential, takes place and also includes some other sectors like leisure, see also *Retail Sector, Office Sector.*

Real Estate Investment Trust: *(P)* A company established for the purpose of owning and operating income producing real estates and development, management and sale of assets like apartments, shopping centres, offices and warehouses.

Real Estate Tax: *(P)* see *Property Tax.*

Real Estate: *(P)* Land and all the natural and man-made elements affixed to it such as buildings, infrastructure, trees, and natural resources like lake, stream, and underground water, also *Real Property, Landed Property.*

Real Property Tax: *(P)* see *Property Tax*, also *Real Estate Tax.*

Real Property: *(H)* see *Real Estate.*

Real-Estate Market: *(P)* The activity of buying and selling of properties that determines the market value and price of the real-estate at a given point of time depending upon the demand and supply situation, also *Property Market.*

Realtor: *(H)* In USA, a real estate agent or broker.

Rebate: *(F)* A sum of money or percentage by which a due payment is reduced under certain conditions such as prompt payment.

Recapitulate: *(ET)* To repeat the main points of an argument in a lecture, technical paper, and research report or seminar presentation.

Receipt: *(F)* A written document establishing that the indicated amount of money has been received for the indicated purpose from the indicated person by the person, agency or department that has issued it.

Recipient: *(F)* An person or body that receives financial assistance directly from the donor to carry out a project or programme.

Reclamation: *(P)* A processes of treating a land in such a manner that brings it back to a desired condition.

Recommendations: *(M)* A set of statements giving suggestions based upon a study or field visit, or experience for consideration of a relevant body or agency

Reconciliation: *(L)* A process of amicable settlement of disputes by the parties with the assistance of a conciliator, also *Conciliation.*

Reconnaissance: *(TQ)* A technique of study of the characteristics of an area by field visits, observation and documentation by photographs and sketches.

Reconstituted Plot: *(P)* see *Land Pooling.*

Reconstruction: *(P)* (a) In disaster management, action of rebuilding structures damaged due to disaster (earthquake and floods), (b) In planning, action of rebuilding structures that are dilapidated due to aging and lack of maintenance.

Recreation (Active): *(P)* see *Active Recreation.*

Recreation (Passive): *(P)* see *Passive Recreation.*

Recreational Area: *(P)* An area designated for activities related to active and / or passive recreation owned by a public agency or private body / individual, also *Recreational Zone.*

Recreational Club: *(P)* A premises with buildings, surrounding open spaces and all related facilities, used for outdoor and indoor recreation purposes by the club members and their family members.

Recreational Facility: *(P)* A designated place that is equipped with all necessary buildings, gadgets and fixtures necessary for a specific recreational activity.

Recreational Zone: *(P)* see *Recreational Area.*

Rectangular Plan: *(P)* see *Grid-iron Pattern.*

Recycling Technology: *(P)* The technology that assists in transforming various waste products into useful new products, and thus, reduce environmental pollution and make environmental management financially attractive.

Recycling: *(P)* In case of waste management, a process of recovery of useful materials from industrial, agriculture, building, or domestic wastes and reusing them or transforming them into new products.

Red Industry: *(P)* Industry that uses processes or produces effluents which are heavily polluting and include distillery, production of sugar, paper, pesticides, cement, iron and steel etc.

Redemption: *(F)* see *Repurchase.*

Redevelopment: *(P)* In an urban renewal programme of a dilapidated area declared unfit for human habitation, a process of (i) temporary or permanent relocation of affected people on the same or to another site, (ii) demolition of buildings, (iii) re-planning the area so cleared having regard to its full potential, (iv) construction of dwellings / other buildings and provision of infrastructure, (v) on completion, allotment of the dwellings to affected people, if located on a temporary site, and (vi) sale of remaining built spaces.

Redundant Labourer: *(EC)* A surplus worker.

Reference Manual: *(M)* A document containing essential, need-to-know information and procedures pertaining to a specific skill or activity.

Refinancing: *(F)* Restructuring a debt by (i) taking a new loan on a favourable terms and clear the old loan, or (ii) by obtaining a new mortgage in place of existing one.

Reforestation: *(E)* see *Afforestation.*

Reformatory: *(P)* A secured, enclosure with necessary buildings and facilities for confinement and reform of offenders.

Reforms: *(M)* To make a system better by introducing changes necessary to improve its performance, accountability and effectiveness, see also *Urban Reforms.*

Refugee: *(H)* A displaced person due to political conflict, war, or disaster seeking refuge and safety in another country.

Refuse Collection: *(S)* The processing of collecting, transporting, treating, and disposing or processing for recycling wastes.

Refuse: *(S)* Any thing that is discarded as worthless or useless and includes municipal, industrial, and other wastes also *Wastes.*

Regeneration: *(P)* see *Renewal.*

Regimental Plan: *(P)* A plan that follows an urban structure where roads and organised spaces form a rigid pattern giving rise to monotony of design, and the loss of identity to the areas, see also *Grid Iron Pattern.*

Region: *(P)* An area defined by a set of attributes. In practice a prefix is added to highlight the attributes on which the region has been defined for example, agriculture region, resource region, city region, planning region, administrative region.

Regional Centers: *(P)* Cities where there is a concentration of economic activities and facilities that serve the entire region.

Regional Cooperation: *(A)* A cooperation among countries of a region for the purpose of mutually beneficial development in economic, social or technical fields.

Regional Core: *(P)* The hub of a city-region comprising the city and its fringe areas, see also *Fringe Area.*

Regional Park: *(P)* A large park that serves as a natural retreat from the urban environment for a population living within one hour driving distance and include rivers, lakes, or other natural features and facilities such as play areas, picnic areas, rain shelters, nature centers, and trails.

Regional Periphery: *(P)* In the context of a city-region, the rest of the urban and rural area in a city-region excluding the regional core and comprising several sub-regions, see also *Regional Core, Sub-Region.*

Registered Contractor: *(M)* see *Panel of Contractors.*

Regulation: *(L)* Legal, regulatory or administrative measures adopted by a competent authority to promote planned development of human settlements.

Rehabilitation: *(M)* (a) In housing and urban development, a process of improving the quality of a blighted area by one or more of the following actions: partial rebuilding, repair, remodeling, renovating, conserving, providing educational, health care and recreational facilities, or augmenting utilities and services, (b) In case of large projects requiring displacement of people, a processes of providing, the project-affected-people, housing, job opportunities, training to enable them to take up new jobs and financial and technical assistance.

REIT: *(P)* see *Real Estate Investment Trust.*

Related Infrastructure: *(P)* In the context of an activity, land use or building type, the infrastructure that is required to support its efficient performance and includes access roads, parking, water supply, sewerage, drainage, solid waste management, public toilets, electricity, telephone, and security.

Relevant Issues: *(P)* Those concerns that are directly related to the objectives or policies being discussed.

Relief: *(P)* In disaster management, financial and other assistance given to affected people.

Religious Building: *(P)* A general term for a building dedicated to the service of the God and may be a temple, mosque, church, *gurudwara, ashram*, and synagogue.

Relocation: *(P)* (a) Temporary or permanent housing of people affected by a redevelopment programme on the same site or to another site, (b) In a slum / *jhuggy*-cluster / squatter area clearance programme, providing a minimum size of plot at subsidised rates, at a designated place, for building a shelter, to each registered household living in such areas..

Remote Area: *(P)* An inaccessible area located away from other settlements generally characterised by traditional customs, beliefs, life style, lack of development, and poverty.

Remote Sensing: *(TQ)* The measurement or acquisition of information of some property or an object or phenomenon by a remote recording device

Remuneration: *(F)* see *Fee*.

Remunerative Projects: *(F)* Development projects that are commercially viable and bankable providing a constant source of income from the assets created, to the local body / developer, in the form of sale, rent, entry fee, charges, etc. also *Commercial Projects*.

Renaissance: *(UD)* A style in urban design that adapts ancient (15th and 16th century) Roman elements and is characterised by symmetry, simplicity, and exact mathematical relationships.

Rendering: *(LA)* The processes of providing landscape treatment to a design or layout plan.

Renewable Energy Resources: *(S)* Sources of energy which do not have a fixed quantity and can be replenished and include sources like biomass, water, sun, and wind, and in future, geothermal, ocean thermal, waves, and tidal action may be added in such sources.

Renewal: *(P)* see *Urban Renewal.*

Renovation: *(H)* Reconstruction of a complete building with or without regard to the existing design, or preservation of architectural features.

Rent Control: *(L)* A statuary provision to limit the maximum rent that can be charged by a landlord to a tenant with a view to make rental housing affordable and regulate eviction.

Rent: *(F)* A mutually agreed charge paid at regular intervals by a tenant to the landlord for use of a piece of land, a building or other real property.

Rental Housing: *(H)* Dwelling units constructed, by the public agencies or private individuals or organisations, for the purpose of letting them out to others after charging a mutually agreed periodic rent.

Repair Shop: *(P)* A place for carrying out of repair of household goods, electronic gadget, automobile, cycles, or such other goods, see also *Service Centre.*

Replacement Value: *(H)* The full value of a real state regardless of depreciation.

Replicability: *(M)* An idea, concept, design, procedure that can be repeated at another place with similar results.

Repurchase: *(F)* (a) To buy back a commodity or property at specific price and terms (b) Right of a property owner to reclaim his property by payment within the statuary period of time after loosing it at the foreclosure sale, also *Redemption.*

Request for Proposal: *(M)* A way to solicit proposals for a new projects, from developers / consultants, through an open public advertisement describing, among other things, the objective of the proposed project, the site description, basic requirements and details of the type of development being sought, and requesting that the interested developers / consultants may submit their technical and financial proposal within a specified time, also *RFP.*

Request for Qualifications: *(M)* A way to solicit information from individuals and firms for getting their professional services on a proposed project, through an open public advertisement describing, among other things, the objective and nature of service to be rendered and requesting that the interested individuals or firms may submit organisational details, experience, and fee charged, explaining why they are or their firm is best qualified to provide the professional service, also *RFQ*.

Research and Development: *(TQ)* Applied research having commercial objectives, see also *Research*.

Research Questions: *(ET)* Based upon literature search and identification of issues, a set of questions posed by a researcher, which guide the research work and the expected outcome, see also *question*.

Research: *(TQ)* A systematic investigation involving data collection, analysis, synthesis, and presentation of results, on a specific subject or issue with a view to achieving a new level of understanding and knowledge.

Resettlement Colony: *(H)* A colony created, on a designated site, for resettlement of a group of displaced persons due to disaster or a large project.

Resettlement: *(P)* A processes of shifting the displaced persons due to disaster or a large project to a new, safe and serviced site and providing them technical and financial assistance for building their shelters.

Residence-cum-work plot: *(H)* A plot accommodating both the dwelling unit and the workspace of the occupant.

Residential Area: *(P)* An area in a settlement where people live and is characterised by residential buildings and related facilities, services and infrastructure, see also *Residential Land Use*.

Residential District: *(P)* A group of residential area linked with network of roads and common facilities and services such as shops, schools,. hospitals, open spaces, recreational areas, and religious buildings.

Residential Flat: *(H)* see *Flat*.

Residential Land Use: *(P)* The land use category in a development or layout plan devoted to residential activity which may be further subdivided into zones / clusters by nature (e.g. primary residential, mixed residential, or unplanned / informal residential), intensity (e.g. high, medium or low density), type (plotted or flatted), ownership (individual or group housing) and / or income (LIG, MIG, HIG).

Residential Plot in Group Housing: *(H)* A plot of specified minimum size, in an area designated for group housing, accommodating residential flats and necessary facilities like parking, open space, convenient shops and utilities as per development control rules.

Residential Plot in Plotted Housing: *(H)* A single plot in a plotted housing scheme accommodating one dwelling unit or more as per development control rules.

Residential Zone: *(P)* A designated area for residential activity where prohibited land uses shall not be allowed to maintain its safety, and environmental quality.

Resolution: *(M)* (a) In GIS and remote sensing, resolution is the accuracy at which a given map scale can depict the location and shape of geographic features where, the larger the map scale, the higher is the possible resolution, (b) In administration, a statement or motion put to a meeting to be resolved after discussion, (c) In administration, a document containing the statement or motion that has been passed by an empowered committee.

Resort: *(P)* A place having rich natural resources and other attractions which is frequently visited by large number of tourists, and depending upon the nature of resources and attractions the resort could be a *Desert Resort, Health Resort, Hill Resort, Seaside Resort, Tourist Resort.*

Respondents: *(P)* The group of people who have been identified, based upon certain considerations, to participate in a survey and constitute the sample.

Responses: *(P)* In a survey, the answers / reactions of the respondents to the questions asked by an enumerator as per the questionnaire.

Restaurant: *(P)* A premises used for cooking and serving, on commercial basis, food items to people seated in the covered or open space or both.

Restoration: *(P)* In case of heritage buildings damaged due to war or disaster, the process of repair work with a view to reconstruct their original form and conditions.

Restricted Zone: *(P)* (a) A zone where entry is restricted to specified persons only and include airports, defense areas, and seaports, (b) A zone within 100m. of a protected monument where all developments are restricted.

Restrictive Policy: *(P)* A policy that aims at controlling or limiting specified activities/ developments/ actions with a view to (i) check their excessive concentration in a city and promote their location in the city region, (ii) retard influx of migration, and (iii) introduce rational and sustainable development.

Retail Shop: *(P)* A premises where sale of commodities, directly to the consumer, takes place and includes space for necessary storage of goods.

Retail Trade: *(P)* Selling of goods and services directly to consumers for their personal or household use.

Retreat: *(P)* A place located in quiet natural surroundings where people go for short period of time to relax and rest.

Retrieval of Data: *(TQ)* A technique of taking out, in raw or processed form, the already stored data or information from a databank or database.

Retrofitting: *(TQ)* Methods of strengthening existing structures with a view to making them resistant and resilient to forces of natural hazard.

Revenue Village: *(D)* (a) The basic unit for rural areas which has definite surveyed boundary comprising one or several hamlets located within the boundary, (b) In case of a village without a surveyed boundary, like one located in a forest area, a habitation area with locally recognised boundary within the forest.

Revenue: *(F)* The total income of a local body from all sources in a year.

Review of Plan: *(P)* A process of evaluation of the performance of a plan as per defined objectives and statutory provisions with a view to get feedback for mid-course corrections, if any.

Revision of Plan: *(P)* Depending upon the results of the feedback and projected requirements, a process of modification of the plan with a view to incorporating changes, if needed, and improving its performance.

Revoke: *(L)* To repeal a law or withdraw a decree.

Revolving Fund: *(F)* An account from which money is continually drawn and replenished by the income from the activities it finances.

RFP: *(M)* see *Request for Proposal.*

RFQ: *(M)* see *Request for Qualifications.*

Rhythmic Pattern: *(UD)* A pattern generated from regular and successive repetition of an element in a composition, a building, or a group of buildings.

Ribbon Development: *(P)* see *Linear Development.*

***Rickshaw*:** *(T)* In Hindi, a vehicle driven manually (as in Kolkata), or with the help of a cycle (cycle rickshaw) or with the help of a petrol, diesel or CNG engine (auto rickshaw) serving a city as a para-transit.

Ridesharing: *(T)* see *Carpool.*

Ridge: *(G)* The upper edge of a hill range on either side of a river forming a watershed.

Right of Way: *(T)* (a) The total width of the strip of land designated as a road, railway, water way, or a public utility, (b) The legal right to pass through the grounds of another under certain circumstances.

Rigid Planning: *(P)* A planning system that does not provide scope for accommodating socio-economic, technological and physical changes.

Risk Analysis: *(M)* (a) In disaster management, a process of analysing and determining the type or scope of difficulty and losses, caused to an organisation / business in case the disaster actually occurs, (b) In finance, a technique of analysis of various seen or unseen factors that may cause loss to a financial institution, see also *risk.*

Risk Coping: *(M)* Measures taken to minimise the adverse effects of risks on a project, see also *Risk.*

Risk Management: *(M)* The action taken to minimise the losses to an organisation / institution incurred due to various risks as identified from the risk analysis and may include risk prevention, risk mitigation and / or risk coping, see also *Risk Analysis, Risk Prevention, Risk Mitigation, Risk Coping.*

Risk: *(M)* A possibility of loss or damage arising from a specific action, processes or situation that could be economic, socio-cultural, environmental or political.

River: *(G)* A natural water body that carries water collected from its catchment area to another river or see and on the way, serves the irrigation, drinking water and other needs of the people.

Road Transport: *(T)* The mode of transport of people and goods that runs on roads and includes 2-wheelers, 3-wheelers, cars, trucks and buses.

Road: *(T)* A common term for a designated way for movement of vehicles, also *Street,* see also *Access Road, Arterial Road, Collector Road/Street, Hierarchy of Roads, Local Road/Street, Sub-Arterial Road, Service Road, Pathway.*

***Rojgar*:** *(EC)* In *Urdu*, employment.

Role-Play: *(ET)* An interactive learning method in which, depending upon the course objectives, participants act out the roles of persons in the real life situation and understand the functions, responsibilities, powers, and risks attached to a post and also the process of taking decisions.

Room: *(H)* A space defined by walls, roof and floor, see also *Habitable Room.*

Roster: *(A)* A list of names of persons working in an organisation indicating the time schedule, functions and duties to be performed by each of them.

Rostrum: *(P)* A raised platform used for public speeches and may be permanent or temporary.

Route: *(T)* The set path followed by a bus or other vehicle.

Row Housing: *(H)* A series of individual dwelling units located together in an unbroken line and having a load bearing common wall with the neighbours on either side, also *Terrace Housing.*

ROW: *(T)* see *Right of Way.*

Run-off: *(G)* The portion of precipitation that flows over the land surface or in open channels.

Rural Belt: *(P)* A stretch of country side around and between towns predominantly serving as agriculture land and park land that may be owned by public or private bodies, also *Agriculture Belt, Country Belt, Rural Zone.*

Rural Housing: *(H)* Public housing, generally for low and economically weaker sections of the society, located in rural area which is different from urban housing in terms of norms, subdivision regulations, dwelling unit design, use of materials and cost.

Rural Zone: *(P)* see *Rural Belt.*

Rural-oriented Regional Plan: *(P)* A regional plan where the main focus is on rural development including agriculture and allied activities.

Rural-urban Migration: *(P)* A pattern of migration where the movement of people is from rural areas to urban centres, see also *Migration.*

S

Safari Park: *(P)* see *Sanctuary.*

Safari: *(P)* An organised journey through natural areas for observing wild life in their natural habitat.

Salary: *(S)* Payment made periodically – monthly, annually – to an employee for the services rendered by him.

***Samiti*:** *(A)* In Hindi, a committee.

Sample Selection: *(M)* The criterion used in selecting a sample and its size for a representative survey.

Sample Size: *(M)* The quantity of a sample of some thing that makes it, with a good degree of confidence, as a representative of that thing.

Sample: *(M)* A part of the whole that can serve as its representative with a good degree of confidence.

***Sampoorna Grameen Rozgar Yojana*:** *(P)* An assured 100 days' wage employment scheme of the 10th Five Year Plan for the rural poor in the identified backward districts, which focuses on generation of wage employment, creation of durable assets and infrastructure, and food security.

Sanction: *(M)* The official permission accorded to a plan / project/ scheme/ bill by a competent authority or designated person after scrutiny, see also *Scrutiny.*

Sanctuary: *(P)* An area of adequate ecological, faunal, floral, geomorphologic, natural, or zoological significance reserved under a Wild Life Protection Act, for the purpose of protecting, propagating or developing wild life and the environment, also *National Park, Safari Park, Wildlife Sanctuary.*

Sandwich Course: *(ET)* A tailor-made course that is shorter in time spent and less rigorous than the formal education, designed especially for the in-service people working on a job for which they are not trained.

Sanitary Landfill: *(S)* A site, located generally on the outskirts of a city, away from residential areas where non-hazardous solid waste is disposed off in layers, compacted and covered with soil.

Sanitation: *(S)* Measures taken to protect public health and include control of insects, rodents, environmental pollution, and management of solid and liquid wastes.

Satellite Town: *(P)* A town, located within the commuting distance from a large city, where the residents are culturally and economically dependent upon the city.

Savings Account: *(F)* An account maintained from small savings of individuals and where interest is paid on such savings, see also *Savings.*

Savings Bank: *(F)* A financial institution that primarily accepts small savings from depositors and invests them in housing mortgage loans, see also *Savings.*

Savings: *(F)* Holding one's income for future use rather than spending it as it is earned and thus forming a basis for accumulation of fiscal resource for further investment.

Scale of Maps: *(P)* Depending upon the size of the planning area and the coverage and extent of information required, the scale of maps vary and it generally is –1:100,000 to 1:250,000 for regional plans, 1:50,000 to 1:100,000 for perspective plan, 1:10,000 to 1:25,000 for development plan (master plan) and 1: 500 to 1:5,000 plans of projects and schemes.

Scale Types: *(P)* There are four types of scales: nominal scale, ordinal scale, cardinal scale (sub-classification: interval scale, rational scale) and scale of maps, see also *Cardinal Scale, Interval Scale, Nominal Scale, Ordinal scale, Rational scale, Scale of maps.*

Scale: *(P) (A)* A system or scheme of relative values or correspondence, (b) In a drawing or model, proportional relationship between an actual object and its representation on paper or as a model, see also *Cardinal Scale, Interval Scale, Nominal Scale, Ordinal Scale, Rational Scale, Scale of Maps.*

Scarcity: *(P)* The state of inadequate supply of a commodity or thing measured against its demand at a given point of time.

Scenario Building: *(TQ)* A method of listing of several possible alternative patterns of future development under varying assumptions and conditions, see also *Scenario.*

Scenario: *(TQ)* A listing of possible sequence of events and the expected pattern of development.

Scene: *(TQ)* In remote sensing or aerial photography, the area on the ground that is covered by an image or photograph.

Scenic Viewpoints: *(P)* Places from where a framed view of the nature can be seen to appreciate its beauty and derive visual pleasure, such points and the development in the line of sight of the view need to be regulated to avoid obstruction.

Schedule: *(M) (A)* In transport, a listing of trips and time points for buses or other transit vehicles for a given route, (b) In quantity surveying, a listing of items and their respective rates, (c) In planning, a listing of various requirements of land under different uses for incorporation in a development plan, (d) A sequential list of events that are planned to take place in a particular time frame.

Scheduling: *(P)* The processes of determining the time frame of commencement and finishing of a project having regard to the various events, constraints, and the time taken for completion of each event.

Schematic Design: *(P)* see *Conceptual Plan.*

Schematic Plan: *(P)* see *Conceptual Plan.*

Scheme Implementation: *(P)* The process of execution or carrying out of the provisions of a scheme.

School: *(P)* An institution located in a building or a campus of several buildings with or without hostel accommodation, managed by public or private institution, for offering education and play facilities at different levels comprising children of different age groups, see also *Integrated School, Kinder Garden, Nursery School, Primary School, Secondary School.*

Scrap: *(E)* Industrial waste material that can be recycled or reused in the same or another processes.

Screen: *(LA)* see *Fence, Hedge.*

Screening: *(LA)* A method of blocking unwanted sight or noise by a barrier using plant materials, berms, fence, or wall or any combination thereof.

Scrub Area: *(G)* An area of land covered with bushes and stunted trees.

Scrutiny: *(M)* Examination of a plan / project / scheme, by a competent person following the policies / objectives / norms / rules / regulations, and a set procedure, for the purpose of according planning permission or sanction of loan / grant, see also *Sanction.*

Seaside Resort: *(P)* see *Resort.*

Season: *(P)* Division of the year according to weather conditions and includes summer, rainy, spring and winter seasons.

Seasonal Migration: *(P)* A pattern of migration where the movement of people is for a specific period during a specific time of the year e.g. agriculture workers moving to urban centres during lean period when there is no job in villages and going back to villages at the start of sowing season, see also *Migration.*

Seasonal Unemployment: *(P)* Unemployment caused due to seasonal nature of some occupation, e.g. agricultural labourer after harvesting and before next sowing or building workers during rainy season.

Secondary City: *(P)* see *Intermediate City.*

Secondary School: *(P)* An institution located in a building or a campus of several buildings with or without hostel accommodation, managed by public or private institution, for offering education and play facilities for children between 11 to 17 years' age studying in VI to XII class / standard.

Secondary Sector: *(EC)* One of the three sectors of economy comprising manufacturing, and household industries, see also *Sectors of Economy.*

Sector Planning: *(M)* (a) The process of planning of a sector of economy such as agriculture, commerce, industry, transport, rural development, urban development, environment etc., (b) In planning, preparation of plan of a sector as a planning unit, see *Sector-(a).*

Sector: *(M)* (a) In physical planning, a particular and distinguishable planning unit forming part of division or sub-division of a city for the purpose of equitable spatial distribution of utilities, facilities and services as per population residing or expected to reside there, (b) In economic planning, it refers to the various components of economy, where each is called a sector, and include agriculture, industry, trade and commerce, transport, urban development, rural development, social development, science and technology, and infrastructure.

Sectors of Economy: *(EC)* The various components of economy classified into three major groups and their sub-groups such as primary sector (agriculture, horticulture, mining, etc.), secondary sector (manufacturing, household industry etc.) and tertiary sector (commerce, trade, transport, services etc.).

Secured Loan: *(F)* A loan that is supported by pledging or mortgaging a property which shall be liquidated in case of default.

Security of Tenure: *(H)* Legal possession of a property that is conferred by legal title.

Seed Money: *(F)* Money paid to an authorised organisation or agency to meet the initial expenses (e.g. for feasibility study, or planning, or down-payment) related to a project with the expectation that it will serve as the basis for generating the required capital.

Self-employed: *(EC)* A person gainfully employed in his own business and not engaged by any employer.

Self-financing: *(F)* A system of financing projects by generating capital from the potential buyers in the form of advance installments in such a way that on payment of the last installment the project is completed and possession is given.

Self-help Housing: *(H)* A process of voluntary participation, with hired support of skilled workers for specialised tasks, in construction of houses of those who are going to occupy them, see also *Aided Self-help Housing.*

Self-help: *(H)* (A) Activities carried out by individuals on their own behalf rather than depending upon others, (b) Activities carried out by the community on its own behalf, see also *Capacity of Self-help.*

Self-reliance: *(EC)* Economic situation of a country, where there are sufficient natural and human resources to meet its needs and make it capable to set the development goals and take decisions independently for their implementation, also *Self-sufficiency.*

Self-sufficiency: *(EC)* see *Self-reliance.*

Semester: *(ET)* One of the two equal divisions of an academic year by number of weeks or months.

Semi-ambulatory Disabilities: *(P)* Impairments that cause individual to walk with difficulty or insecurity and include persons using braces or crutches, suffering from arthritis, pulmonary and cardiac ills or those who are spastic.

Semi-arid Area: *(G)* see *Semi-arid Region.*

Semi-arid Region: *(G)* An area characterised by less than 40 cm. per year precipitation that allows only limited agriculture and growth of short, sparse grasses, also *Semi-arid Area.*

Semi-detached Housing: *(H)* An arrangement of houses using pairs of dwelling units in such a way that two houses are attached by a common wall between them leaving the remaining three sides of each house detached.

Semi-literate: *(P)* An adult person who can read but not write and may have acquired some skills.

Seminar: *(ET)* (a) A discussion among a group of advanced level students on a specific subject under the guidance of a teacher. (b) A deliberation on a specific subject by a group of persons, having similar professional interests, through formal presentation of papers followed by discussion.

Semi-skilled Worker: *(EC)* A worker who is partially trained for the job.

Sensitive Environmental Features: *(E)* Features that are endangered or will cause a danger or are part of eco-system and need special protection and include habitats of rare, threatened and endangered species, water bodies and 50-year floodplains, snow covered peaks, and glaciers, and protected forests.

Separate System of Drainage: *(S)* A system in which the foul water (sewage) and surface water are conveyed by separate sewers and drains.

Service Centre: *(P)* In the context of a region, a town or large village having linkages with its rural hinterland and providing commercial, education, health, communication and recreational facilities and agriculture-related services to the group of villages in the service area.

Service Frequency: *(T)* The total number of buses or other transit vehicles on a given route, passing a specific point within a given time period.

Service Garage: *(P)* A building or a portion thereof designed or used for servicing and repairing of vehicles.

Service Industry: *(P)* A labour intensive economic activity that provides services rather than production of goods and includes printing, photography, health care, film and TV serial making, cold storage, laundry, dry cleaning, repair, servicing and maintenance of equipments and machineries.

Service Latrine: *(S)* A latrine from which the excreta is removed manually and not by water carriage.

Service Pipe: *(S)* The water pipe that runs between the distribution main in the street and the riser in case of a multi-storeyed building or the water meter in case of an individual house and is subject to water pressure from such mains.

Service Road: *(T)* (a) A road, 7 to 10 m right of way, running at the rear side of residential or commercial buildings dedicated for providing services, scavenging in residential areas, or loading and unloading of goods in commercial areas (b) A 2-lane road forming a part of highway, arterial or sub-arterial road on its either sides and dedicated to providing direct access to properties.

Serviced Land: *(P)* A parcel of land that has been appropriately leveled and provided with off-site infrastructure, also *Serviced Site,* see also *Off-site Infrastructure.*

Serviced Plot: *(P)* A plot of land in a subdivision that has direct access from a road, and has been provided with on-site infrastructure, see also *On-site Infrastructure.*

Serviced Site: *(H)* see *Serviced Land.*

Services: *(P)* Include transportation by rail, road, air, waterways, telecommunication, police protection, fire fighting, postal, and such other services, not covered under utilities or facilities, see also *Utilities, Facilities.*

Set-back Line: *(P)* A line parallel to the plot boundaries or centerline of the road facing the plots, at a distance, as per building bye-laws, beyond which nothing can be constructed towards the plot boundary.

Setback: *(P)* Mandatory open space between a building and the front, side or rear boundary of the plot as per local bye laws.

Settlement Hierarchy: *(P)* see *Hierarchy of Settlements*, see also *Urban Hierarchy.*

Settlement: *(P)* Any settled colony of people, having a specific location on ground, that may be urban or rural in character and large or small in population size.

Severe Slope: *(P)* A terrain where the cross slope is greater than 25 per cent (e.g. 25 m. change in elevation in a 100 m. horizontal distance).

Sewage Disposal: *(S)* A system of collection, treatment, and safe disposal of sewage.

Sewage Effluent: *(E)* Effluent from any sewerage system or sewage disposal work and includes sullage from drains.

Sewage Pumping Station: *(S)* A pump house used for pumping sewage to a higher gradient.

Sewage Treatment: *(TQ)* The various techniques through which the sewage is subjected to for removing its hazardous contents before safe disposal.

Sewage: *(S)* Waste water from all sources - residential, commercial. and industrial or other areas, also *Waste Water.*

Sewer: *(S)* A conduit pipe or channel, open or closed, carrying sewage or trade effluent.

Sex Ratio: *(D)* Number of females per 1000 males.

Sex: *(E)* Classification of human beings into male and female.

SGRY: *(P)* see *Sampoorna Grameen Rozgar Yojana.*

SGSY: *(P)* see *Swarnjayanti Gram Swarozgar Yojana.*

Shack: *(H)* A shelter made of makeshift materials.

***Shahar*:** *(P)* In Persian, a city.

Shanty Town: *(P)* Low-income group settlement where shelters are made of temporary make-shift materials.

Shared Ride: *(T)* A trip, other than by public transit, where more than one person occupies the same vehicle.

Shell Housing: *(H)* see *Core Housing.*

Shelter: *(H)* A structure that provides bare minimum space for living and a cover for protection from sun and rain, which may not always be adequate, see also *Adequate Shelter.*

Shooting Range: *(P)* A large open space equipped with facilities for shooting practice or game with place for seating spectators and having parking, public toilets, and other facilities for players.

Shopping Centre: *(P)* A place with concentration of a variety of retail shops and commercial services and related infrastructure.

Short Notice Question: *(A)* A question of an urgent character, relating to a matter of public importance, asked in the House of Parliament with notice shorter than clear 10 days.

Short-term Plan: *(P)* (a) A plan, formulated having regard to immediate and short-term issues, needs and priorities that may form part of a long-term plan (b) An action plan to tackle immediate and short-term issues.

Shrub: *(LA)* A woody plant of low to medium height, deciduous or evergreen, generally having many stems.

***Shulka*:** *(F)* In Hindi, a general term for cess, or fee payable to a public agency for using its premises or services e.g. *mandi shulka* paid by farmer to enter the agriculture market and sell the produce.

Sidewalk: *(T)* see *Footpath.*

Sight Disabilities: *(P)* Total blindness or impairment affecting sight to the extent that the individual functioning in public areas is insecure or exposed to danger.

Signage: *(P)* A well designed display mechanism, located strategically along the channel of movement of vehicle and people, indicating (i) direction to important places, facilities and services, (ii) name of roads, buildings, and sites, (iii) information of tourist interests, or (iv) traffic regulations.

Signature: *(TQ)* In aerial photography or remote sensing, any characteristic or series of characteristics by which a material may be recognised.

Simulation Model: *(TQ)* A model that reproduces the behaviour of a system without reproducing the system itself and includes computer-aided 3–dimensional perspective of buildings, structures and objects or true-to-life representation of a process like driving an automobile, or flying an aeroplane.

Simulation: *(TQ)* Generally a computer aided method of reproducing the behaviour of a system without reproducing the system itself.

Single Storey: *(P)* A structure comprising just a floor on the ground and the roof above it.

Single-family Dwelling: *(H)* A dwelling unit located on a plot with setbacks on all the four sides generally used for occupancy by a single family, also *Single-family Housing.*

Single-family Housing: *(H)* see *Single-family Dwelling.*

Single-occupancy Vehicle: *(T)* Vehicle containing only the driver.

Site Development: *(P)* The process of rendering a sit fit for building construction and includes clearing, leveling, demarcation as per site plan and provision of essential infrastructure such as water supply, sewerage, drainage, power supply, roads and road-side plantation..

Site Layout: *(P)* see *Layout Plan.*

Site Management: *(H)* see *Construction Management.*

Site Plan: *(P)* see *Layout Plan.*

Site Planning: *(P)* A process of arranging buildings, open spaces, roads, pedestrian pathways, facilities, and services, having regard to physical features of the site, land use requirements, planning and urban design principles, landscape considerations, and subdivision regulations.

Site: *(P)* A well-defined parcel of land or area intended or suitable for development and building construction purposes, the various types of sites by accessibility are *Corner Site, Double-Frontage Site,* and *Interior Site.*

Site-and-Services: *(H)* A system of providing low-cost housing for low-income households, where plots of minimum size (20-25 sq.m.)

equipped with minimum basic services such as access road, community water faucet, common latrine, electricity, common open space, and other facilities, as per norms, are provided and the beneficiaries build their own shelter on the allotted site according to their needs and means.

Skilled Labour: *(EC)* see *Skilled Worker.*

Skilled Worker: *(EC)* A worker having training and experience in a specific trade or occupation, also *Skilled Labour.*

Slaughter House: *(P)* see *Abattoir.*

Sliding Rates: *(P)* A schedule of rates for utilities wherein the rates per unit of consumption are less for less consumption and increase, in slabs, when consumption is more.

Slip Road: *(T)* A road forming part of a road junction design that provides free access to left turning traffic.

Slop Hopper: *(S)* A hopper shaped sink, with a flushing run and outlet similar to those of a water closet pan, for the reception and discharge of human excreta.

Slope: *(P)* A raise in elevation within a specific distance generally expressed in percentage, e.g. one per cent slope means a rise of one metre in elevation over a horizontal distance of 100 metre, also *Grade.*

Slum Clearance: *(P)* Removal of a slum by demolishing buildings and clearing the site to be used for the designated purpose.

Slum Improvement: *(P)* Provision of adequate access road, and basic services such as drainage, water supply and toilets on the slum site with a view to improving the quality of life of people living there, also *Slum Upgradation,* see also *Upgradation.*

Slum: *(P)* (a) That portion of a city where the quality of life of people is very poor because of dilapidated buildings, overcrowding, faulty design, lack of ventilation, light or sanitary facilities or a combination of any of these factors, (b) In large cities, areas lacking in basic infrastructure and occupied by poor people living in shelters made of temporary materials, see also *JJ Colony.*

Small Farmer: *(AG)* A farmer holding 2 ha non-irrigated or 1 ha irrigated land, see also *Marginal Farmer.*

Small Industry: *(P)* An industry that has fixed assets without depreciation, or project cost of less than or equal to Rs. one crore.

Small-Scale Project: *(P)* A project having a very limited scope and investment..

Smog: *(E)* (a) A general term used to describe the irritating haze produced by photochemical reactions in the atmosphere, (b) Urban atmospheric conditions caused by the combined effect of smoke and fog generated from various sources.

Soak-away: *(S)* A pit dug into permeable ground lined to form a covered perforated chamber to which waste liquid after treatment is led and from which it soaks away into ground.

Social Benefits: *(P)* The gains accrued to the society as a whole or a section thereof as a result of an economic policy, programme or a development project.

Social Change: *(P)* A transformation in the social organisation, structure, behaviour, value system or patterns resulting from continued changes due to change in technology, modernisation, pace of urbanisation, or population growth.

Social Cost: *(P)* A cost, in terms of ill health due to air pollution caused by industrial emissions, borne by the society and not the polluter by way of appropriate treatment and environmental management.

Social Housing: *(H)* Heavily subsidised housing provided by the government for economically weaker sections of the society.

Social Infrastructure: *(P)* Social facilities needed for a community and include health care, education, recreation, communication, security, safety, religious and cultural activities, old-age homes, night shelters, cremation and burial grounds and cemeteries.

Social Planning: *(P)* A process of planned improvement in the economic conditions and quality of life of identified social groups such as the elderly, handicapped, and economically or socially disadvantaged communities, with their active participation.

Social Service: *(P)* Activities of individuals, groups, NGOs, or government agencies that aim at well-being of society especially the poor, deprived and disadvantaged and may include education, health care, recreation, mother and child care, and provision of employment opportunities.

Social Structure: *(P)* The social arrangements and relationships evolved out of cultural values, social behaviour, class composition, and distribution of wealth.

Social Welfare: *(P)* Economic and social well-being of a community as a whole advanced through public policies, programmes or non-governmental actions

Socio-cultural Constraints: *(P)* Social behaviour, customs and beliefs that sometimes act as hindrance to developmental efforts.

Socio-economic Development: *(P)* A process of development where planned actions aimed at social improvement tend to reinforce economic well-being and *vice versa* (e.g. improvement in the level of education leads to better job and hence better economic well-being).

Soffit: *(S)* The highest point of the internal surface of a sewer or culvert at any cross-section, also *Crown.*

Soft Landscape: *(LA)* The animate or living component of landscape planning and design.

Soft Loan: *(F)* A loan that bears no or low rate of interest which is below the true cost of capital loaned and it generally has a long repayment period with slow amortisation rate.

Soil Pipe: *(S)* In plumbing, a pipe that conveys the discharge of water closets.

Soil Pollution: *(E)* see *Ground Pollution.*

Soil Waste: *(S)* The discharge from water closets, urinals, slop hopper, stable yard or cowshed gullies and similar appliances.

Solid Waste Disposal: *(S)* The process of collecting, transporting, processing, recycling, and disposing solid wastes safely in landfills or incinerators.

Solid Waste Management: *(S)* A holistic approach to the issue of solid wastes and includes reduction of waste generation at source, segregation, collection, transportation, recycling, and safe disposal.

Solid Waste: *(S)* Solid materials discarded from houses, business establishments, industries, gardens and forests, construction sites and other places and it does not include excreta.

Sparse Development: *(P)* A pattern of development of a settlement characterised by buildings located in a scattered pattern with large fields or incidental open spaces in between them.

Spatial Conceptual Model: *(TQ)* A model that provides an analysis of generalised spatial patterns of social, economic or physical change in an area.

Spatial Development Strategy: *(P)* Physical development approach having regard to socio-economic and environmental issues, local potentials and fiscal resources.

Spatial Equilibrium: *(P)* A pattern of balanced development in which shifting of location of one activity will affect the entire system.

Spatial Model: *(TQ)* A model that provide spatial variations of social, economic or physical change in an area, see also *Model Types. (b), Supra-National Model, National, Sub-National Model, Spatial Conceptual Model, or Spatial Mathematical Model.*

Spatial Organisation: *(P)* Physical structure of a city or region evolved out of location of all types of activities and their interrelationship.

Spatial Planning: *(P)* see *Physical Planning.*

Spatial Planner: *(P)* see *Town Planner.*

Spatial System: *(P)* The hierarchical system of settlements in a region together with their functional linkage among themselves as well as the surrounding rural areas.

Spatial Mathematical Model: *(TQ)* Mathematical equations evolved with specified assumptions that calculate the spatial variations of social, economic or physical change.

Special Areas: *(P)* (a) In city planning, areas designated as such that need unique and specific development norms, rules and regulations and include city core requiring redevelopment, or a heritage area needing conservation, (b) In regional planning, areas designated in the regional plan that require unique and specific policies and programmes and approaches for their planning and development and include hill areas, coastal areas and tribal areas, and environmentally sensitive areas.

Specialised Park: *(P)* A park designed and landscaped for a specific special purpose, such as public meeting, social gatherings, and entertainment, where the activity may or may not be of a permanent nature, see also *Fun Park, Wonder Land, Water Park.*

Specifications: *(H)* see *Building Specifications.*

Spectral Band: *(TQ)* An interval in electromagnetic spectrum defined by two wave lengths, frequencies or wave numbers.

Speculation: *(P)* see *Land Speculation.*

Spin-off Effect: see *Multiplier Effect.*

Sponsor: *(P)* A person or agency, public or private, that assumes the financial responsibility of planning and implementation of a project or programme.

Spontaneous Settlements: *(P)* A settlement that is characterised by irregular and unplanned pattern of spatial growth, see also *Organic Growth.*

Spot Elevation: *(LA)* An existing or proposed elevation of a point on ground shown as dot on the plan.

Sprawl: *(P)* The haphazard outward physical growth around a large city in a disorderly fashion.

Spread Effect: *(P)* (a) In the context of a metropolitan region, socio-economic and physical growth of metro-periphery due to the effect of the developmental impulse generated by the metro-core, (b) Between rich and poor regions, evolution of forces that generate a process of socio-economic and physical growth of the poor region due to demand of its resources generated by the rich region, see also *Dispersal, Decentralisation.*

Squatter Area: *(P)* see *Squatter Settlement.*

Squatter Settlement: *(P)* An unplanned, illegal settlement where the occupants do not have title to land or permission from the landowner and shelters are made of make-shift materials without basic services, also *Squatter Area, Marginal Settlement.*

Squatter: *(P)* (a) A person who occupies a piece of land unlawfully without any title and settles there, (b) A person who takes unauthorised possession of a building.

Squatting: (P) A process of occupying land illegally, and in many cases, with the intention of gaining title of another piece of land at the time of relocation, see also *Relocation-(b).*

Stadium: *(P)* A place used for outdoor field and track games with pavilion and other structures for seating spectators and having parking, public toilets, and changing rooms for players, also *Outdoor Stadium* see also *Indoor Stadium.*

Stagnant Settlement: *(P)* A settlement that is characterised by very insignificant or no demographic, spatial and economic growth.

Stagnant Water Body: *(P)* A water body that is characterised by very insignificant or no flow of water making it stale, static, polluted, and stinking.

Stakeholder: *(P)* An individual or group of individuals who has an interest in and can influence the decisions pertaining to the government activities, programs and objectives.

Stamp Duty: *(P)* A tax levied on sale and purchase of all properties.

Standard of Living: *(EC)* The level of material well-being of a society as indicated by level of economic output, or pattern of consumption of goods and services, or income of individuals, groups or the society as a whole.

Standard Rent: *(H)* A rent of a property worked out on the basis of the value of land and cost of construction when built.

Standard Urban Area: *(D)* An area comprising a core town of at least 50,000 people and a number of dependent smaller towns and villages that will, in all probability, be urbanised within the next couple of decades.

Standardisation: *(M)* (a) In industry, a system of production of various components by different manufacturers following standard dimensions and specifications that can be effectively incorporated in design and construction of buildings, (b) In administration, a system of making set procedures for effective functioning, (c) In planning, a system of evolving, procedures, norms and standards for rational planning and efficient plan implementation.

Standards: *(M)* Technical specifications based on accepted practice and approved by a recognised agency for repeated and continued use.

Staple Food: *(AG)* The principle food of a majority of people living in an area.

Starred Question: *(A)* A question to which a member of Parliament wishes to have an oral answer on the floor of the house and which is distinguished by an asterisk.

State Government Office: *(P)* A building or group of buildings used for performing functions and activities related to the state government.

Static Model: *(TQ)* A model comprising variables, which do not change with respect to time.

Station: *(T)* A major facility servicing one or more transit mode.

Statute: (L) The law book or the written law.

Statutory Authority: *(M)* An authority that has been established by an Act to perform certain specified functions and has powers to implement them.

Statutory Body: *(M)* A body that has been established by an Act to perform certain specified functions and has powers to implement them.

Statutory Document: *(M)* A document that has been authorised by law or has been issued under the provisions of a law.

Statutory Plan: *(P)* A plan prepared under a relevant Act, approved by a competent authority after following the procedure laid in the Act and notified in the official gazette. Such plan becomes a legal document from the date of its notification in the gazette.

Statutory Resolution: *(A)* A resolution passed in pursuance of a provision of the Constitution or an Act.

Statutory Town: *(D)* A settlement having an urban local body such as a municipality, corporation, cantonment board or notified area committee that may not qualify the population, occupation or density norms of a census town, see also *Census Town.*

Statutory: *(L)* A prefix to a document, agency, body, indicating that the same has been authorised / established by law, see also *Statutory Authority, Statutory Body, Statutory Document.*

Steep Terrain: *(P)* A terrain where the cross slope is greater than 60 per cent (e.g. 60 m. change in elevation in a 100 m. horizontal distance).

Stereopair: *(TQ)* A pair of photos which overlap in area and are suitable for stereoscopic examination.

Stereoscopic Image: *(TQ)* The mental impression of a 3-dimensional object which results from stereoscopic vision.

Stochastic Model: *(TQ)* A probability model that indicates the degree of probability that a set of events, ordered in time together, will take place at another time.

Stop Tap: *(S)* see *Stopcock.*

Stop Valve: *(S)* see *Stopcock.*

Stopcock: *(S)* A device fitted in a pipeline for controlling the flow of water at will, also *Stop Tap, Stop Valve.*

Storage Tank: *(S)* A container used for storage of water that is connected to the water main or tube-well by means of supply pipe.

Storage: *(P)* A place, where goods of non-hazardous nature are stored.

Storey: *(H)* The portion of a building included between the surface of any floor and the surface of the floor next above it, and if there is no floor above it then the space between the floor and the ceiling next above it.

Storm Water Management: *(S)* The collection, conveyance, storage, and disposal of storm water runoff with a view to meet water demands, maintain water quality, and minimise erosion and flooding.

Strategic Centres: *(P)* In a region, places having strategic location characterised by, for example, nodality of major transport routes, availability of economic resources, or existence of features of architectural, historical, or religious significance.

Strategic Framework: *(P)* A tool for communicating the development strategy and a basis for measuring, analysing, and reporting results of various programmes.

Strategic Goals: *(P)* The milestones or the specific performance targets to be achieved by an organisation or a development plan.

Strategic Issues: *(P)* The basic issues and challenges that need to be addressed on a priority basis in order to achieve the objectives of an organisation or a development plan.

Strategic Objectives: *(P)* Within the framework of the strategic goals, these are the operational means to achieve them.

Strategic Plan: *(P)* A vision of development that includes the strategic issues, goals and objectives and a description of how resources will be deployed to accomplish them.

Strategic Planning: *(M)* (a) In planning, a processes of evolving a development-vision and a mission based upon anticipated changes in future and scenarios of the possible alternatives with a view to responding to the emerging trends, events, challenges, and opportunities, (b) In management, development vision and mission evolved by the top-level management, and incorporates broad policy decisions to achieve the organisation goals and resource mobilisation.

Strategic Thinking: *(P)* An interactive process to build reflection on action by people who are active, involved, connected, committed, alert, and stimulated.

Strategy: *(P)* An overall approach to achieve a set goal.

Stream: *(M)* (a) In geography, a small river, (b) In transport, line of steadily moving vehicles on a road.

Streamlining: *(P)* A process or procedure of making an action more simple, smooth running, efficient and effective.

Street Furniture: *(LA)* Outdoor elements include signage, advertisements, tree grates/ guards, utility lines, bus stands, kiosks, booths etc. located on the central verge or side walks that are required along streets in a city.

Street Vender: *(P)* see *Hawker.*

Street: *(T)* (a) A means of access to abutting properties, (b) A transport link connecting various areas of a city.

Streetscape: (UD) The visual quality and ambiance of a street created by, (i) composition, design and colour of adjacent buildings, pavements, street furniture, (ii) nature of activities, (iii) intensity use of the public right-of-way, and (iv) presence of people.

Structure of a City Region: *(P)* A city-region consists of the regional core and regional periphery.

Structure Plan: *(P)* A plan intended to provide a broader and strategic framework of development of housing, transportation, economic activities and physical growth of an urban area to guide preparation of subsequent action plans, see also *Action Plan.*

Structure: *(M)* In civil engineering, the basic frame of a building comprising foundation, columns, and beams, (b) In administration, the organisational set up of an institution, office or department.

Student: *(ET)* An individual receiving education, also see *Learner*

Sub-arterial Road: *(T)* A road having for intra-urban through traffic with frontage access but no standing vehicles having a right-of-way of 30 to 40 m., very high cross traffic at high-capacity intersections spaced at least 300 m. apart.

Sub-committee: *(M)* A committee constituted by a main committee to perform certain assigned functions and, on completion of the task, report back to it (the main committee).

Sub-contract: (L) An agreement between a main contractor and another contractor for performing an agreed specific service related to the original contract.

Sub-division: *(P)* see *Land Sub-division.*

Subletting: *(H)* Transfer of occupancy of a rented property by the tenant to another person for a specific period on payment of agreed rent.

Sub-national Model: *(TQ)* A spatial model covering part of a country that provides spatial variation of social, economic or physical change in the area

Sub-region: *(P)* A well-defined sub-division of a region, served by a sub-regional centre, comprising sub-regional core and sub-regional periphery, see also *Sub-regional Centre, Sub-regional Core, Sub-regional Periphery.*

Sub-regional Centre: *(P)* A medium size city having linkages with both the service centres, on the one hand, and the higher order cities on the other, and serving the entire sub-region as the centre of education, health, communication and recreational facilities as well as trade, commerce, industrial and administrative functions.

Sub-regional Core: *(P)* The area in a sub-region comprising the sub-regional centre and its fringe areas which may be urban or a mix of urban and rural character, see also *Sub-regional Centre.*

Sub-regional Periphery: *(P)* The rest of the urban and rural area in a sub-region excluding the sub-regional core and comprising several micro-regions, see also *Sub-regional Core, Micro-regions.*

Subsidised Housing: *(H)* Housing that is subsidised by the public funds or cross subsidy to make the dwellings affordable for occupation by low-income group households, see also *Cross Subsidy, Subsidy.*

Subsidy: *(F)* (a) Direct or indirect financial support by the government for serving a public purpose, (b) Direct or indirect financial support by the government, in the form of tax concessions and other incentives and inducements, to the property owners to provide housing for low-income households, (c) Direct or indirect financial support by the government, in the form of allowances, to individuals to pay the rent of the house they occupy.

Subsistence Farming: *(EC)* A farming operation where the produce is just enough to meet the food requirements of the members of a household and where there is no surplus to meet their other requirements.

Sub-soil Water: *(G)* Water occurring naturally in the sub-soil.

Substandard Housing: *(H)* (a) A housing that does not meet the design and building standards, (b) A housing that is dilapidated or structurally unfit for human health and safety.

Substantially Built-up Area: *(P)* A site where more than 75 per cent of its area is covered with buildings.

Sub-urban Areas: *(P)* see *Sub-urbs.*

Sub-urban Sprawl: *(P)* see *Urban Sprawl.*

Sub-urbs: *(P)* Fringe areas of a city where development of housing and commercial activity takes place to counter the high cost of land and other problems the city, also *Sub-urban Areas.*

Sullage: *(S)* Domestic waste water excluding water from WC that is contaminated from excreta.

Sunk Cost: *(EC)* A cost that has already been incurred, and therefore cannot be avoided by any strategy.

Support Paper: *(P)* A document produced to justify the provisions of a plan or project.

Supra-national Model: *(TQ)* A spatial model covering continents, international zones, or even the world that provides spatial variation of social, economic or physical change in the area.

Surface Water Drain: *(S)* A drain carrying surface water including storm water.

Surface Water: *(G)* Natural water occurring on the ground surface – water in a river / lake, see also *Run-off.*

Surveillance Control and Communication: *(TQ)* A system, operated remotely, that allows communication with motorists for monitoring and managing transport facility.

Survey: *(TQ)* A technique of systematic collection of information, its analysis, interpretation and presentation.

Surveyor: *(M)* A person, qualified in the techniques of systematic data collection, analysis, interpretation, and presentation, see also *Survey.*

Sustainability: *(E)* The ability of an ecosystem to maintain ecological processes and functions, biological diversity, and productivity over time.

Sustainable Agriculture: *(AG)* Adaptation of alternative agriculture and animal husbandry practices that minimise the resultant pollution of land, water and air.

Sustainable Architecture: *(UD)* Design of buildings that creates pleasing and healthy living and working environment and minimises the use of energy, water and other resources required for lighting, heating, cooling, movement (lifts) building construction and other activities.

Sustainable Development: *(P)* (a) According to Brundland Report, a development which meets the needs of the present without compromising the ability of future generations to meet their own needs and aspirations, (b) A development that can be, physically, socially, economically, technologically, environmentally, financially, and politically sustained for a longer time, (c) A development that judiciously uses country's resources, conserves economic, cultural, and natural environment, generates income, creates enterprises and indigenous institutions, improves quality of life in such a manner that can be extended or prolonged over many generations.

Sustainable Forestry: *(AG)* Management of goods and services provided by forests to meet the demand of present in such a way that they (the forests) remain equally or more useful to future generations.

Swale: *(LA)* (a) A grassy area in a low lying land, (b) An appropriately graded drainage trench through a park or a lawn.

***Swarnjayanti Gram Swarozgar Yojana*:** *(P)* A programme of the 10th Five year Plan, for the poor with focus on formation of self-help groups for micro financing, training and capacity building, development of infrastructure and establishing market linkages.

SWOT Analysis: *(TQ)* An analysis that highlights the strengths, weaknesses, opportunities and threats pertaining to an area, project, or policy initiative.

SWOT: *(TQ)* strengths, weaknesses, opportunities and threats, see also *SWOT Analysis.*

Symposium: *(ET)* A congregation of persons for intellectual discussion to get various views on a specific issue or subject, see also *Colloquium, Conference, Workshop-(b).*

Synergy: *(M)* The quality of a place, an organisation or group of persons that indicates its collective potential.

Synopsis: *(M)* An outline of a plan, project, research study, or thesis work highlighting the need, aims, objectives, scope and limitations, methodology, and summary of findings and recommendations.

Synthesis: *(TQ)* The technique of combining results of different surveys into an integrated whole having regard to objectives and requirements of the plan or project being formulated.

System of Drainage: *(S)* A system designed for removal of any liquid and includes combined, separate, and partially separate systems of drainage, see also *Combined System of Drainage, Separate System of Drainage, and Partially Separate System of Drain Age.*

System: *(TQ)* A set of interconnected elements functioning together, as an entity, in a regular and interdependent manner following a specific relationship.

Systematic Approach: *(A)* In a process of information gathering and its evaluation in a systematic manner before arriving at any decision.

Systems Analysis: *(TQ)* A scientific, logical, step-by-step method of doing something.

T

Tactical Planning: *(P)* In management, a short-term (up to 12 months) planning processes, by the mid-level management, that supports the overall strategic planning and includes formulation of specific alternative plans, checking of the soundness of different alternatives with respect to specific resource allocation and approved strategies, and identifying an alternative for consideration for implementation.

Tactics: *(P)* The specific and measurable actions needed to achieve the strategic goals and implement the strategic plans.

***Taluka*:** *(A)* In Hindi, an administrative subdivision of a district comprising a number of villages, also *Tehsil*.

Target Group: *(M)* A group of people, identified on the basis of certain specified parameters, who qualify for being beneficiary of a programme or scheme.

Target Population: *(M)* The number of persons in a target group qualifying for a programme or scheme.

Task Analysis: *(TQ)* An examination and identification of the major responsibilities, duties and activities, related to a task, which are to be carried out by an individual worker, with a view to assess the requirements of the worker's knowledge, attitudes and skills as well as the resources required and risks involved.

Task Force: *(M)* A committee of experts appointed by the government or any agency to deliberate upon a specific problem or issue and report the findings and recommendations to the appointing body for consideration and necessary action.

Task: *(M)* An assignment or work to be accomplished.

Tax Base: *(F)* In case of real estate, the value of all properties under the jurisdiction of a local body for the purpose of determining the tax rate and the amount of property tax.

Tax Benefits: *(F)* Benefits accrued to a tax payer due to reduction in tax levies for certain socially desirable activities.

Tax Burden: *(F)* The effect of increase in taxes on a group or individual in the form of additional amount to be paid.

Tax Penalties: *(F)* Penalties on misuse, over-use or non-use of a property as per regulations.

Tax Rate: *(F)* The rate at which taxes, on various items, are levied depending upon the taxation policy.

Tax-exempt Properties: *(F)* Properties that are released from the tax net as a privilege accorded to them and include public buildings, religious buildings and properties of non-profit organisations.

Taxi Cab: *(T)* see *Taxi.*

Taxi Stand: *(T)* A place designated as such for parking of taxies for hiring.

Taxi: *(M)* (a) A car available for hire, (b) A para-transit hired mode of transportation run by a private operator, available on demand for hire, also *Taxi Cab, Cab.*

TDM: *(T)* see *Transport Demand Management.*

TDR: *(P)* see *Transferable Development Rights.*

Teacher: *(ET)* A person who has knowledge, skills, ability and preparation to teach a subject or a set of subjects to others.

Teaching: *(ET)* A process of transferring knowledge, attitudes and skills.

Technical Assessment: *(P)* An examination and certification of a technical soundness of a project as per specifications, norms and standards, or conditions of the agreement.

Technical Assistance: *(P)* An aid or cooperation, extended by a donor country to a developing country, in the form of training and professional guidance in use of materials, processes, techniques, and equipments in fields like agriculture, industry, housing, environmental management, and sanitation, also *Technical Cooperation.*

Technical Cooperation: *(P)* see *Technical Assistance.*

Technique: *(TQ)* A processes used to perform an action derived from theory and its testing in practice.

Technological Innovation: *(P)* see *Innovation.*

Technology Transfer: *(P)* The process of transferring, from one country to another, the technological know-how, production techniques and equipments to be used in production.

Technology Upgradation Scheme: *(P)* A scheme of the 10th Five Year Plan that aims at improving competitiveness of Indian industries vis-à-vis global players through procurement of benchmark technology.

***Tehbazari*:** *(F)* In *Urdu*, a charge collected generally on a daily basis, by local authority, from small traders for allowing them to sell their wares in a public place.

***Tehsil*:** *(A)* In Hindi, see *Taluka.*

Telecommunication: *(TQ)* Communication of voice, data and images through telephone and other methods.

Telephone Exchange: *(P)* A building with all necessary equipments and office space to provide telephone service to an area.

Temperate Zone: *(G)* A zone characterised by (i) climatic conditions ranging between the semi-polar and semi-tropical, (ii) topographic variation from mountainous areas to arid and semi-arid areas, and (iii) existence of a wide variety of plant and animal life.

Temple: *(P)* A building or a complex of building with related infrastructure including parking and serving the public as a place of worship.

Temporal Analysis: *(TQ)* An analysis where time is one of the variable, e.g. decadal growth of population.

Temporary Housing: *(H)* Housing with basic infrastructure intended for occupation for a limited period of time and may be provided in response to (i) an emergency situation, or (ii) a periodic influx of people due to tourism / pilgrimage, or (iii) a stop-gap arrangement before shifting to a permanent accommodation in an urban renewal programme.

Tenancy: *(H)* (a) Possession or occupation of a premises under lease. (b) Duration of a tenant's occupancy.

Tenant Farming: *(AG)* Farming on another person's land by a farmer on payment of rent in cash or kind (sharing the produce on an agreed basis).

Tenant Participation: *(H)* Participation of tenants in the management of the housing complex.

Tenant: *(H)* A person who possesses or occupies a premises under lease.

Tender: *(M)* An offer to supply goods and services at a fixed price.

Tenements: *(H)* Dwelling units generally characterised by low cost, poor maintenance, inadequate infrastructure and location in slum areas.

Tenure: L (a) The permanent right of occupancy of a land or building, (b) The duration and terms of the use or possession of a land or building, (c) The rights, terms and mode of occupying a property, whether owner-occupied or rented.

Terminal Project: *(ET)* A guided research / design work, generally by an individual under-graduate student, conducted during the final phase of a course of study, and submitted, in the form of drawings, and written report, for the award of a degree from an university, see also *Dissertation, Thesis.*

Terrace Farming: *(AG)* A system of farming in hill areas where beds are made on slopes in level tiers after cutting and filling.

Terrace Garden: *(LA)* see *Hanging Garden.*

Terrace Housing: *(H)* see *Row Housing.*

Terrace: *(M)* (a) A paved area, open to sky, next to a house forming its integral part, (b) Steps in a stadium or theatre for seating arrangement with uninterrupted view.

Terrain: *(G)* A stretch of land having somewhat uniform physical features.

Tertiary Sector: *(EC)* One of the three sectors of economy comprising commerce, trade, transport, construction, and services, see also *Sectors of Economy.*

Texture: *(TQ)* In a photo image, the frequency of change and arrangement of tones.

***Theka*:** *(P)* In Hindi, (a) a contract, see *Contract,* (b) A country liquor shop which is allowed on yearly contract (*theka*) by the authorities.

Thekedar: *(P)* In Hindi, a contractor, see *Contractor*.

Thematic Map: *(P)* A map representing information pertaining to an area on a specific theme like soil characteristics, or land use and the like, see also *Map*.

Theory of Human Behaviour: *(A)* Theories related to likes, dislikes, work culture, aspirations, attitudes and expectations of workers and include, as evolved by McGregor, Theory X, Theory Y, and Theory Z, see *Theory X, Theory Y, Theory Z*.

Theory X: *(A)* According to this theory of human behaviour, an average person dislikes work and will avoid it if he can, he needs to be forced, compelled, controlled, directed and threatened with punishment to perform on job, he avoids responsibility, has relatively little ambition and wants job security above all.

Theory Y: *(A)* According to this theory of human behaviour, when people feel committed to a specific objective or target, they work with dedication and show self-control as well as desire to learn and shoulder greater responsibilities, it also highlights that motivation can introduce a sense of commitment in such persons.

Theory Z: *(A)* According to this theory of human behaviour, the motivation that inculcates the sense of commitment in people is 'culture related' that changes with change in quality of life of the person and therefore, there is a need to reviewing the essential nature of man and the factors that motivate him.

Theory: *(P)* Reasoned supposition put forward to explain a set of facts or events that has been confirmed by observations or experiments and is accepted as accounting for the known facts.

Thesis: *(ET)* A guided research / design work, by an individual post-graduate student, conducted during the final phase of a course of study, and submitted, in the form of drawings, and written report, for the award of a degree from an university, see also *Dissertation, Terminal Project*.

Thinking Approach: *(A)* In decision-making, it refers to logical reasoning by the decision-maker before arriving at the decision.

Thinking in Time: *(TQ)* A process of mental analysis that strategically links the past events to the present, and paints alternative future scenarios.

Third World: *(M)* The underdeveloped countries of the world.

Three level organisation: *(A)* An organisation where the organisational-structure comprises three-level hierarchy with manager at the top level, a set of mid-level managers to assist the top level management, and a set of personnel below each mid-level manager to assist him by performing operational level tasks where the employees at each level have a clear cut understanding of the hierarchy of functioning, decision making, authority, responsibility and accountability.

Three-wheeler Stand: *(T)* A place designated as such for parking of three wheelers for hiring, also *Auto-Rickshaw Stand.*

Threshold Analysis: *(TQ)* An analysis of the major physical constraints (thresholds) to urban growth followed by a further analysis of the alternative methods of overcoming major constraints supported by a cost benefit analysis.

Threshold Population: *(P)* Minimum population necessary to support an activity in a settlement e.g. 4,000 population for a primary school of 500 students in plane areas or a population of 250,000 for a general hospital of 500 beds.

Throughput: *(T)* The volume of vehicles or passengers passing a specific point during a predetermined period of time.

Ticket: *(M)* A device bearing the evidence of the holder's right to use a service or facility.

Tidal Energy: *(S)* A non-conventional source of energy generated by the natural phenomenon of tide in oceans.

Time Management: *(P)* A conscious effort to find appropriate time to accomplish professional, social and personal needs.

TIS: *(T)* see *Traffic Impact Study.*

Toll: *(M)* (a) A charge on all vehicles passing a road or a bridge, with a view to recover its cost, (b) The total damage to life and property in a disaster.

Ton: *(M)* (a) A measuring unit of weight equal to 2240 pounds (1016 kg) (b) In USA, a measuring unit of weight equal to 2000 pounds (907 kg), see also *Tonne.*

***Tonga*:** *(T)* In Hindi, a horse driven two-wheel passenger carrier.

Tonne: *(M)* A measuring unit of weight equal to 1000 kg.

Top-down Approach: *(P)* A method of planning where policies and programmes decided at the top-level dictate the planning efforts at the lower levels, also *Top-down Procedure.*

Top-down Procedure: *(P)* see *Top-down Approach.*

Topographic Survey: *(TQ)* Survey and mapping of the physical features and relief of an area.

Topography: *(G)* The shape of the surface of the earth in a given area.

Topology: *(TQ)* In GIS, the spatial relationships between connecting or adjacent coverage features, e.g. arcs, nodes, polygons, and points.

Topsoil: *(LA)* The uppermost layer of the soil.

Tot Lot: *(P)* An outdoors, safe play facility for children of less than 10 years of age, located in residential area and serving a population of about 250 persons.

Total Fertility Rate: *(D)* The total of the age specific fertility rates for the entire reproductive age span and it provides the average number of children that will be born to a woman under the fertility levels indicated by the age specific fertility rates assuming that there is no mortality of women till the completion of reproductive period.

Tourism Industry: *(EC)* A service industry to support tourism and comprises hotels, motels, restaurants, transport, and tourist-related trade, commerce, recreation and information.

Tourism: *(P)* A socio-economic activity initiated by desire to travel and enjoy the places of natural beauty and / or architectural, historical, religious, and socio-cultural significance.

Tourist Resorts: *(P)* see *Resort.*

Tourist Zone: *(P)* An area of tourists' interest, that has buildings, monuments, and / or sites of architectural, socio-cultural, or archaeological significance or natural beauty, which has been developed, with necessary supporting infrastructure, to serve as a tourist place.

Town Centre: *(P)* see *City Centre.*

Town Planner: *(P)* A person, professionally qualified by education and experience and membership of Institute of Town Planners,

India, to pursue the profession of urban and regional planning, also *Physical Planner, Spatial Planner*, see also *Physical Planning.*

Town Planning: see *Physical Planning.*

Town: *(P)* A small urban settlement in the hierarchy – mega-city, metropolis, city, and town, functioning as a service centre to the surrounding rural areas and housing people engaged in non-agricultural activities, see also *Census Town, Urban Centre.*

Township: *(P)* An urban extension to a large city that may be within or outside its administrative boundary and may have both urban and rural characteristics.

Townscape: (UD) The visual scene of an urban area and the image of a city.

Track: *(T)* A path made by frequent use.

Trade Effluent: *(P)* Any liquid, gaseous or solid substance which is discharged from any premises used for carrying any industry, operation, or process, or treatment and disposal system other than the domestic sewage.

Traditional Leadership: *(A)* A leadership pattern which is authoritarian and dictatorial in nature and where the leader thinks, takes all decisions and responsibilities and directs the group members to perform the task with no question asked.

Traffic Assignment: *(T)* The planning and modeling process of allocating trips by different modes and to different origins and destinations including routes.

Traffic Congestion: *(T)* Overcrowding of vehicles and other activities that obstruct free flow of traffic along a route at a given point of time.

Traffic Control Device: *(T)* Devices that help in efficient flow of traffic and include road markings, signals, and road signs.

Traffic Impact Study: *(T)* An analysis of the impact of new developments on traffic in the surrounding area.

Traffic Management: *(T)* Measures taken to ensure free-flow of traffic during the morning and evening peak periods and includes transportation system as well as demand management, see also *Transportation System Management.*

Traffic Volume: *(T)* The number of vehicles, in passenger car units, passing a road in both directions, see also *Passenger Car Unit.*

Traffic: *(T)* To and fro movement of people or vehicles in an area, or along a route that could be a road, rail, waterway, or airway.

Trainee: *(ET)* see *Learner.*

Trainer: *(ET)* (a) A person who possesses the knowledge and skills in a specified subject area and has the ability and training to transfer them to others, (b) The person who imparts training.

Training Centre: *(ET)* A public or private establishment equipped with all necessary physical facilities and technical, administrative and financial resources, for imparting training, also *Training Institute.*

Training Institute: *(ET)* see *Training Centre.*

Training Programme: *(ET)* A programme designed to provide training in specified fields depending upon the training needs assessment.

Training: *(ET) (A)* Process of transferring or obtaining the knowledge, attitudes and skills needed to carry out a specific activity, (b) Depending upon need, a processes of imparting awareness, knowledge or skill in a particular occupation or activity to the participants.

Trans-boundary Movement: (E) Any movement of hazardous waste or any other waste from an area under the national jurisdiction of one country to or through an area under the national jurisdiction of another or several other countries.

Transfer of Property: (L) The legal conveyance of title of a real estate from one person/party to another.

Transferable Development Right: *(P)* A land management tool where the potential of a plot of land, identified by the permitted FAR, has been separated from the plot itself and can be made available to the plot-owner in the form of transferable development right (TDR). In case a plot is required for a public purpose, the owner of such plot may be given, in lieu of compensation of the plot, the TDR, which can be utilised as additional FAR on another plot owned by him and located in the designated outer areas of the city. TDR is given in the form of certificate and it can be freely traded, in full or in parts in the designated area like any share certificate.

Trans-frontier Pollution: (E) Pollution that adversely affects the area in other countries by crossing the boundaries of the country in which it originates.

Transit System: *(T)* see *Transit.*

Transit: *(T)* General term referring to all vehicles and systems that move more than one person and includes carpools, vanpools, minibuses, buses, coaches, LRT, heavy rail, and commuter rail, also *Transit System.*

Transitional Area: *(P)* (a) An area, located normally on the fringes of a city, that is undergoing change from rural to urban character, (b) An area, located within a city, that in undergoing change in activities or character as influenced by the processes of invasion of an activity or the socio-economic changes in conditions of the inhabitants e.g. growth of commercial activity in residential area located near a commercial centre or improvements / renovations in middle class residential areas as a result of changes in economic status of the inhabitants of the area.

Transmission Tower: *(P)* An area used for installation of towers for communication purposes, also *Wireless Station.*

Transplant: *(LA)* To move a sufficiently grown plant, with its roots, from nursery to another location in such a manner that it continues to grow at the new location.

Transport Corridor: *(T)* A strip of land reserved in a development plan for providing one or more parallel transport routes between two nodes.

Transport Demand Management: *(T)* The measures taken to influence demand and indirectly supply to manage congestion and minimise travel in short and long terms and includes car-pooling, subsidising bus fare, parking management, and introduction of flexible office timings.

Transport Network: *(T)* The pattern of transport routes, links and facilities in an area.

Transport Planning: *(T)* The process of analysis of travel demand in a city or region having regard to socio-economic, land use and other factors and formulation of policies, programmes, plans, and projects for its efficient management.

Transport Policy: *(T)* The long-range goals, strategies and institutional setup that a country / state / region intends to follow for development of transport system based upon population growth, transport demand of the sectors of economies, and available and projected resources.

Transport System Management: *(T)* The techniques used to make best use of existing infrastructure to increase the efficiency of the existing transport system through lower cost solutions like, improvement of traffic (both vehicular and pedestrian) circulation through redesigning signals and turning lanes, introduction of one-way traffic, and removal of encroachment.

Transport System: *(T)* The total transport network in an area including all modes of transportation to cater to the movement of goods and people.

Transport Terminal: *(T)* The end point of a transport route by road, rail, air or waterway, including the facilities for passenger and parking of vehicles.

Travel Time: *(T)* The length of time taken to travel between two points.

Tree Grate: *(LA)* A metal grill installed at the base of a tree, otherwise surrounded by pavement, that allows free passage of air, water and nutrients to the tree, but does not interfere with pedestrian traffic.

Tree Guard: *(LA)* A protection constructed around a tree using metal, concrete, wood, bamboo or such other material to prevent it from damage caused by people or animals, also *Plant Guard.*

Tree: *(LA)* A woody plant, generally taller than 2 metre, with well-distinguished trunk.

Trend: *(P)* General pattern or tendency of some physical, social or economic activities or event based upon past regularities.

Trespass: (L) To enter in the property of someone else without the permission of the owner.

Tribal Area: *(P)* An area inhabited by tribal people having special problems and issues needing special attention to improve their quality of life, see also *Tribe.*

Tribe: *(P)* A group of people or families, or a clan having a common ancestor, customs, beliefs, and atypical way of life.

Tributary: *(G)* A small river merging into a larger river and together forming a part of a wider system of rivers.

Tricycle: *(T)* A three-wheeled cycle.

Trip Generation Rates: *(T)* The number of vehicular trips to and from a residential area, per unit of measure such as 100 sq. m., acre, or hectare.

Trip: *(T)* One-way travel from one point (origin) to another (destination) for a specific purpose, the destination of one trip becomes the origin of the next.

Trophy: (E) In relation to wild life, means the whole or any part of any captive animal or wild animal which has been kept or processed by any means and includes rugs, skins, and specimens of such animals mounted in whole or part through the process of taxidermy and antlers, horns, hairs, feathers, nails, teeth, musk, eggs, and nests.

Tropical Rainforests: *(G)* Heavily forested equatorial areas characterised by high humidity, heavy annual rainfall and rich bio-diversity.

Tropical Regions: *(G)* Regions of equatorial latitudes characterised by dry seasons, relatively short period of rains, high temperatures throughout the year, a great variety of plants and animals, rainforests, and savannah of grasslands.

Trunk Line: *(S)* The main channel of utility that connects the terminal or central distribution facility to the distributory network.

Trunk Roads: *(T)* A main road in an settlement connecting its different activity areas.

Trunk Sewer: *(S)* The main sewer line collecting flows from two or more branch sewers and carrying it to the sewage treatment plant.

TSM: *(T)* see *Transport System Management.*

Twin City: *(P)* Two administratively separate urban centres growing, or designed to develop, side-by-side e.g. Hyderabad and Seccundrabad.

Two Level Organisation: *(A)* An organisation where the organisational structure consists of a manager at the top and a set of personnel below him performing operational level tasks assigned to them by the manager.

U

UDA: *(P) Urban Development Authority.*

UDPFI Guidelines: *(P)* see *Urban Development Plan Formulation and Implementation Guidelines.*

ULA: *(A) Urban Local Authority.*

ULB: *(A) Urban Local Body.*

Umland: *(G)* The area around a city that supplies resources, agriculture produce and manpower to the city.

UN Development Programme: *(M)* A programme of the UN that provides assistance to developing countries for their socio-economic and physical development.

UN Educational, Scientific and Cultural Organisation: *(M)* A specialised agency, joined to the UN through special agreement, which promotes education for all, cultural development, protection of world's natural and cultural heritage, and international cooperation in science, press freedom and communication.

UN Industrial Development Organisation: *(M)* A specialised agency, joined to the UN through special agreement, which promotes the industrial advancement of developing countries through technical assistance, advisory services, and training.

UN: *(M)* see *United Nations.*

Unauthorised Colony: *(P)* (a) Any residential development that does not conform to an approved master plan, zonal plan, or layout plan for that area, (b) Any residential area that does not conform to land use, sub-division regulations and building bye-laws.

Unauthorised Development: *(P)* (a) Any development that does not conform to an approved master plan, zonal plan, or layout plan for that area, (b) Any development that does not conform to land use, sub-division regulations and building bye-laws, see also *Non-conforming Use, Unauthorised Colony.*

Unauthorised Regularised Colony: *(P)* Any residential colony that did not conform to an approved master plan, zonal plan, or layout plan for that area but has been regularised with certain conditions, after following the prescribed procedure, as a regularised colony.

UNCHS: *(P)* United Nations Centre for Human Settlement.

Underdeveloped Area: *(P)* see *Underdeveloped Region.*

Underdeveloped Region: *(P)* An area having poor attributes related to development and generally characterised by inaccessibility, stagnant or negative economic growth due to poor and primitive agricultural practices, slow or no resource utilisation, industrialisation and urbanisation, also *Underdeveloped Area.*

Underdevelopment: *(EC)* A stage in economic development of an area characterised by mass poverty, low per capita income, and inadequacy of social infrastructure due to poor and primitive agricultural practices, slow or no resource utilisation, industrialisation and urbanisation.

Underemployment: *(EC)* (a) Employment of a worker on a job below his level of education, skill or training, (b) Employment of a worker for a part time, (c) Employment of a worker on a salary / wage lower than the one with same qualification and experience.

Under-five Mortality: *(D)* see *Child Mortality.*

Underground Railway: *(T)* A mass transit running under the ground in tunnels generally passing through and serving heavily built-up and high-density areas of a city.

Underground Tank: *(S)* A tank constructed below the ground level for storage and distribution of water to its service area.

Underground Utility Network: *(S)* Network of utility lines such as electricity, water supply, and sewage disposal running under the ground and requiring special attention in their planning having regard to location, safety, and horizontal and vertical spacing between different networks.

Underprivileged: *(EC)* see *Poor and Disadvantaged.*

Undertaking: *(A)* (a) A registered or unregistered body, institution, business or enterprise established for performing a specified function, (b) An agreement to do something.

Undeveloped Area: *(P)* An area of land in its natural state, before development, also *Undeveloped Land.*

Undeveloped Land: *(P)* see *Undeveloped Area.*

UNDP: *(M)* United Nations Development Programme.

Unemployment: *(EC)* A state of joblessness of workers within the economy caused by inadequate demand, or excess supply of labour.

UNESCO: *(M)* United Nations Educational, Scientific and Cultural Organisation.

Unfit for Human Habitation: *(P)* A condition of an area, caused by unsafe and unhealthy buildings, see also *Unsafe Building.*

UNIDO: *(M)* United Nations Industrial Development Organisation.

Union: *(A)* (a) A registered or unregistered association of workers for a common cause, (b) An association of individuals or group of individuals for pursuance of a common purpose.

Unit Area Rates: *(F)* As a part of urban sector reforms, a transparent system of property tax assessment, made by the owners / occupiers themselves, using the procedure and unit area rates as approved by the local body, taking into account factors like nature of the area, quality of construction, age of building, use, width of abating road, location of property near a bus / railway station, commercial centre and nature of occupancy.

Unit Cost: *(F)* (a) The total cost of producing any product at per unit basis, e.g. cost of construction of a building per square metre or development cost of an area per hectare.

United Nations: *(M)* An international organisation of 191 member countries of the world working under the UN Charter and committed to preserving peace, developing friendly relations among nations, evolving solutions to international problems and promoting the respect for human rights.

University: *(P)* (a) A campus comprising teaching and research blocks, assembly hall, library, administrative offices, sports and recreational facilities, students hostels, staff housing, and guest houses, (b) An institution established by law to impart higher education and research with authority to award degrees.

Unlinked Trip: *(T)* A direct trip from origin to destination without any intermediate stops or waiting or walking time.

Unplanned Industrial Area: *(P)* An area characterised by haphazard growth or mixed residential-industrial use where the dominance of the residential area is invaded by the industrial use making it predominantly industrial in nature and requiring redevelopment.

Unsafe Building: *(P)* A building that is dangerous to human life due to faulty structure, inadequate access, bad maintenance, old age, non-compatible land use or inadequate provision of fire safety measures..

Unsecured Loan: *(F)* A loan that is not backed by any kind of collateral or insurance against loss.

Unskilled Labourer: *(EC)* see *Unskilled Worker.*

Unskilled Work: *(EC)* A job that does not require any training or experience in its performance.

Unskilled Worker: *(EC)* A worker, who does not have any training, skill and experience in a specific trade or occupation, also *unskilled labourer.*

Un-Starred Question: *(A)* A question, raised by a member of Parliament, placed on the list of questions for supply of written answers by concerned department / ministry and such answers are deemed to be laid on the table in the House of Parliament at the end of the question hour.

Upgrading: *(P)* The processes of improving the quality of housing and the residential area through planning, designing of building, strengthening of structures, augmenting of infrastructure and strictly enforcing of building bye-laws.

Upland: *(G)* A high ground.

Upward Transitional Area: *(P)* An area having potential and propensity to upward change - from rural to urban or stagnating state to developed state or slow development state to fast growing state.

Urban Agglomeration: *(P)* (a) A city with contiguous out growth outside the statutory limits but falling within the boundaries of the adjoining village or villages, (b) Two or more towns with their outgrowths, (c) A city and one or more adjoining towns with or without outgrowths and forming a contiguous urban spread. An urban agglomeration is treated as one continuous urban spread for the purpose of overall population size classification and analysis of urban data.

Urban Area: *(M)* (a) In demography, an area that fulfils the following conditions – has a municipal council or corporation, municipal board, cantonment board or notified town area committee etc., (b) An area that fulfils the following conditions: (i) has a minimum population of 5, 000, (ii) at least 75 per cent of male working population is engaged in non agricultural pursuits, and (iii) has a density of population of at least 400 persons per sq. km., (c) In planning, a common term for all hierarchies of settlements, also *Urban Centre.*

Urban Blight: *(P)* see *Blight.*

Urban Centre: *(P)* see *Urban Area (b).*

Urban Core: *(P)* see *City Centre.*

Urban Decay: *(P)* see *Blight.*

Urban Design: *(UD)* The discipline that fosters and promotes aesthetic and functional urban form in human settlements.

Urban Development Plan Formulation and Implementation Guidelines: *(P)* Guidelines, issued by the Government of India, for the urban local bodies providing innovative planning system and approaches to formulation of development plan of a city and its implementation as envisaged by the Constitution (Seventy-fourth Amendment) Act 1992.

Urban Development: *(P)* A process of spatial expansion of urban areas through effective planning of socio-economic activities and infrastructure, plan implementation and urban management.

Urban Dynamics: *(P)* The study of those socio-economic and physical parameters that attract people to move to a city and also those that cause a city to evolve, grow, age, and decay over time.

Urban Ecology: (E) Temporal study of complex interaction between people and the natural and man-made environment created by urban activities, socio-cultural behaviour, and standard of living.

Urban Economy: *(EC)* Temporal study of complex interrelationship between urban development and growth of secondary (manufacturing) and tertiary (commerce, trade, transport, and services) sectors.

Urban Fabric: *(P)* The configuration of all physical element (buildings, structures, network of roads, open spaces, water bodies, flora and fauna) of an urban area at a given point of time, also *Urban Pattern.*

Urban Form: *(P)* The three dimensional shape of an urban area evolved out of the urban design characteristics and the spatial arrangement of land uses and activities.

Urban Fringe: *(P)* A physically defined transitional area bordering a city, characterised by a mix of both rural and urban form and functions, also *Fringe, Fringe Area,* and *Peri-Urban Area.*

Urban Functions: *(P)* The non-agriculture functions performed by an urban area and include those related to industrial, commercial, education, research, health care, socio-cultural, and administrative activities as well as provision of infrastructure and services.

Urban Geography: *(G)* The branch of geography that concentrates upon the study of socio-economic and environmental processes that (i) determine the location, spatial arrangements and evolution of towns and cities in a region and (ii) establish the spatial arrangements of urban activities in a city.

Urban Growth Management: *(P)* Actions taken for planning and promoting growth of a city to equip it to meet the socio-economic and spatial needs at a right time and a right place.

Urban Growth: *(P)* Physical expansion, generally unplanned, of a city as a result of increase in its population and socio-economic activities.

Urban Hierarchy: *(P)* Ranking of urban settlements by population size, functions, and socio-economic importance ranging from megalopolis, metropolis, city, and town, or regional centre, sub-regional centre, and service centre.

Urban Housing: (H) Public housing, generally for low and economically weaker sections of the society, located in an urban area.

Urban Indicators: *(TQ)* see *Indicators.*

Urban Land Economy: *(EC)* The study of the pattern of activities and intensity of development on a parcel of land in urban areas as a consequence of its market price.

Urban Management: *(P)* The process of ensuring efficient, equitable, and sufficient provision of urban services in a city through appropriate policies, programmes, investment decisions and governance.

Urban Pattern: *(P)* see *Urban Fabric.*

Urban Perception: *(P)* The image of the city as perceived by the people living and working there as well as those who visit there as tourists and these two perceptions may not be the same.

Urban Planner: *(P)* see *Town Planner.*

Urban Planning: *(P)* see *Physical Planning.*

Urban Population: *(D)* Population residing in an urban area and enumerated in a census or projected based upon demographic techniques.

Urban Poverty: *(P)* (a) A condition, generally in large cities, that results in wandering homeless people, informal commercial activities, and slums, (b) A condition in urban areas, characterised by severe deprivation of basic human needs, safe drinking water, sanitation facilities, health care, shelter, education and information, (c) A condition in urban areas where the people live on earnings less than US $2 per capita per day (World Bank), see also *Extreme Poverty, Poverty.*

Urban Reforms Incentive Fund: *(P)* A fund created in the 10th Five Year Plan to support state governments to undertake specified reforms in urban sector, see also *Urban Reforms.*

Urban Reforms: *(P)* Legal, fiscal and planning related reforms introduces in the urban sector and include repealing Urban Land (Ceiling and Regulation) Act, rationalisation of stamp duty rates, computerisation of property transaction, improvement in system of property tax and its collection, levy of realistic user charges for water supply and other schemes, adopting the double entry book keeping system by municipalities, urban planning system, land assembly systems, and simplification / harmonisation of development promotion rules.

Urban Region: *(P)* see *City Region.*

Urban Renewal: *(P)* A process of rejuvenation of a dilapidated area in a city having physical decay and economic stagnation caused by old age of buildings, poor accessibility, loss of real estate value, and changes in technology, transportation systems, land use and activity patterns, through improvement of buildings, accessibility, circulation system, augmentation of facilities and services and reassignment of compatible land uses, also *Renewal.*

Urban Sanitation Mission: *(P)* A mission that focuses on improvement of drainage system in urban areas and also setting up sanitary landfills and composting plants for urban solid waste management.

Urban Settlement: *(P)* see *Urban Area-(b).*

Urban Sprawl: *(P)* A process of growth of urban area or sub-urban area in an unplanned manner having no regard to social infrastructure and subsequent needs for transport and other facilities and services, also *Sub-Urban Sprawl.*

Urban Structure: *(P)* The configuration and relationship among various planning units of an urban area e.g. 3 to 5 housing clusters form a neighbourhood, 3-5 neighbourhoods constitute a community, 3-5 communities form a district and 3-5 districts comprise a city where each planning unit has a centre such as cluster centre, neighbourhood centre, community centre, district centre, and city centre/CBD respectively accommodating commercial and socio-cultural activities as per respective hierarchy and population served.

Urban System: *(P)* A set of interconnected urban settlements extending over a designated area – regional, national, or international - serving a role in the development process depending upon their functional hierarchy.

Urban: *(P)* (a) Belonging to a city, (b) An area that has a concentration of population normally engaged in non-agriculture occupation and different countries have different norms to define an area as urban e.g. in New Zealand, a place with population of 1,000 persons is considered urban, in Ireland this population is 1500, in France, Israel and Argentina 2,000, in USA, Mexico 2,500, in Belgium and Ghana, India 5,000, in Greece and Senegal 10,000, see also *Urban Area.*

Urbane: *(P)* Pertaining to or influenced by a city and its positive way of life and mannerism.

Urbanisation: *(P)* A process of urban growth guided by socio-cultural, economic, political and physical factors and spatio-economic planning interventions.

Urbanised Area: *(P)* (a) When referring to existing situation, the built-up area of a city occupying various urban functions, (b) When referring to the proposals in a development plan, the proposed area designated for various urban activities and may extend beyond the municipal boundary of the city.

Urbanism: *(P)* Urban way of life evolved by the socio-cultural, economic and political factors in a city, it is not a process of urban growth rather it is the result of urbanisation.

Urban-oriented Regional Plan: *(P)* A regional plan where the main focus is on development of region as guided by the problems of major urban centres located therein and where rural development is of secondary concern.

Urban-urban Migration: *(P)* A pattern of migration where the movement of people is from one urban centre to another urban centre, see also *Migration.*

URIF: *(P)* see *Urban Reforms Incentive Fund.*

USAID: *(F)* United State Agency for International Development.

Use of Land: *(P)* see *Land Use.*

Use Permissible: *(P)* see *Permissible Use.*

Use Permitted: *(P)* see *Permitted Use.*

Use Premises: *(P)* One of the several subdivisions of a use zone designated in a layout plan for a specific purpose or type of development related to that use zone, e.g. in residential use zone there could be use premises for plotted housing, group housing, hostels, *dharamshala* etc.

Use Prohibited: *(P)* see *Prohibited Use.*

Use Zones: *(P)* Areas designated in a development plan or layout plan for a specific land use that could be residential, commercial, industrial, recreational, and related to transport, and facilities and services.

User Charges: *(F)* Charges levied by the local body for the services like water supply, sewerage, and garbage collection, provided to people with a view to recover a part or full amount of investment on the service, also *User Fees.*

User Fees: *(F)* see *User Charges.*

User Survey: *(TQ)* A technique of identifying from the users themselves the need, perception, reaction, acceptance or rejection of a project, product, or service as well as their willingness to pay for the same, also *Users' Evaluation.*

Users' Evaluation: *(TQ)* see *User Survey.*

Utilities: *(P)* The basic public services like water supply, sewerage, drainage and electricity supply in a settlement.

V

Vaastu Purush Mandala*: *(H) In Hindi, a term that signifies metaphysical plan of a building. In this term, *vaastu* means a surrounding, environment, matter or nature; *purush* means energy, work power, vigor or soul; and *mandala* means the astrological chart-which relates the layout to the orientation. The essential and basic form of *Vaastu Purush Mandala* is a grid of 64 squares with a man lying with his head-pointing North-East, the legs in the South-West, right hand in North-West, left hand in South-East and other parts of the body fill the square.

Vaastu Shastra: *(H)* In Hindi, the ancient Indian treatise of *Vedic* origin on the science and art of planning villages and designing houses based on principles close to the nature.

Vaastu: *(H)* In Hindi, the dwelling of human beings and Gods.

Vacant Developed Land Tax: *(F)* A tax levied on vacant developed land to control land speculation and speed-up development.

Vacant Developed Land: *(P)* A vacant parcel of land located in a developed area, see also *Developed Area, Developed Land.*

Vacant Land: *(P)* A public or private parcel of land that is not used for any purpose or has not been designated in an approved development plan for a specific use at a given point of time.

Vacant Undeveloped Land: *(P)* A vacant parcel of land located in an undeveloped area, which is in its natural state, before development, see also *Undeveloped Area.*

Valedictory Session: *(ET)* The concluding session of a training programme or seminar generally devoted to assessment and evaluation of training and in case of a seminar, presentation of the findings and recommendations followed by valedictory speech by the chief guest.

Valid Plan: *(P)* A legally binding and effective plan that is good or adequate in law at a given point of time.

Validation: *(TQ)* The process of testing a model or regression equations with actual field data to ensure its accuracy and reliability.

Valley: *(G)* A stretch of land between hills or mountains often with a river flowing through it.

Valorisation Charges *(F)* A tax levied, generally along with property tax in the affected area, to recover the cost of development schemes such as street improvements, and sewer extensions.

Value Addition: *(EC)* The increase in the value of a material due to its further processing and packaging.

Vanpool: see *Carpool.*

Variable: *(TQ)* An indicator that is changeable and affects other indicators in an equation or relationship.

VCR: *(T)* see *Volume to Capacity Ratio.*

Vector: *(TQ)* In GIS, a coordinate-based data structure commonly used to represent linear geographic features where each linear feature is represented as an ordered list of vertices.

Vegetation: *(L)* see *flora.*

Vehicle Occupancy: *(T)* The number of people traveling in a car, bus, or other vehicle.

Vehicle: *(T)* Any means of transportation of people and goods that may be driven by any source of power – human, animal, petrol, diesel, gas, electricity and others.

Vehicular Capacity: *(T)* The maximum number of vehicles that can pass in both directions, during a given period of time over a given section of a road under a given level of service and it is expressed as number of vehicles per hour.

Vending Booth: *(P)* A small stall where commodities of daily need are sold either through mechanical device or otherwise, see also *Vending Machine.*

Vending Machine: *(P)* A mechanical device for selling commodities of daily use.

Venture: *(EC)* An undertaking in which there is a risk of say, profit and loss.

Vermin: *(E)* Any wild animal.

Vernacular Architecture: *(M)* The indigenous architectural style that is typical of a specific place, era, or tribe.

Vertical Aerial Photography: *(TQ)* The technique of taking photographs from a camera mounted in an airplane or balloon in a vertical position with respect to the Earth's surface at the time of exposure, and is used for photogrammetric mapping requiring a high degree of accuracy, also *Orthophotography.*

Vertical Mixing of Land Uses: *(P)* In a single building, a pattern of mixing where its different floors may have different uses e.g. store in the basement, shop on the ground floor, and office / residential use on the upper floors, also see *Mixed Use Zoning.*

View: *(M)* (a) In landscape, a section of natural or manmade or combined scene seen from a specific point, (b) In case of education and training, an opinion of an author on some issues, (c) In sociology, the belief of a group of persons, community, tribe, on certain issues or matters.

***Vikas Pradhikaran*:** *(P)* In Hindi, a Development Authority, see *Development Authority.*

Village: *(P)* A human settlement with basic utilities, facilities and services comprising cohesive community and simple organisational structure where a majority of population is engaged in agriculture and allied activities, see also *Habitat, Human Settlement, Abadi.*

Vine: *(LA)* see *Climber.*

Violation: *(L)* An infraction of the rules and regulations.

Virtual Water: *(S)* Water that a country would require to domestically produce food that it imports, Japan is the biggest consumer of virtual water as it imports 60 per cent of its food requirements.

Vision Statement: *(P)* A written document highlighting the future course of development of different sectors of economy having regard to the political ideology, socio-economic and physical conditions and resources.

Vision: *(P)* A perception, a foresight of the future course of changes in a given situation, see also *Development Vision, Goals.*

Vista: (UD) A beautiful, pleasing, long and narrow view in natural or manmade surroundings, also *View-(a).*

Visual Study: (TQ) A method of study of the characteristics, problems, issues, changes, or potentials of an area with the help of site visits and documenting the observations through, photographs, sketches, maps, and written notes.

Vital Record: *(P)* A record that must be preserved and available for retrieval when needed e.g. land records.

Vital Statistics: *(D)* Record of death and birth maintained by a municipality.

Viva-voce: *(ET)* An examination of thesis, project through audiovisual presentation by the student / candidate and oral questioning by the examiners.

Vocational Training Institute: *(P)* An institution located in a building or a campus of several buildings with or without hostel accommodation, generally managed on non-commercial basis by public or private institution, for offering diploma courses and practical training preparatory to employment in certain professions or trades.

Vocational Training: *(ET)* A process of imparting awareness, knowledge or skill required for employment in a particular occupation.

Volume to Capacity Ratio: *(T)* The ratio between the actual volume of traffic in PCUs to the designed capacity of a road, see also *PCU.*

Voluntary Organisation: *(A)* A registered or unregistered non-profit organisation dedicated to a social cause.

W

Wages: *(EC)* Payment made periodically – hourly, daily, weekly, monthly – to workers for the services rendered by them.

Walking Distance: *(P)* A distance that can be comfortably covered by most people of all ages and normally covers a distance that can be covered in 5 to 10 minutes (350 m. to 700m.).

Walkway: *(T)* see *Footpath.*

Want: *(EC)* A desire of person or a community to do something, possess some object or be benefited by a facility or service which may or may not be fulfilled, see also *Need.*

Ward: *(M)* Subdivision of a city into physically identifiable boundaries based upon population for the purpose of municipal elections, collection of property taxes, and grassroots participation in local development process as envisaged under Constitution (Seventy-fourth Amendment) Act 1992, (b) A large room in a hospital for caring indoor patients, (c) A minor child under the care of a guardian.

Ward Committee: *(P)* A committee constituted under a Municipal Act for the assigned purposes.

Warehouse: *(P)* A premises that is exclusively used for storage of goods and commodities transported by rail and / or road and has loading and unloading facilities and other supporting uses, also *Storage, Godown.*

Waste Collection: (S) A system of removal of solid waste from residential, commercial, or industrial areas, also *Waste Removal, Refuse Collection.*

Waste Conversion: *(E)* The processes of utlising urban or agriculture wastes for generation of energy in the form of steam, electricity or biogas.

Waste Disposal System: *(S)* A mechanism of collection, segregation, treatment and disposal of solid waste at designated sites or facilities.

Waste Management System: *(S)* The technical, administrative and fiscal arrangement for collection, segregation, recycling, treatment, transportation and disposal of solid waste in a city.

Waste Removal: *(S)* see *Waste Collection.*

Waste Separation: *(S)* The processes of removing, at the source, and setting aside each specified (e.g. paper, glass. metals etc) type of waste materials in different containers, as per colour code, so as to facilitate their efficient disposal/recycle.

Waste Utilisation: *(S)* Use of fully, partially treated or untreated municipal solid waste or sewage for agriculture, horticulture or other purposes.

Wasteland: *(G)* Barren land not fit for agriculture purposes and not occupied by any other use.

Wastes: *(S)* see *Refuse.*

Wastewater: *(S)* see *Sewage.*

Water Bound Macadam Road: *(T)* A road with surface made of crushed stones, mud and water.

Water Closet: *(S)* A water-based toilet system.

Water Conservation: *(E)* Protection, development, sustainable use, and efficient management of water resources.

Water Consumption: *(S)* Amount of water used in an area for different purposes such as domestic, industrial, commercial, and agriculture.

Water Districts: (E) An administrative division of a city for the purpose of water supply to the population residing there.

Water Main: *(S)* The principal pipe in a water supply system.

Water Management: *(S)* The technical, administrative and fiscal arrangement for procurement, processing and distribution of water in an area.

Water Park: *(P)* A specialised park designed with all related infrastructure, predominantly for water sports and water-based active recreation, see also *Specialised Park*.

Water Pollution: *(E)* Contamination of water or alteration of its physical, chemical or biological properties caused by discharge of any sewage or any other liquid, gaseous or solid substance therein, that may, or is likely to, create a nuisance or render such water harmful to public health, or to the life of animals, plants, and aquatic organism, or to domestic, commercial, industrial, agriculture, or other legitimate use.

Water Supply: *(S)* (a) The quantity of water available from all sources to meet the water demand of a community for all purposes, (b) The processes of provision, treatment, storage and distribution of water to a settlement for domestic, industrial, commercial and other purposes.

Water Supply System: *(S)* The entire arrangement for supply of water from a source at one end to an outlet at the other and includes water reservoir, treatment facility, pumping facility, storage, and network of pipes for distribution, control valves, fittings and fixtures.

Water Table: *(S)* The upper surface of groundwater in an area at a given point of time.

Water Transport: *(T)* The mode of transport of goods and people that runs on water surface in rivers, canals, sea and other water bodies and includes boats, ships, and other vessels.

Water Transport System: *(T)* The entire system of water transport including vessels, terminal facilities, ports and jetties.

Water Treatment: *(S)* The processes of cleansing water for human consumption.

Water Treatment Plant: *(S)* The facility for treatment of water to ensure that it is potable.

Watershed: *(P)* The area, identified by joining the ridge-lines, which drains into a single stream, river, lake or a water body and serves as an appropriate spatial eco-systems for planned development of resources, system of settlements, distribution of infrastructure, control of floods and protection of environment.

Watershed Hierarchy: *(P)* The hierarchy of rivers form a hierarchy of watersheds which are classified as main watershed, sub-watersheds, and micro-watersheds.

Waterway: *(T)* A water body that is navigable, provides access to different areas and can be used for water transport.

Way: *(T)* (a) A passage to a building or site, which may or may not be motorable, (b) A manner, system or method of doing some thing.

Wayside Facilities: *(P)* Amenities, conveniences and services located along highways for the benefit of the motorists and other road-users and include motels, restaurants, eating places, restrooms, petrol pumps, service stations, and repair shops.

WBM Road: *(T)* see *Water Bound Macadam Road.*

WC: *(S)* see *Water Closet.*

Weather: *(M)* Condition of atmosphere characterised by temperature, humidity, rainfall, sunrise, sunset, daylight hours, and wind direction and speed.

Weed Tolerance: *(TQ)* The minimum allowable distance between any two vertices along an arc.

Weekly Market: *(P)* A designated open area where a number of informal shops assemble on a day of the week (and move to another locality the next day) and form a temporary market to sell with permission under *tehbazari* system, a variety of commodities ranging from vegetables, crockery, garments, cloth to plastic and food items.

Weights and Measures Systems: *(M)* There are two types of such systems: the FPS and CGS system, see *FPS, CGS.*

Welfare: *(P)* The state of well-being defined by health, education, income of people.

Welfare State: *(A)* A country where the government takes the responsibility of well-being of all its citizens through social programmes like free health care, education and social security.

Wet Latrine: *(S)* Water borne sanitation system.

Wetland Function: *(G)* The biological, chemical and physical process that wetlands perform, such as storing floodwaters, removing nutrients or providing bio-diversity.

Wetland Value: *(P)* The worth of a wetland or a particular function performed by it as perceived and decided by a society, or specific community.

Wetlands: *(G)* Areas that are partially of completely covered by water and are swampy or marshy in character that provide natural habitat for a variety of wild life and assist in flood control.

Wharf: *(T)* A series of platforms with equipments for loading and unloading of goods from ships in a harbour.

WHO: *(M)* see *World Health Organisation.*

Wholesale Market: *(P)* A place where goods and commodities are sold in bulk to the retailers and includes shops, storage and godown, loading and unloading platform, parking of trucks, offices of forwarding agents and other facilities.

Wild Animal: *(E)* Any animal found wild in nature.

Wild Life: *(E)* Includes animals, bees, butterflies, crustacean, fish, and moths, and aquatic or land vegetation, which form part of any habitat.

Wildlife Sanctuary: *(E)* see *Sanctuary.*

Wind Breakers: *(LA)* Natural or artificial barrier, created by trees or walls respectively, serving as shelter from wind.

Wind Energy: *(S)* The energy generated by harnessing kinetic force of the wind, also *Wind Power.*

Wind Power: *(S)* see *Wind Energy.*

WIPO: *(M)* see *World Intellectual Property Organisation.*

Wireless Station: *(P)* see *Transmission Tower.*

WMO: *(M)* see *World Meteorological Organisation.*

Wonder Land: *(P)* A park designed and landscaped with all necessary infrastructure, for entertainment in a variety of ways covering both indoor and outdoor recreation activities, also *Wonder Park.*

Wonder Park: *(P)* see *Wonder Land.*

Work: *(EC)* Participation in any economically productive activity, which may be physical or mental in nature, and includes supervision and direction of work also.

Work Force: *(D)* The total number of persons in the age group of 15 to 55 years, available at a given point of time for employment in an city / region, which may or may not be employed, comprise the work force, also *Labour Force.*

Working Capital: *(F)* The part of capital of an establishment that is available for conducting daily business, which is continuously circulating.

Working Place: *(P)* The premises, including the house, where a person works.

Workload: *(EC)* (a) The amount of work defined by number of hours per week and indicated on the time table, (b) The expected performance and job assigned to a worker.

Workshop: *(M)* (a) In planning, a premises in which production or servicing work is done with the aid of machines, (b) In education and training, a congregation of experts to discuss and evolve consensus on a given issue or theme.

World Health Organisation: *(M)* A specialised autonomous organisation, joined to the UN through special agreement, which coordinates programmes aimed at solving health problems and the attainment by all people of the highest level of health through working in areas such as immunisation, health education, and provision of essential drugs.

World Intellectual Property Organisation: *(M)* A specialised agency, joined to the UN through special agreement, which promotes international protection of intellectual property and foster cooperation on copyrights, trademarks, industrial design and patents.

World Meteorological Organisation: *(M)* A specialised agency, joined to the UN through special agreement, which promotes scientific research and the earth's atmosphere and climate change, and facilitates the global exchange of meteorological data.

WTO-GATS: *(M)* World Trade Organisation's General Agreement on Trade in Services.

Y

Yard: *(M)* (a) Central open space in a building, (b) An open air storage space for building materials, equipments, machines and such other things, (c) A measure of length equal to three feet.

Yardstick: *(M)* A norm or standard to evaluate the quality of performance of some action, policy or programme.

Yield: *(EC)* (a) Return on an investment, (b) Production per unit area.

Yoga and Meditation Centre: *(P)* A building having facilities for practicing yoga and meditation for self-attainment and achieving higher quality of mind and body.